Madness on trial

Manchester University Press

SOCIAL HISTORIES OF MEDICINE

Series editors: David Cantor and Keir Waddington

Social Histories of Medicine is concerned with all aspects of health, illness and medicine, from prehistory to the present, in every part of the world. The series covers the circumstances that promote health or illness, the ways in which people experience and explain such conditions and what, practically, they do about them. Practitioners of all approaches to health and healing come within its scope, as do their ideas, beliefs and practices, and the social, economic and cultural contexts in which they operate. Methodologically, the series welcomes relevant studies in social, economic, cultural and intellectual history, as well as approaches derived from other disciplines in the arts, sciences, social sciences and humanities. The series is a collaboration between Manchester University Press and the Society for the Social History of Medicine.

Previously published

The metamorphosis of autism: A history of child development in Britain *Bonnie Evans*

Payment and philanthropy in British healthcare, 1918–48 *George Campbell Gosling*

The politics of vaccination: A global history *Edited by Christine Holmberg, Stuart Blume and Paul Greenough*

Leprosy and colonialism: Suriname under Dutch rule, 1750–1950 *Stephen Snelders*

Medical misadventure in an age of professionalization, 1780–1890 *Alannah Tomkins*

Conserving health in early modern culture: Bodies and environments in Italy and England *Edited by Sandra Cavallo and Tessa Storey*

Migrant architects of the NHS: South Asian doctors and the reinvention of British general practice (1940s–1980s) *Julian M. Simpson*

Mediterranean quarantines, 1750–1914: Space, identity and power *Edited by John Chircop and Francisco Javier Martínez*

Sickness, medical welfare and the English poor, 1750–1834 *Steven King*

Medical societies and scientific culture in nineteenth-century Belgium *Joris Vandendriessche*

Managing diabetes, managing medicine: Chronic disease and clinical bureaucracy in post-war Britain *Martin D. Moore*

Vaccinating Britain: Mass vaccination and the public since the Second World War *Gareth Millward*

Madness on trial
A transatlantic history of English civil law and lunacy

James E. Moran

Manchester University Press

Copyright © James E. Moran 2019

The right of James E. Moran to be identified as the author of this work has been asserted by him in accordance with the Copyright, Designs and Patents Act 1988.

Published by Manchester University Press
Oxford Road, Manchester M13 9PL
www.manchesteruniversitypress.co.uk

British Library Cataloguing-in-Publication Data is available

ISBN 978 1 5261 3303 8 hardback
ISBN 978 1 526 16379 0 paperback

First published by Manchester University Press in hardback 2019

This edition published 2022

The publisher has no responsibility for the persistence or accuracy of URLs for any external or third-party internet websites referred to in this book, and does not guarantee that any content on such websites is, or will remain, accurate or appropriate.

Typeset by Toppan Best-set Premedia Limited

Contents

List of tables	vi
Acknowledgements	vii
Note on sources	ix
List of abbreviations	xii
1 Introduction: civil law and madness in transatlantic context	1
2 Suing for a lunatic: lunacy investigation law, 1320–1890	31
3 Indefinite mental states: negotiating the legal definition of madness	49
4 Trials of madness: family struggles over property in England	71
5 Care and protection: managing madness in England	97
6 Atlantic crossing: lunacy law as colonial inheritance	117
7 Family, friends and neighbours: localising madness in New Jersey	140
8 Asylum in the community: managing madness in New Jersey	171
9 Orders of insanity: lunacy investigation law and the asylum reconsidered	206
10 Conclusion	232
Bibliography	237
Index	246

Tables

8.1 Symptoms described in the lunacy commissions in order of frequency — 181

8.2 'Assertions and pretences': types of delusion described in the New Jersey lunacy commissions in order of frequency — 185

9.1 Patient population of the New Jersey State Lunatic Asylum, 1848–60 — 208

9.2 Population of Newark County, New Jersey, 1840–80 — 224

Acknowledgements

The impetus for this book came in the mid-1990s when I was digging around in the New Jersey State Archives at Trenton. I was hoping to conduct research on the New Jersey State Lunatic Asylum. However, at the time of my visit, documents relating to asylum development in New Jersey were difficult to access. Upon further inquiry, the helpful archivists at the Trenton archives suggested that I take a look at a collection of manuscripts that had been deposited, unprocessed, in several boxes that were destined for recycling. These files proved to be a rare treasure trove of civil legal documents relating to madness in New Jersey, dating from the 1790s to the early twentieth century. But it took time – years in fact – to unpack them, literally and figuratively. Although there is still much historical potential in these trials of madness awaiting the next brave soul who relishes reading thousands of hand-written documents at the Trenton archives, I think that I have made myself familiar enough with them to articulate in this book the arguments that I wish to establish about their importance. The origins of these New Jersey civil trials of lunacy lie in English precedent, and this fact encouraged me to add to the good work of a few other historians by writing chapters on the formation and development of lunacy investigation law into what, I argue, was the most important and enduring formal response to madness in England. Finally, the connections between the development of lunacy investigation law in England and in New Jersey required a consideration of this body of law in transatlantic imperial context. This, in a nutshell, is the background and rationale for the book.

As befits a book that took many years to complete, I owe a debt of gratitude to a great many individuals. In my initial excitement about the New Jersey lunacy trial documents, Susan Houston challenged me to realise their potential. I was encouraged by Charles Rosenberg to keep pushing at what he termed the 'un-asylum' history of madness that these sources seemed to represent. Archivists Betty Epstein and Joseph Klett at the New Jersey State Archives have given me good counsel about archival collections and have been wonderfully open minded about keeping and preserving hitherto unappreciated manuscript sources. Many conference presentations and many discussions with historians of mental health about lunacy investigation law and madness have helped to clarify the analysis in this book. In particular, I would like to thank Jonathan Andrews, Barbara Brookes, Erika Dyck, Waltraud Ernst, Marjory Harper, James Muir, Thomas Muller, Thierry Nootens, Isabelle Perreault, Jim Phillips, Andrew Scull, Len Smith, Sally Swartz, Marie-Claude Thifaut, Barbara Todd and Leslie Topp. The long-distance and long-term friendship of Akihito Suzuki, a pioneer historian of English lunacy investigation law, has been of major benefit to my thinking on the subject. Closer to home, at the University of Prince Edward Island, I am grateful for the support of colleagues Ian Dowbiggin, Scott Lee, Edward MacDonald and Sharon Myers who kept politely asking, 'so, how is the book coming along?' Undergraduate researchers Cassandra Armsworthy, Kathryn (Morell) Doucette, Jennie (Palmer) Mutch, Norah Pendergast and Marilyn Sweet gave excellent assistance at earlier stages of the research. Their professional and personal successes since graduation are a reminder of their good research skills and also of the time that has passed in my efforts to complete the book!

David Wright has been instrumental in my musings about how to write a book about the history of lunacy investigation law. This has entailed many conversations, house visits, coffee-shop debates and discussions, along with his willingness to read and review several draft chapters of this book. My father, Jim Moran, has read every word of every chapter with his professional editorial eye. For this, and the wonderful academic conversations that ensued, I am grateful. This book has benefited from some crucial early-stage funding from the Social Sciences and Humanities Research Council and from Associated Medical Services. I would also like to acknowledge the good work of editorial staff at Manchester University Press and the insightful suggestions of the anonymous referees.

My partner, Lisa Chilton, has been in on this book project since the beginning. It is impossible to overestimate the privilege of a lifelong academic friendship with one so wise.

Note on sources

Although historians have for a long time known about the existence of lunacy investigation law, the sources relating to the law's use have remained elusive and underappreciated.[1] Specifically, while there are many sources about the functioning of lunacy investigation law, the trial testimony, judges' statements, lawyers' interventions, appeals and witness statements have been difficult to locate for most jurisdictions in which this trial process took place. In order to write a history of lunacy investigation law in transatlantic perspective, this book has exploited two major sources: reports on lunacy trials that are found in the *English Reports* (see below), and a largely intact set of lunacy trial manuscripts found in the New Jersey State Archives.

The most comprehensive published interpretation of English lunacy trials for the early nineteenth-century period is Akihito Suzuki's *Madness at Home: The Psychiatrist, the Patient, and the Family in England, 1820–1860*. Suzuki's analysis is based on 196 commissions of lunacy that were published in *The Times* newspaper. Finding the original manuscript sources for these and earlier commissions of lunacy has so far proved next to impossible.[2] However, case reports of many lunacy trials are now available online. The *English Reports* is a 179-volume compilation of case reports dating from 1220 to 1866. As Peter Bartlett notes, 'the vast bulk of the cases date from the seventeenth to the mid-nineteenth centuries.'[3] A convenient way to access *English Reports* relating to lunacy trials is through the search engine Justis, which, among other resources, provides an extensive online library of legal sources for the United Kingdom.[4] Using the Justis search engine, I have collected case reports for over two hundred cases in lunacy, dating from Beverley's landmark case in 1598 to the beginning of the period covered by Akihito Suzuki's book in 1823. These reports vary in length and in the quality of their content, depending on their usefulness to the legal system at various subsequent periods in English history. But many of them are detailed, containing case summaries, the perspectives of the various participants and the observations and explanations of the Lord Chancellors. Although the majority of case reports on trials in lunacy pertain to the Court of Chancery, some describe trials played out in the Court of King's Bench and the ecclesiastical courts.

The paperwork that is largely absent from the case reports on lunacy trials in England is fully on display in the extant sources for New Jersey. Approximately 1,800 lunacy trials were found in boxes in the basement of the New Jersey State Courthouse, collected together at some point at the turn of the twentieth century into 'lunacy bundles'. Although intended for destruction, they have subsequently become part of the New Jersey State Archives' permanent manuscript collections.[5] These hand-written sources, though uneven in length and quality, offer extensive witness testimonials from neighbours, friends and local authorities, lawyers' arguments, judges' deliberations, the machinations of the guardianship process and, occasionally, full retrials of earlier verdicts of *non compos mentis*. These sources allow for the reconstruction of the complex dynamics of the trial process and the equally complicated community and familial contexts within which the legal recourse to madness took place.

Notes

1 See the discussion in P. Bartlett, 'Legal madness in the nineteenth century', *Social History of Medicine*, 14:1 (2001), 107–31.
2 Suzuki notes that the original manuscripts for the period covered in his study 'were destroyed, unavailable, or scattered'. A. Suzuki, *Madness at Home: The Psychiatrist, the Patient, and the Family in England, 1820–1860* (Berkeley: University of California Press, 2006), p. 26. He refers to a few records at The [British] National Archives, but the vast majority of the lunacy trials seem to have been lost. In 1998 I was informed by an archivist at The National Archives that, although the index to the commissions of lunacy was extant, the thousands of pieces of paper with the content of most trials was considered expendable during the First World War and had been recycled for the war effort.

Note on sources

3 Bartlett, 'Legal madness', 113.
4 See http://www.justis.com/about/what-is-justis.aspx. Cases referenced in this volume are cited by volume number in *English Reports* (abbreviated as E.R.), followed by the case name and year(s) and page numbers. E.g. 88 E.R., Bennett and His Wife and Spencer and His Wife against Vade and Several Others, 1742, pp. 474–83.
5 A fuller discussion of these sources as they compare with asylum documents can be found in J. Moran 'A tale of two bureaucracies: asylum and lunacy law paperwork', *Rethinking History*, 22:3 (2018), 419–36.

Abbreviations

CC, LCF   Chancery Court, Lunacy Case Files
EC, CCP   Essex County, Court of Common Pleas
E.R.   *English Reports* (London: Stevens & Sons, 1900–32, 178 vols)
NJSA   New Jersey State Archives

1

Introduction: civil law and madness in transatlantic context

The madness of James B.

From the early modern period to the First World War the importance of the civil law in the history of madness was dramatically played out in the life experiences of countless English and American subjects and citizens. In the case of James B., the entanglements of civil law and madness began with his first major employment with his uncle's diamond import company. In 1875, by the age of twenty-two, James B. had sufficiently impressed his uncle to be put in charge of the company's office in London, England. Just before he moved to London, he was married to Carrie B. Soon afterwards the couple had their first and only child. At a certain point in London, perhaps from the pressures of a new family and from being in charge of the London branch of his uncle's diamond import business, James B. began to drink heavily. According to James B., he was recalled to New Jersey from London in 1891 after correspondence between his wife and his uncle in which Carrie stated that she could no longer live with James on account of his heavy drinking. James B. freely admitted that he was also suffering from 'nervous depression', and that he had consented, at the request of his uncle, 'to go to a retreat, and remain until [he] was better'.[1] However, the next five years of James B.'s engagement with mental health institutions, and with the New Jersey civil courts, were marked by controversy and acrimony.

The details of James B.'s life, and the context of his mental troubles, are made available through civil legal documents of the New Jersey Court of Chancery. A lunacy trial was filed against him in July 1893. This civil trial in lunacy, launched against James B. by his wife, found him to be *non compos mentis* – mentally incapable of governing himself or his property. James B. fought back against the decision of the civil court by attempting to traverse, or overturn, the verdict of *non compos mentis*. Together, these legal proceedings created over six hundred pages of documentary evidence. The verdict of the twelve 'good and lawful men' summoned as jurors to the trial was that James B. was 'of unsound mind' with 'no lucid intervals'. The proceedings of the trial were transmitted to the Orphans Court, whereupon guardianship arrangements were made, placing James B.'s wife in charge of his person and of his considerable income, valued at $200 per year, and fixed property of about $28,000.

One year and one month after this verdict, in August 1894, James B. filed for a traverse (a new trial to re-examine his mental state) in an attempt to regain his legal status as a sane man and to take back control of his property. At this trial, James B. claimed that, upon returning from London, he had taken the 'Keeley cure' in Philadelphia, which cured him of his drinking habit. However, still suffering from a 'nervous depression', James B. had consulted Dr Banker, who recommended that he start taking 'bromide of soda or sodium' to help him sleep. Despite James B.'s concerns about becoming addicted to this new substance, his doctor reassured him that the chances of this happening were remote. Shortly thereafter, he became addicted to bromides, and it was at this point that he agreed to his uncle's request that he find a retreat in which to recover. But, James B. claimed, 'I was decoyed to [an] asylum after I had consented to go to a retreat, had consulted with a doctor about it; under the pretext of taking me to such a place for inspection, he landed me like a felon into the asylum.'[2] The asylum, to which James B. was committed on 7 May 1893, was the publicly funded New Jersey Morris Plains Lunatic Asylum. It was during James B.'s five-month stay at the Morris Plains asylum that his wife launched the lunacy trial against him. In his trial of traverse, James B. testified that he had not been made aware of the original lunacy trial proceedings and thus had had no ability to defend himself against the accusation or the verdict. Upon his release from the Morris Plains asylum, James B. was admitted to the private Long Island Home at Amityville.

The trial of traverse was largely a consideration of whether or not James B., who was originally diagnosed with paresis when he was committed to the Morris Plains asylum, could have sufficiently recovered from this condition to take back control of his person and property. Opinion on this matter was divided among medical professionals, and

Introduction

these divisions were further exacerbated by the tough questioning of well-paid lawyers acting on behalf of James B. and on behalf of his wife. For instance, Dr Orville Wilsey, the physician in charge of the Long Island Home at Amityville, argued that 'no case of paresis ever recovered yet. Once to have paresis is always to have it until you die, although perhaps frequently there are remissions when the disease is not as marked or is not making rapid progress as it did before … I think [James B.'s] is a case of paresis passing through a remission where the mental symptoms of dementia and loss of will power are most marked.'[3] Mr Hardwicke, James B.'s lawyer, was so aggressive in his questioning of Dr Wilsey's expertise in the mental condition of paresis that the Master in Court intervened to caution the lawyer. Hardwicke countered that he wanted 'simply to show by this witness that he keeps an asylum where patients are put by relatives in order to get their money and by wives to get rid of their husbands'.[4]

Despite these kinds of contentious comments, characteristic of most of the trial proceedings, most medical witnesses agreed that James B. suffered from paresis. What was not so clear about James B.'s condition, until Dr Edward Spitzka gave his testimony towards the end of the trial, was that James B.'s paresis was brought on by syphilis. When asked by Mr Guild, the lawyer acting on behalf of Carrie B., 'what the supposed or claimed nature of [James B.'s] malady' was, Spitzka replied, 'I found out'.[5] When pressed by the lawyer about what Spitzka had found out, the doctor replied, 'There is a lady present [in the court room]; of course it was aggravated by intoxicants.'[6] Like most of the other medical experts on the witness stand, Spitzka concluded: 'I should think [James B.] was able to mind his own affairs. I might not counsel him to rush into feverish activity, but in regard to the ordinary every-day affairs of business, I see nothing at all objectionable to his entering into them.'[7]

Yet, the weight of the long and drawn-out testimony of the trial of traverse did not convince the Special Master in Chancery, Frank Bergen, that James B. had 'sufficiently recovered to make it proper to give him complete control' of himself and property. On 18 August 1894 the Master declined James B.'s attempt at traverse. For James B., this was clearly not acceptable because, in his opinion, 'my wife is … a very strong-minded woman, and I have always had a great respect for her, but she is very determined, and I am very determined, and we neither of us like to yield, and, under such circumstances there will be times when there is friction when neither of us wants to give in.'[8] True to his remarks, through repeated appeals to the Special Master in Chancery, by 12 March 1898, James B. finally regained full control over his property and person.

In many respects, the civil trials of James B. relating to his mental state encapsulate key aspects of this book. His increasing mental trouble in London, and his return to the town of Elizabeth, New Jersey, underline the transatlantic nature of lunacy investigation law. This body of law that encompassed trials in lunacy, chancery court proceedings, proceedings in guardianship and trials of traverse had its origins in fourteenth-century England. Its development in England included its successful migration across imperial pathways to several colonial and post-colonial contexts, including New Jersey. James B.'s five-year engagement with lunacy investigation law, from 1893 to 1898, came towards the end of the real influence both in England and in New Jersey of this legal response to madness – a period that marks the end point of this study. His trials also highlighted the melding of lunacy investigation law with various medical responses, including those from physicians, asylums and specialty institutions for the mentally unwell. The ability of James B. to use traverse proceedings to challenge the verdict of *non compos mentis* also bore witness to the enduring legal principle, grounded in the civil law of lunacy, that those considered insane had the potential to recover their mental faculties and to regain control over themselves and their property. Finally, the detail provided by evidence from legal investigations into the madness of individuals like James B., both in England and in transatlantic settings like New Jersey, allows for a close reading of the importance of civil law in the response to madness, and of the complex dynamics of family and community in this civil legal process.

This book examines civil law responses to madness in England and in the North American territory of New Jersey. In England, by the eighteenth century, the law governing trials in lunacy had become a sophisticated legal response to those among the propertied classes who suffered from madness. This response included the famous *writs de lunatico inquirendo*, the investigations into the mental state of individuals by trial (often with a full jury), the participation of lawyers, judges and witnesses in these trials and the establishment of a tradition of precedent which Lord Chancellors drew upon in their considerations of what madness was and how it should be dealt with. A trial verdict of *non compos mentis* resulted in the establishment of guardianship both for the individual deemed legally mad and for his/her property.

As Akihito Suzuki has pointed out, there were over three thousand lunacy trials in England between 1660 and 1853.[9] This bears some statistical testimony to their importance but does not, as Suzuki notes, address how these trials also permeated English society's understanding of the problem of mental breakdown.[10] This book shows that the development of this body of law was central to understandings of and responses to madness in England over several centuries, before, during and after the emergence of the large public asylums of the nineteenth century. Lunacy investigation law helped to structure approaches to madness among England's elite, but its reach was broader than that. By investigating the evidentiary fragments of this legal process that have been left behind, largely through a study of case reports, a sense is gained of English familial and community approaches to madness, especially for the eighteenth and nineteenth centuries. So too is the extent to which familial and community understandings of madness were structured around the civil law in England over a considerable period of time.

Next, the book considers how lunacy investigation law was transplanted into the colonial and post-revolutionary context of New Jersey. Like other English institutional and cultural imports, the law of lunacy investigation was successfully adopted into the colonial contexts of North America and elsewhere.[11] Drawing on a large evidentiary base of lunacy trials and other legal documents for New Jersey, it is possible to study in detail the development of this law. Lunacy investigation law planted deep roots in New Jersey, developing, from the mid-eighteenth century to the end of the nineteenth century, into the most important formal response to madness, not just for the well-to-do but also for families across the economic spectrum. In so doing, it formed a major force both in the determination of madness and in the response to it. Furthermore, the largely intact and extensive New Jersey lunacy trials often contain detailed accounts of madness that allow for a thorough investigation into the ways in which witnesses described madness and how they reacted to it at the local level. Although these rich testimonials to madness can be studied on their own for what they say about everyday understandings and responses, I argue that they are best considered as closely tied to the legal process of lunacy investigation. Civil law and custom were connected in important and, at times, surprising ways in New Jersey, and their relationship is closely considered in this book. Finally, the archived lunacy trials available for study were produced before, during and after the institution of the asylum was introduced in New Jersey. This allows for an examination both of the relationship between lunacy investigation law and asylum development and of how neighbours and family members of the mad – and sometimes the mad themselves – responded to the introduction of the asylum as an alternative to care in the community.

Madness, the asylum and the family

A primary aim of this book is to show that the focus on lunacy investigation law over a long period of time, and in transatlantic context, adds to historical understandings of the relationship between madness, the family and the asylum. As far back as Andrew Scull's 1979 book *Museums of Madness: The Social Organization of Insanity in Nineteenth-Century England*, the crucial relationship between the family and the asylum was acknowledged, although not explored in detail.[12] For Scull, the relationship between asylum development and family transformation formed part of his broad analysis of changes in the social relations of capitalist production, the professionalisation of psychiatry and the social reform movement in Britain. More specifically, the transition from the old paternalist social order to a fully capitalist social system 'destroyed the traditional links between rich and poor' while, at the same time, 'sharply reducing the *capacity* of the lower orders to cope with economic reverses'.[13] Scull argued that 'while the family-based system of caring for the insane and other types of deviants may never have worked especially well', these changes in capitalist social relations probably left it 'functioning particularly badly'.[14] Under these circumstances, the asylum was a possible solution for individuals who could no longer be cared for by their families.[15]

In several books and articles from the late 1970s to the early 1990s, the study of the relationship between the family and the asylum gave more sustained attention to specific geographical contexts and to specific factors in the disruptions to family dynamics that prompted the institutionalisation of the insane. These scholars looked between the broad lines of capitalist transformation, industrialisation and modernisation to see what, in specific locations of the transatlantic world and in specific social strata of society, motivated the impulse to asylum committal. This, in turn, led to the investigation of hitherto undiscovered primary sources for investigation and to important alterations to the understanding of the family/asylum relationship. In many respects, this new scholarship challenged earlier accounts and, in so doing, intensified historiographical tensions as to the asylum/family relationship. For example, John Walton's 1979 article on asylum admissions in Lancashire, England attempted to nuance historians' earlier claims about the asylum.[16] Walton described Lancashire as a county that, at mid-century, was home to traditional agricultural practices (in the north), robust urbanisation and industrialisation (in Manchester and Liverpool) and an important area of mid-sized textile towns. Drawing on the work of labour historians and on his own analysis of the relationship between asylum admission and working-class migration patterns, Walton concluded that 'large cities whose growth was fuelled by long-distance migration, and whose inhabitants lacked the solidarity which soon arose from shared work experiences and, perhaps, a disciplined industrial environment, were generous providers of lunatics for the new custodial institutions'.[17] On the other hand, 'in the smaller towns and industrial villages, where kin and migrants from the same village were accessible and the workplace built up a supportive friendship network of its own, the working-class family was better able to deal with the problem of what was coming to be seen as insanity than it had been in a countryside dominated by scattered smallholdings'.[18] As Walton suggests, this detailed examination of admission practices in Lancashire indicated the need to pry deeply into the specific contexts of social and economic development in order to see what forces of capitalism were fuelling asylum growth. Moreover, in this sort of analysis, understanding changes in the family economy and structure became essential to understanding asylum development. The working-class were no longer seen as an amorphous mass drawn to a state response to madness over which they had little or no control. The concept of agency among the working-class now formed part of the family/asylum equation.

Richard Fox's 1978 examination of madness and asylum development in turn-of-the-century California further challenged earlier arguments about the asylum/family relationship in the context of capitalist development by arguing against any simple equation between the family's capacity to care and the twin processes of urbanisation and industrialisation. Fox pointed out that the city was, in fact, 'a center of ethnic, religious, and familial groups that have preserved for many residents some of the organic, personal relationships typically attributed to rural living alone'.[19] Moreover, Fox believed that some of his revisionist colleagues made the mistake of assuming that 'institutions [like the asylum] are imposed by that elite or that society upon a passive, malleable "lower class"'.[20] In Fox's account, families (and community officials) made use of the asylum on their own terms in order to deal with people who 'seemed to threaten family stability or public tranquility'.[21]

By the mid-1980s, interpretive battle lines were further drawn by a drifting of the perspectives of madness studies away from a respect for broad structures of power, towards so-called complexity theory, and/ or towards more sustained attention to the micro-powers of everyday life. Also, the concept of working-class agency now formed part of the family/asylum equation. This nuanced approach to the relationship between the family and the asylum is exemplified in Mark Finnane's path-breaking 1981 study, *Insanity and the Insane in Post-Famine Ireland*. Finnane devoted a whole chapter of his book to the 'contexts of committal' of the insane to Irish state asylums. In this chapter he used institutional records to draw a picture of patient characteristics (another feature of these studies of the late 1970s and 1980s), noting that there were noticeable regional variations in the use of the asylum. Finnane suggested that the higher usage in the western seaboard of Ireland reflected a region 'fragmented by the two-fold impact of emigration and a decline in marriage' as a result of the famine. More significantly, Finnane examined several individual committal cases to assess how family conflicts 'were translated into forms of madness'.[22] He concluded that 'those committed to the asylum, could as equally be victims as dangers within the family structures. Some threatened violence, some even used it. But it was also the case that the insane were the objects of violence, particularly if they were women. And the lunacy committal was in many hands an instrument of domination, to reinforce a position of power in the family or an expectation of certain behaviour.'[23] Moreover, towards the end of the nineteenth century the use of the asylum by families was also 'bound up with a set of cultural expectations that the asylum was the appropriate place for those who were "out of their mind"'.[24]

For Finnane, this aspect of the study of madness – the family dynamics precipitating asylum committal – was essential to a full understanding

Introduction

of how 'the asylum's history reflected the realities of social power – whether manifested in the priorities and preoccupations of national and local politics, in professionalism [or] in family life'.[25] In this formulation of the relationship between the family and the asylum, the asylum becomes 'an institution whose role and function was mapped out by a lengthy process of popular usage and custom as much as by the legal and financial imperatives which the state erected around it'.[26] In bringing the micro-power politics of familial relationships into the context of asylum development, Finnane was envisioning not so much a *layering* of social powers along professional and class lines, as had earlier revisionist writers, but, rather, a *web* of social powers that made the decisions of ordinary people, including those who committed and those who were committed, crucial to the success of asylum development. The working-class/popular classes/masses weren't merely 'done to' in this analysis – they were active in the domestic responses to madness and to asylum development.

The work of Fox, Finnane and Walton led to a flurry of research that devoted considerable attention to the familial contexts of committal. This literature further enhanced our understanding of the importance of class, gender and power within families to the development of the asylum. At the same time, these arguments in favour of an even closer scrutiny of the family/asylum nexus profoundly altered interpretations of the wider analysis of power. For example, in her 1984 exploration of the Pennsylvania Hospital for the Insane, Nancy Tomes demonstrated how this private hospital's 'patrons' were at the centre of asylum development. Tomes probed pre-committal treatment strategies within families; the specific familial dynamics that eventually led to asylum committal as a last resort; and the influence on psychiatric practice of families' perceptions of insanity and of their concerns about the asylum. This analysis led her to conclude that 'asylum medicine reflected a shared consensus [between families and asylum doctors] regarding the origins and treatment of mental disorders'.[27] For families with means, like those whose members predominated at the Pennsylvania Hospital for the Insane, Tomes suggests that a combination of the growing 'cult of domesticity', along with a concern about the disorder being created by 'complex modern society', may have led to decreasing tolerance for domestic care of the insane and an expansion of the definition of insanity.[28] Similar conclusions were drawn by historians assessing the history of public asylums designed for a more mixed clientele, or exclusively for pauper patients.[29]

The focus of these monograph studies on family/asylum connections was reflected in a growing article literature. Scholars on both sides of the Atlantic, like Mary Ellen Kelm, Wendy Mitchinson, Patricia D'Antonio, Geoffrey Reaume, Patricia Prestwich, Richard Adair, Joseph Melling and Bill Forsythe, Terry Nootens, Marjorie Levine-Clark and David Wright have tackled the relationship between family and asylum development, further positioning decisions to commit within specific geographic, economic, cultural and social contexts.[30] Migratory patterns, urbanisation, family structure, work, ethnicity, gender and institutional proximity were all factors which, these authors discovered, could combine at specific historical conjunctures to promote asylum growth. In many cases, the influence that these historians saw exerted by the family extended from pre-asylum management, through the committal process right to discharge and (in certain cases) to readmission.

The sheer volume of this literature has shifted attention 'downwards' from the aspirations and fears of state officials, psychiatrists and middle-class reformers, to the motivations and circumstances of those who cast forth the asylum patient. Notwithstanding important nuances in individual contributions to this growing body of work, in general it considered the asylum to be as much the product of family agency as it was the product of parliamentary or professional fiat. Moreover, for many authors, nineteenth- and early twentieth-century asylum medicine incorporated the diagnoses of families upon whose accounts psychiatrists relied heavily in the creation of their patient records and disease nosologies.[31]

Linking micro or case studies into broader contexts of social and political power is indeed a difficult task. But, as much of the above-cited literature demonstrates, many who write this sort of history do, in fact, recognise power differentials, despite their focus on the agency of families and communities in the response to madness and the decision to commit. Moreover, these studies are now numerous enough to be read for what they *do* reveal about 'imbalances of power' among state officials, mad-doctors and family members, among family members, and between family and community. One of the aims of this book is to show that a more sustained consideration of what many scholars are writing about at the local level – changing family dynamics; alterations in family structure in the face of developments in capitalism; family decisions

Introduction

about asylum committal and discharge; familial and community practices outside of the asylum's sphere of influence – can fundamentally alter the ways in which we consider the linking-up of power and madness in historical context at the micro and macro levels.

The importance of lunacy investigation law

Part of that task for this book is to consider the under-researched civil legal response to madness (a response that certainly was, in large measure, a structured understanding of madness) and the important place that it held in the management of perceived irrational behaviour. Including the role of lunacy investigation law as an integral component of the historiographical mix certainly alters our understanding of the history of madness. For example, as in the case of James B. outlined at the beginning of this chapter, although the asylum was important to many who experienced mental troubles in the Anglo-transatlantic context, this institution was not the principal mechanism over the longer dureé. That mechanism was lunacy investigation law.

The influential body of lunacy investigation law on both sides of the Atlantic needs to be considered much more seriously in terms of how it structured understandings of and responses to madness. We need to understand the law's development over time, communities' and families' response to it and their strategic manipulations of the law to suit their own needs. James B.'s case, and the hundreds of other cases that form the basis of this study, do clearly confirm many aforementioned historians' arguments about the close connections between asylum committal and family dynamics. James B.'s experiences included time in the publicly funded Morris Plains Lunatic Asylum,[32] and at the privately run Long Island Home at Amityville, New York. His stay in both institutions was fraught with the machinations of family decisions about his mental state, conflict over family fortunes and debates among medical professionals about how to best respond medically to James B.'s condition. However, if we include attention to how the civil law in lunacy contributed to this dynamic in James B.'s case and in the cases of many others, the situation gets a great deal more complex.

Lunacy investigation law was influential in the determination of mental status for a great number of individuals. In England, the civil law played an important role primarily, though not exclusively, for wealthy people.

In New Jersey, the law was significant for individuals across a much broader socio-economic spectrum. Moreover, lunacy investigation law became a long-standing institutional response to madness, but operated in a way that was very unlike the asylum. It was a mechanism for shoring up familial property under threat and for establishing the care and management of the mad person on a more permanent basis, through specific legal steps. These included guardianship over the person deemed to be *non compos mentis* and guardianship over the property of that individual. This legal response had a much longer tradition than the asylum both in England and in colonial and post-colonial settings like New Jersey. By the time that the asylum came on the scene, families had been using the legal workings of lunacy law for decades and centuries, along with myriad other non-institutional responses that, as historians have noted, are much harder to recover.

While families did come to understand the civil law in lunacy as a means to shore up anxieties about family members whose behaviour was considered beyond the pale, this law also developed as a very public process, involving witnesses who were drawn from the community, jurors who were property-owning men, also from the community, and trials that were open to the public. This legal process established a 'community of understanding' about madness that deeply influenced how families and neighbours understood the problem, and the range of options that were available in responding to it, including, eventually, the asylum. Finally, embedded in lunacy investigation law over the entire period of its existence was the concept that a person found by trial to be insane could recover. With this in mind, the right of 'traverse', or the right to overturn the decision of the lunacy investigation of *non compos mentis*, although not often used, was always, technically, at the disposal of the individual. This recourse to traverse, used by James B. in an attempt to re-establish his status as mentally fit to govern himself and his property, needs to be considered as a powerful additional feature of the legal structure that affected the ways in which families in England and in North America responded to madness.

Getting out of the asylum

Much of the recent literature on the family and the asylum, and my research for this book on lunacy investigation law, points towards a

Introduction

more radical reconceptualisation of the family/asylum relationship. This reconceptualisation suggests a 'decentring' of the asylum from pride of place in the responses to madness for much of the nineteenth century. This shift was anticipated historiographically by David Wright's landmark (and suitably entitled) article 'Getting out of the asylum: Understanding the confinement of the insane in the nineteenth century'.[33] In his synthesis of the substantial research on the history of the role of the family in asylum confinement that had been published prior to 1997, Wright offered a methodology with which to reconsider the family/asylum relationship. He advocated the use of nominal record linkage in the study of asylum records in order to reconstruct patient profiles, and a 'household economics' approach to get at the familial circumstances precipitating committal. Wright cautioned the would-be researcher to consider the changes in the family's *ability* to care for their alleged insane as well as its changing *willingness* to care.[34] Strikingly, he noted that although the asylum did become more 'important as the nineteenth century drew to a close ... the abundance of institutional sources, and the paucity of material on informal caring networks, should not mislead us into accepting uncritically the primacy of the mental hospital itself'.[35] For instance, just under half of patients in public asylums in Britain were institutionalised for twelve months or less, while many of these same patients had a recorded history of madness prior to their committal that had lasted for many months or years. Moreover, despite the growing asylum population in nineteenth-century Britain, government officials were convinced that many more mad people were being cared for and managed outside the walls of the asylum. This research suggested that the function of the family in the response to madness was alive and well, and running parallel to the development of the asylum response. This points to a more modest reassessment of the asylum's role as a singular response to madness. To Wright, this just made sense, as the lay public was unlikely to have 'cast off centuries-old cultural and popular ideas about insanity [and familial responses that went with them] when confronted by the medical gaze' of institutional psychiatry.[36] But a key set of questions remains. What exactly were these cultural and popular ideas about insanity, and what kind of less formal, if not routine, responses to madness did these ideas generate?

Wright's article presaged a momentum in family-centred/asylum-decentred perspectives on madness that assess the response to madness through the lens of familial and community management and care.[37] This perspective is well developed in Akihito Suzuki's book *Madness at Home: The Psychiatrist, the Patient, and the Family in England, 1820–1860*, in which Suzuki discovers a 'domestic psychiatry' that 'existed and even flourished' at least for the more privileged members of Victorian English society.[38] Drawing on the work of historians of the middle-class English family, Suzuki argued that the cult of middle- and upper-class domesticity that developed in the face of the uncertainties and demands of political and economic change included an enduring 'flexible fabric of strategies' for dealing with the insane. Far from being wiped out by asylum growth, this 'domestic psychiatry' endured, at the same time that it profoundly influenced the nature of psychiatric medicine. Suzuki's findings, drawn largely from civil legal trials in madness, have been consistent with those of other researchers such as Thierry Nootens and R. A. Houston, who have been working with similar primary sources.[39]

More sustained investigation into the decentring of the asylum, such as that provided by Akihito Suzuki in his book *Madness at Home*, also reveals certain analytical tensions and conundrums that are embedded in the historiographical consideration of the subject. Suzuki allows his powerful thesis about the development and perseverance of 'domestic psychiatry' among England's elites to pry open the door to major revision to the history of the asylum and of psychiatry. But he is reluctant to push the door open very far – perhaps, as he states, because the state of the field does not yet allow it. For Suzuki:

> Although considerable nuances have been made to the chronology, dynamics, and causes of this momentous change [of asylum and psychiatric ascendancy], none has refuted the core thesis of the rise of the asylum and psychiatry in Victorian England. Nor do I intend to dispute it. It is true that the family became less frequently the locus of care for those recognized as suffering from mental disease, and the family's role in providing care and in organizing a therapeutic or controlling regime diminished during the course of the nineteenth century.[40]

However, in the next paragraph Suzuki notes that 'caution is necessary', for 'historians have not so much verified as assumed the diminishing role of the family vis-à-vis that of the asylum and the psychiatric profession.'[41] Moreover, citing the considerations of Wright and Bartlett, Suzuki states, 'we still do not know the number of men and women who were "recognised" as insane during the nineteenth century.'[42] I would add

Introduction

that we still do not know how these figures stack up against asylum and population statistics in given areas at given points in time. The collective weight of recently published literature focusing on madness and the family at the turn of the asylum era, including that of Suzuki, points to the fact that, for much of Britain and, in particular, North America, the lunatic asylum did not become the dominant response to madness, nor did it replace or undermine family and community care for the insane until well past the mid-nineteenth century.

This debate is partly resolved by recognising the great geographical diversity of the asylum's influence. In this book, the focus on England aims to establish the importance of lunacy investigation law, even in the face of an increasingly prominent private and public asylum system. For New Jersey, a more sustained focus of the book is the extent to which lunacy investigation law operated as the principal means by which the formal response and understanding of madness was structured (in the absence of any institutional response) until the opening of the New Jersey State Lunatic Asylum in 1848. Indeed, the numbers of asylum patients in the state were relatively low until well after the American Civil War. It may well be that the resort to lunacy investigation law helped to temper the appetite for asylum development in New Jersey and elsewhere. An equally likely scenario is that the successful migration of lunacy investigation law from England to New Jersey, and its development into an effective response to madness in what was a primarily agricultural society, rendered the asylum option less dominant for a longer period in this territory. Finally, as the trial of James B. suggests, the depth of detail provided by the testimonials of friends and family at the trials of lunacy in New Jersey reveal the rich repertoire of responses to madness at the local level. By mining the details of New Jersey lunacy trials, it becomes clear what some of the content of the 'centuries-old cultural and popular ideas about insanity' actually was, at least in this part of North America. These local cultural understandings and responses to madness are described in this book in order to further the argument that, when it arrived on the scene, the asylum was but one of many options to madness.

Madness and colonisation[43]

A study that purports to trace the history of civil lunacy investigation law from its origins in England, through its migration into the colonial setting in English New Jersey, and on to its continuing development in the post-revolutionary American state, requires some consideration of how the relationship between civil law and madness was tied to colonialism and empire. The transatlantic history of madness and civil law intersects with empire and colonialism in significant ways. First, the civil law of lunacy was, by definition, designed to test the mental state of those who were suspected of not being able to rationally manage either their property or themselves. This struck at the heart of property-holding English society over a considerable period of time. Despite major changes in the economic structure of England from the origins of lunacy investigation law in the 1300s until its decline in the late 1800s, this law remained important because it was situated at the axis of power, property and self-governance in England.

It is no surprise, therefore, that during the first colonial era England sought to reproduce the law of lunacy investigation in its colonial settings. The important relationship between lunacy law and colonialism was both practical and theoretical. Practically, this body of law was placed into the hands of colonial rulers by English authorities as a mechanism for dealing with propertied colonists who were considered mentally incapable of managing their property. If lunacy investigation law was of major significance to how madness was understood and responded to in England, its introduction and development into the colonial context of New Jersey was of even greater importance. In part, this was due to the fact that in colonial and post-revolutionary state contexts the law helped to structure the response to madness in a transatlantic world that was predominantly rural and that had not developed institutional responses to madness at pace with the private and public asylum system in the 'mother country'. The case of James B. shows that the colonial inheritance of lunacy investigation law persisted in New Jersey until at least the late nineteenth century.

At a more abstract, theoretical level, early exponents of the laws of *non compos mentis*, as well as some early eighteenth-century English legal intellectuals, drew heavily on the uneasy juxtaposition of the concept of *non compos mentis* with the rights (or lack thereof) of those peoples discovered in new lands who were judged not to have the intellectual capacity to govern themselves or the lands which they happened to inhabit. In particular, those newly discovered indigenous people without any concept of property or property ownership (as defined by English legal tradition) were compared to English citizens who had become *non compos mentis* – both were in need of guardianship and protection by the English Crown. Indeed, this protection was considered (rather perversely for the former group) to be a natural right of rational rule. In this sense, the colonial extension of lunacy investigation law can be seen as an essential aspect of colonisation, for, as Diane Kirkby and Catharine Coleborne put it: 'Law, the rule of law, was at the heart of the English colonial enterprise.'[44] Early protagonists of the imperial importance of the laws of *non compos mentis* thus rationalised the dispossession and guardianship of indigenous peoples who had no (western) concept of property with the same logic with which they rationalised the dispossession and guardianship of mad English colonists who had lost their mental capacity to govern their property. In ensuring that 'new' lands were being rationally organised, developed and inherited in the 'new world', where threats were being posed by 'savages' and mad colonists alike, lunacy investigation was an obvious colonial carry-over.[45]

This early colonial connection between those considered naturally dispossessed of their mental capacity of property ownership and self-governance, and colonists in need of the long-standing traditions of lunacy investigation law in the event that they became *non compos mentis*, has a corollary in more contemporary periods of psychiatry and madness in a variety of colonial contexts.[46] In an editorial analysis of some of this work, Megan Vaughan notes that 'in the new and burgeoning literature on the history of psychiatry and empire … we are continually returned to this theme: the analogy (or for some, homology) between the alleged madness of colonialism and the madness of the mad'.[47] In this analysis, Vaughan notes that 'colonialism's severely disruptive effects upon the societies in which it developed created individual and collective forms of madness, the imposition of Western notions of mental illness through the establishment of psychiatric institutions labelled traditional behaviours and cultural practices of indigenous peoples as mad, and these precedents created complex and, at times equally challenging post-colonial relationships between madness and psychiatry'.[48]

As Vaughan notes, for the most part, 'the existing literature on psychiatry and empire concentrates on the history of institutions. This not only reflects the influence of Michel Foucault on historians of colonialism, but also, more prosaically it reflects the availability of historical documentation. Institutions leave records; the day-to-day struggles of communities to deal with the problems raised by mental illness generally do not.'[49]

In its examination of surviving civil trial evidence in New Jersey, the research for this book allows for a reconstruction of such 'day-to-day' struggles. The book also places these examples within the context of structured responses to madness that predate the asylum by centuries. To be clear, this historical detail allows for an exploration of how New Jersey English white colonists (and their Dutch, Swedish and Finnish colonial predecessors whose offspring stayed on after English takeover) and, more especially, subsequent generations of their post-revolutionary kin, understood madness and how they responded to it day-to-day. By definition, the trial process that generated all of this extraordinarily rich evidence happened only when someone in New Jersey who was considered mad had some property at stake.

It was very unlikely that indigenous people during the period under study would have property under scrutiny in this manner. I have found no trial in which a member of the Lenape/Delaware First Peoples of the New Jersey region is the focus. This, as Peter Wacker states, is likely due to several factors resulting from two centuries of contact with Europeans:

> A major point of contention between European and aborigine was the notion of permanent individual land ownership. Whites attempted, with success, to alienate Indian lands permanently, quickly, and with as little expense as possible. Generous quantities of rum were made available, often technically illegally, to hasten the process and through liquor as well as the lack of resistance to European diseases, the Lenape began to decline in numbers. Land alienation and the increasing tide of whites also served to encourage most surviving Indians to leave for the west. Those who remained, even though a reservation of sorts was provided for them, were generally treated so badly that they left in a body in the early nineteenth century.[50]

The theoretical positioning of *non compos mentis* law as part of the justification for colonisation and the exercise of English imperial power over indigenous peoples did not mean that indigenous peoples in New Jersey would be subject to this law in a literal sense.[51] However, this did not preclude lunacy investigation law from playing its part in the broader ambit of Anglo North American colonialism.

Madness on trial: civil law and lunacy in a transatlantic world

This book takes a new approach to these historiographical considerations by developing a case study in the transatlantic history of madness with a focus on civil law. It elaborates the civil law's important role in the history of madness in England, the reconstitution of this law in English colonial settings and its development in the white settler society of New Jersey. This sustained view of madness in transatlantic context through the lens of civil law opens the door to reinterpretation. Chapter 2 of the book traces the history of lunacy investigation law from 1320 to 1890 in England. It demonstrates the longevity and the importance of this law. This legal overview is essential in order to illustrate how the law was structured and how it evolved over the centuries. The verdicts in these trials of *non compos mentis* were concerned with the mental incapacity to manage property and with the recognition of the need to appoint a guardian to keep personal and family property intact. The definition of madness was embedded in laws governing commissions of lunacy and guardianship. Included in this legal approach to madness was the appointment of someone who would oversee the care and management, as well as the material wellbeing, of those deemed to be *non compos mentis*. The law also provided for the restoration of control over property and person in cases where individuals could successfully convince the courts that they had regained their ability to control their property rationally. In this legal context, the response to madness was primarily concerned with providing for the rational control over property by removing it from the hands of those who risked compromising it through their irrational behaviour and, occasionally, by giving it back to those who had proved, some time later, that they could once more use it wisely. In this chapter, I argue that the development of lunacy investigation law for the preservation of property in the face of irrational behaviour was not incidental but, rather, central to the definition and response to madness for centuries in England. It was a socio-legal context for understanding and responding to madness that would eventually be situated in parallel with laws that signalled a growing emphasis on institutional confinement and inspection in England and, later, in parts of North America.

Through an exploration of the content of specific cases, Chapter 3 assesses how claimants, defendants and lawyers in lunacy trials and Lord Chancellors occasionally challenged the definitions of insanity embodied in lunacy investigation law. The cases in this chapter encompass individuals who, during the course of the trial, were considered to be on the borderlands of madness – that is, they were understood to be mentally 'weak' and/or 'incapable', but not necessarily *non compos mentis* enough to fit neatly into the laws related to commissions of lunacy. The chapter shows how legal struggles around these more ambiguous cases further shaped the definition of madness both inside and outside the courts. The decisions of judicial authorities, along with other peculiarities of the chancery court, enabled Lord Chancellors greater latitude for settling cases in lunacy that were at the boundaries of madness. However, legal authorities were also challenged by the circumstances of some cases – ones, for example that included physical debilitation, eccentric behaviour or the challenges of old age – which made clear verdicts difficult to determine. The testimony of families and of other witnesses with conflicting views of an individual's mental state further militated against clear-cut outcomes in these trials. An examination of these cases of indefinite mental state highlights the flexibility of lunacy investigation law. It also shows how legal authorities attempted, not always successfully, to shape the law to conform more closely to their legal outlook on madness.

Chapter 4 evaluates how families used lunacy investigation law as a strategic response to the unsettling circumstances created by the mad behaviour of their relatives. This included the management of the mad and their property, the safeguarding of inheritance and the regulation of marriage. The chapter shows how lunacy trials served as a powerful and enduring mechanism by which families of the mad attempted to reorder the disorganisation created by madness. However, the interventions of legal authorities in these trials, along with the competing interests of family members, did not always make the resort to lunacy investigation law as satisfying an option as families had hoped. On one level, the Lord Chancellors can be seen as the arbiters of this social and economic cohesion, the law of lunacy investigation being an imperfect legal instrument through which they attempted to impose their broad outlook. But these principles were at times inconsistent with the wishes of family members who often had more specific pecuniary interests in mind. As late as the early nineteenth century, the principle of the 'king's conscience' was still guiding Lord Chancellors' outlooks on these cases. More specifically, Lord Chancellors prioritised the protection and wellbeing of those deemed *non compos mentis*. This, they argued, had always been the responsibility of the law. The protection of those found insane through commissions of lunacy included maintaining the integrity of the lunatic's estate, but not always in ways that met the interests of individual family members.

Chapter 4 also shows how lunacy investigation trials highlight the relationships of gender and class in England in the eighteenth and early nineteenth centuries. While the structure of English law made women unequal participants in these trials, they were far from invisible. Women participated at these trials as the subjects of investigations and also as witnesses. At various trials they appeared as the appointed guardians of the person and, sometimes, of the estate of those found to be mad; as the victims of opportunistic men who took advantage of their mental weakness; and, occasionally, as opportunistic women who took advantage of the mental eccentricities of others. While men dominated these legal processes and, for the most part, retained more economic power in their outcomes, at least as the subjects of lunacy trials they could also find themselves in the unusually weak position of having lost their male identity as figures of power and authority. Indeed, the finding of *non compos mentis* and the attendant lunacy investigation and guardianship processes guaranteed for these men a loss of male privilege and power. Although the law structured family fortunes in gender-specific ways, trials in lunacy highlight how madness could both affirm and complicate conventional relationships between men and women.

Chapter 5 highlights the ways in which lunacy investigation law shaped the management and care of the mad in England. This chapter argues that lunacy investigation law was the oldest institution that was, in theory, invested in the care and management of madness in England. Built into the law was the principle that the outcome of the trial process was supposed to protect and safeguard the person and property of an individual considered to be mad. This was achieved by appointing a committee to take guardianship of the mad person, and another committee to take guardianship of his/her property. The legal assumption that the mad individual could eventually recover shaped the responses of legal authorities. The right of an individual found *non compost mentis* by lunacy trial to challenge and overturn this decision upon his/her mental recovery through a trial of traverse further attests to the assumptions about care and management upon which this law was based. Over the course of the eighteenth and early nineteenth centuries, in their attempts to uphold these principles of good management and caring, Lord Chancellors heavily influenced the course of the trials in a variety of ways in England. Sometimes the decisions of Lord Chancellors and other legal authorities were not in accord with the wishes of family members of the mad, whose motives were frequently at odds with the welfare and safekeeping of their mad relations. This tension between legal authority and families (and other acquaintances) over the course of trial processes frequently compromised the legal outcomes for those on trial for madness. Over the course of its long-standing influence, lunacy investigation law developed alongside a much wider context of understandings of and responses to madness. During the period that marks the focus of this chapter (1700–1830) mad-doctors and other medical practitioners were also forging their professional outlook on madness through the establishment of a mad-doctor profession and the creation of private madhouses. These mad-doctors, and other medical practitioners, also appeared as expert witnesses in some lunacy trials. In this chapter, the growth of lunacy investigation law is evaluated in relation to this broader professionalising medical context.

Chapter 6 begins with a consideration of how the transatlantic history of madness and civil law intersects with empire and colonialism in significant ways. Lunacy investigation law was seen as a suitable transplant into colonial settings such as New Jersey because this law fitted well with more general assessments of the role of law in the exercise of imperial power. The civil law of lunacy was, by definition, designed to test the mental state of those who were suspected of not being able to rationally manage either their property or themselves. It is no surprise, therefore, that during the first colonial era England sought to reproduce the law of lunacy investigation into its colonial settings, where a premium was placed upon the rational organisation of newly acquired property. The rest of Chapter 6 explains how this law was successfully ensconced in New Jersey, despite the region's tumultuous transformation from British colony to fledgling American state. The law of lunacy investigation was a very successful legal transplant, taking root in ways that could not have been anticipated by those who had shaped the law in England. In New Jersey, the law applied to a much broader socio-economic group. It served as a formidable regulatory, managerial and caring mechanism for madness. This democratisation of the application of lunacy investigation law enabled it to play a major role in the determination of madness, its management and treatment in nineteenth-century New Jersey long after the establishment of an asylum option there.

Much as in the case of England, lunacy trials were an essential vehicle by which families in New Jersey attempted to sort out the disruptions to property and social relationships created by their mad relations. Unlike the English case reports, the extensive collection of hand-written manuscript lunacy case files in New Jersey includes, in many instances, court recordings of witnesses' testimonies, many of which are long and descriptive. This allows for a more comprehensive analysis of the social dynamics of law and madness, which is the focus of Chapter 7. In New Jersey, lunacy investigation law provided a legal scaffolding upon which families and communities could build responses to the challenges of madness – scaffolding that was shaped by legal tradition inherited from England, by customary use of the law over time in New Jersey, by the decisions of legal officials and by the public. In many cases, it served as a means of protecting those individuals experiencing mental troubles. At the same time, it allowed their families to shore up interests that were being threatened by their troubled family members. In some cases, these interests were not shared, and the unresolved tensions among family and community members over property and control of the mad are plainly evident. Overall, however, lunacy investigation law served a regulatory function not unlike that found in its transatlantic cousin, albeit in a context that allowed it to thrive in ways that it could not in England.

Chapter 8 argues that lunacy investigation law largely shaped antebellum New Jersey's response to madness. As in England, the legal process was used in many cases to safeguard the interests of the insane by ensuring that funds would be available for long-term care, to minimise the exploitation of the insane and to provide for the possibility of legal recourse for those who recovered their sanity. In this chapter, the New Jersey records are mined for details about the relationship between lunacy investigation law and other aspects of the care and treatment of the insane. Witnesses' testimonies offer insight about the ways in which families cared for the mad at home, about the role of physicians and other caregivers and about other forms of rehabilitation established in the community. The focus here is on how these forms of care intersected with the civil law of lunacy. Lunacy investigation law was not just an important legal response to madness in New Jersey. Its long-standing influence at the legal and local levels knitted it tightly into the everyday understandings of and responses to madness in local communities in the state.

Chapter 9 probes the relationship between the well-entrenched legal process of lunacy investigation law – along with the customs of community care and understanding that revolved around it – and the lunatic asylum as it emerged as a purpose-built institutional response in New Jersey. A close reading of a sample of longer trials uncovers great detail about local views of the asylum and its role in the everyday decision making in the community about madness. These trials reveal a broad spectrum of attitudes toward the asylum – some negative, some ambivalent and some more positive. After its opening at Trenton in 1848, the New Jersey State Lunatic Asylum became an increasingly logical option to the difficulties posed by madness. Yet, the patient population of the new institution remained modest until the turn of the century. Moreover, patients who found themselves committed to the asylum in its early years were also subject to a range of alternative responses to madness. The detailed testimony of lunacy trials highlights the ways in which the asylum was integrated into the longer-standing civil law of lunacy, and into the customs of community management and care of the mad in New Jersey. This chapter also explains how the structure of lunacy investigation law was adapted in the mid-nineteenth century to the challenges posed by the asylum committal of individuals in difficult socio-economic circumstances. As the state's population grew and its economic base began to change, the relationship between the asylum and lunacy investigation law began to shift. While lunacy trials in their traditional form were still used in New Jersey (at least until as late as the 1893 trial of James B.) an alternative hybrid form of legal investigation into madness clearly signalled a change in the balance of legal and institutional responses in New Jersey. This hybrid legal mechanism, referred to as the 'order in lunacy', is examined and explained in order to consider the eclipse of lunacy investigation law in the later part of the nineteenth century.

Introduction

The civil law was of major importance in the consideration and determination of madness in the transatlantic world over several centuries. In fact, the power of civil law in the history of madness cannot be overestimated. Like any other formal regulatory mechanism, the civil law was entangled with prevailing attitudes about madness and the myriad responses to it emanating from medical, familial, community and broader cultural quarters. These entanglements, which are a focus of this book, serve as a reminder of just how complex the exercise of power in the face of madness can be. However, in order to begin to appreciate the complexities of civil legal power in the face of madness, the following chapter outlines the history of lunacy investigation law in England in broader strokes from 1320 to 1890.

Notes

1 New Jersey State Archives, Trenton (hereafter NJSA), Chancery Court, Lunacy Case Files (hereafter CC, LCF), Case of James B., 1893–8. The names of the subjects of court cases in lunacy have been made anonymous according to NJSA policy.
2 *Ibid.*
3 *Ibid.*
4 *Ibid.*
5 *Ibid.*
6 *Ibid.*
7 *Ibid.*
8 *Ibid.*
9 Suzuki, *Madness at Home*, p. 23.
10 *Ibid.*
11 Research into this legal colonial export, and its effects, is still in its infancy. However, it is clear that lunacy investigation law was operating in the North American colonies of Massachusetts, New York, New Jersey, Upper Canada (present-day Ontario), New Brunswick and Prince Edward Island. There is also evidence of an English version of lunacy investigation law operating in Jamaica, India and Australia. A French version of this law thrived in the colonial context of Quebec. For the law's importance in Quebec, see, A. Cellard *Histoire de la folie au québec de 1600 à 1850* (Montreal: Boréal, 1991).

12 A. Scull, *Museums of Madness: The Social Organization of Insanity in Nineteenth-Century England* (New York: St Martin's Press, 1979).
13 *Ibid.*, p. 34.
14 *Ibid.*
15 Similar analyses of the relationship between the family and the asylum can be found in other books written during the same period. See for example, K. Doerner, *Madmen and the Bourgeoisie: A Social History of Insanity and Psychiatry* (Oxford: Basil Blackwell, 1986), pp. 165–6, 71 and 291; D. Rothman, *The Discovery of the Asylum: Social Order and Disorder in the New Republic* (Boston: Little Brown, 1971), pp. 70–8, 120–2 and 127.
16 J. Walton, 'Lunacy in the Industrial Revolution: A study of asylum admissions in Lancashire, 1848–1850', *Journal of Social History*, 13.1 (1979).
17 *Ibid.*, 18.
18 *Ibid.*
19 R. Fox, *So Far Disordered in Mind: Insanity in California, 1870–1930* (Berkeley: University of California Press, 1978), p. 6.
20 *Ibid.*, p. 9.
21 *Ibid.*, p. 77.
22 M. Finnane, *Insanity and the Insane in Post-Famine Ireland* (London: Croom Helm, 1981), p. 166.
23 *Ibid.*, p. 168.
24 *Ibid.*
25 *Ibid.*, p. 17.
26 M. Finnane, 'Asylums, families and the state', *History Workshop Journal*, 20:1 (1985), 136.
27 N. Tomes, *A Generous Confidence: Thomas Story Kirkbride and the Art of Asylum Keeping, 1840–1883* (New York: Cambridge University Press, 1984), p. 123.
28 *Ibid.*, pp. 126–8. For a similar analysis see C. Warsh, *Moments of Unreason: The Practice of Canadian Psychiatry and the Homewood Retreat, 1883–1923* (Montreal: McGill Queen's University Press, 1989), pp. 64, 71 and 91 and Chapter 6, passim.
29 E. Dwyer, *Homes for the Mad: Life inside Two Nineteenth-Century Asylums* (New Brunswick: Rutgers University Press, 1987), pp. 6, 86–7, 97 and 116; J. Moran, *Committed to the State Asylum: Insanity and Society in Nineteenth-Century Quebec and Ontario* (Montreal: McGill Queen's University Press, 2000), pp. 99 and 140. See also the excellent study by Catharine Coleborne, *Madness in the Family: Insanity and Institutions in the*

Australasian Colonial World, 1860–1914 (Hampshire: Palgrave Macmillan, 2010).

30 R. Adair, J. Melling and B. Forsythe, 'Migration, family structure and pauper lunacy in Victorian England: Admissions to the Devon county pauper lunatic asylum', *Continuity and Change*, 12:3 (1997), 373–401; M-E. Kelm, 'Women, families and the provincial hospital for the insane, British Columbia, 1905–1915', *Journal of Family History*, 19:2 (1994), 177–93; G. Reaume, 'Mental hospital patients and family relations in Ontario, 1880–1930', in L. Chambers and E-A. Montigny (eds), *Family Matters: Papers in Post-Confederation Family History* (Toronto: Canadian Scholar's Press, 1998), pp. 271–87; P. D'Antonio, 'The need for care: families, patients, and staff at a nineteenth-century insane asylum', *Transactions and Studies of the College of Physicians of Philadelphia*, 12:3 (1990), 347–66; D. Wright, 'Family strategies and the institutional confinement of "idiot" children in Victorian England', *Journal of Family History*, 23:2 (1998), 190–208; M. Levine-Clark, 'Dysfunctional domesticity: Female insanity and family relationships among the West Riding poor in the mid-nineteenth century', *Journal of Family History*, 25:3 (2000), 341–61; P. Prestwich, 'Family strategies and medical power: "Voluntary" committal in a Parisian asylum, 1867–1914', *Journal of Social History*, 27:4 (1994), 799–818; A. Cellard and M-C. Thifault, 'The uses of asylums: Resistance, asylum propaganda, and institutionalization strategies in turn-of-the-century Quebec', in J. Moran and D. Wright (eds), *Mental Health and Canadian Society: Historical Perspectives* (Montreal: McGill Queen's University Press, 2006), pp. 97–117; D. Wright, J. Moran and S. Gouglas, 'The confinement of the mad in Victorian Canada', in R. Porter and D. Wright (eds), *The Confinement of the Insane, 1800–1965: International Perspectives* (Cambridge: Cambridge University Press, 2003), pp. 175–222; J. Parle, 'Family commitments, economies of emotions, and negotiating mental illness in late-nineteenth to mid-twentieth-century Natal, South Africa', *South African Historical Journal*, 66:1 (2014), 1–21.

31 See Suzuki, *Madness at Home*, pp. 41 and 64; D. Wright, 'The certification of insanity in nineteenth-century England and Wales', *History of Psychiatry*, 9:35 (1998), 267–90. Not all historians of madness have been pleased with these reinterpretations of the relationship between the family and the asylum. See, for example, A. Scull, *The Insanity of Place/The Place of Insanity: Essays in the History of Psychiatry* (London: Routledge, 2006), pp. 109–11; A. Scull, *The Most Solitary of Afflictions: Madness and Society in Britain, 1700–1900* (New Haven: Yale University Press, 1993), pp. 362–74.

32 The Morris Plains Asylum was opened in 1876, in part to help take pressure off the overcrowded conditions of the state's first asylum, the New Jersey State Lunatic Asylum, which opened its doors in 1848.
33 D. Wright, 'Getting out of the asylum: Understanding the confinement of the insane in the nineteenth-century', *Social History of Medicine*, 10:1 (1997), 137–55.
34 *Ibid.*, p. 152.
35 *Ibid.*, p. 155.
36 *Ibid.*, p. 144.
37 See the articles in P. Bartlett and D. Wright (eds), *Outside the Walls of the Asylum: The History of Care in the Community, 1750–2000* (London: Athlone Press, 1999). For similar conclusions, see the introduction to P. Horden and R. Smith (eds), *The Locus of Care: Families, Communities, Institutions and the Provision of Welfare Since Antiquity* (London: Routledge, 1998); A. Suzuki, 'Lunacy in seventeenth and eighteenth-century England: Analysis of Quarter Session records, Part I', *History of Psychiatry*, 2:8 (1991), 437–56; A. Suzuki, 'Lunacy in seventeenth and eighteenth-century England: Analysis of Quarter Session records, Part II', *History of Psychiatry*, 3:9 (1992), 29–44.
38 Suzuki, *Madness at Home*, p. 3.
39 T. Nootens, *Fous, prodigues et ivrognes: familles et déviance à Montréal au XIXe siècle* (Montreal: McGill Queen's University Press, 2007); R. A. Houston, *Madness and Society in Eighteenth-Century Scotland* (Oxford: Clarendon Press, 2000); J. Moran, 'The architecture of madness: Informal and formal spaces of treatment and care in nineteenth-century New Jersey', in L. Topp, J. Moran and J. Andrews (eds), *Psychiatric Spaces: Architecture and the Built Environment, 1600–2000* (Routledge, 2007), pp. 153–72; J. Moran, 'Asylum in the community: Managing the insane in antebellum America', *History of Psychiatry*, 9:34 (1998), 217–40.
40 Suzuki, *Madness at Home*, p. 2.
41 *Ibid.*
42 *Ibid.*, pp. 191–2, fn. 2.
43 This subheading is borrowed from the stimulating analysis in R. Keller, 'Madness and colonization: psychiatry in the British and French empires, 1800–1962', *Journal of Social History*, 35:2 (2001), 295–326.
44 D. Kirkby and C. Coleborne, 'Introduction', in D. Kirby and C. Colborne (eds), *Law, History, Colonialism: The Reach of Empire* (Manchester: Manchester University Press, 2001), p. 3.

Introduction

45 For one view of the extent to which a farmer's life in early America was bound up with legal affairs, see R. L. Bushman, 'Farmers in court: Orange County, North Carolina, 1750–1776', in C. Tomlins and B. Mann (eds), *The Many Legalities of Early America* (Chapel Hill: University of North Carolina Press, 2001), pp. 388–413.

46 This can be seen in a growing historiography that includes: W. Ernst, *Mad Tales from the Raj: The European Insane in British India, 1800–1858* (New York: Anthem Press, 1991); G. el-Khayat, *Une psychiatrie modern pour le Maghrib* (Paris: Harmattan, 1994); J. McCulloch, *Colonial Psychiatry and 'the African Mind'* (New York: Cambridge University Press, 1995); J. Sadowsky, *Imperial Bedlam: Institutions of Madness in Colonial Southwest Nigeria* (Berkeley: University of California Press, 1999); J. H. Mills, *Madness, Cannabis, and Colonialism: The 'Native Only' Lunatic Asylums of British India, 1857–1900* (New York: St Martin's Press, 2000); S. Swartz, 'Madness and colonial spaces: British India, c. 1800–1947', in L. Topp, J. Moran and J. Andrews (eds), *Madness, Architecture and the Built Environment: Psychiatric Spaces in Historical Context* (Routledge, 2007), pp. 215–38; J. Parle, *States of Mind: Searching for Mental Health in Natal and Zululand, 1868–1918* (Scottsville: University of KwaZulu-Natal Press, 2007); W. Ernst and T. Mueller (eds), *Transnational Psychiatries: Social and Cultural Histories of Psychiatry in Comparative Perspective c. 1800–2000* (Newcastle: Cambridge Scholars, 2010); M. Sloan and M. Vaughan, *Psychiatry and Empire* (Basingstoke: Palgrave Macmillan, 2007); L. Smith, *Insanity, Race and Colonialism: Managing Mental Disorder in the Post-Emancipation British Caribbean, 1838–1914* (Hampshire: Palgrave Macmillan, 2014); C. Coleborne, *Insanity, Identity and Empire: Immigrants and Institutional Confinement in Australia and New Zealand, 1873–1910* (Manchester: Manchester University Press, 2015).

47 Sloan and Vaughan, *Psychiatry and Empire*, p. 1.

48 Ibid., pp. 1–3.

49 Ibid., pp. 3–4.

50 P. Wacker, *Land and People: A Cultural Geography of Preindustrial New Jersey: Origins and Settlement Patterns* (New Brunswick: Rutgers University Press, 1975), p. 119.

51 Histories of the Lenape/Delaware peoples who inhabited what became the Colonies and State of New Jersey can be found in: C. A. Weslager, *The Delaware Indians: A History* (New Brunswick: Rutgers University Press,

1972); and Wacker, *Land and People*. For an innovative gender analysis of the Lenape in colonial contexts see G. Fur, *A Nation of Women: Gender and Colonial Encounters Among the Delaware Indians* (Pennsylvania: University of Pennsylvania Press, 2009). By the mid to late nineteenth century a more developed psychiatric analysis would posit that Native Americans, like indigenous peoples elsewhere, were less likely to become mentally ill, due to their relatively underdeveloped societies. See, A. M. Oda, C. Banzato and P. Dalgalarrondo, 'Some origins of cross-cultural psychiatry', *History of Psychiatry*, 16:2 (2005), 155–69.

2

Suing for a lunatic: lunacy investigation law, 1320–1890

In his compendious work on the state of English law and lunacy in 1890, lawyer Danby P. Fry observed that, technically, 'the law does not require that every lunatic should be brought necessarily under its control; in fact, it takes no cognisance of private lunatics until application is made on their behalf, unless they are dangerous to others, or are not under proper care'.[1] The law, Fry continued, left the mentally troubled 'to take care of themselves, or to be taken care of by their relatives or friends, until occasion arises for its active intervention'.[2] However, despite what was, in theory, an absence of obligatory legal intervention in this respect, Fry concluded that 'it is probable that, in consequence of the great attention which has been paid to this subject for some years past, a large majority of these afflicted persons are at present brought, in some way or other under legal supervision'.[3] Fry's observations are consistent with the work of several historians of madness and psychiatry who have described the wide array of legal protocols and institutional responses that together constituted a major intervention into the lives of mad people. This included the development of private madhouses, charitable hospitals with mad wards, a network of public asylums for the mad and a system of inspection of the mad by state-appointed lunacy commissioners, all of which entwined legal procedure with inspection, surveillance, management and care.[4]

According to Chris Philo, the legal origins of this identification of the mad for special consideration and treatment lay in the watershed 1714 Act for the More Effectual Punishment of Rogues, Vagabonds, Sturdy Beggars and Vagrants.[5] The significance of this law was that, for the first time, it made 'plain in national statute that certain categories of mad person should be removed from public space, the everyday streets of living and working, and transferred to set-apart secure places elsewhere'.[6] Philo sees the amendments to this statute thirty years later in the 1744 Justices Commitment Act as even more significant, in so far as they called for '"the reasonable charges of removing, and of keeping, maintaining and curing such person", thereby including "a small but possibly significant particular" which entailed "the first reference in legislation to treatment of the insane".'[7] According to Philo, the sequestering and treatment of the mad underwrite the significance of these two statutes, respectively, for they suggested an emerging consensus around modern trends of confinement and cure.

Yet the 1714 and 1744 laws are even more significant because, when examined in their entirety, both statutes represent a historical bridge between the emergence of an incipient tradition of institutional management (as Philo suggests) and a much older legal tradition of lunacy investigation and guardianship. The persistence of this older tradition can be seen in the last articles of both statutes, which read as follows:

> Provided always, That this Act, or any Thing therein contained, shall not extend, or be construed to extend to restrain or abridge the Prerogative of the King or the Power or Authority of the Lord Chancellor, Lord Keeper or commissioners of the Great Seal of Great Britain for the Time being ... touching or concerning such Lunaticks, or to restrain or prevent any Friend or Relation of such Lunaticks from taking them under their own Care and Protection; any thing in this Act contained to the contrary notwithstanding.[8]

What is significant about the last section of these laws is that they maintain the legitimacy, and in some respects the primacy, of the law of lunacy investigation (or commissions of lunacy), a long-standing body of law that stretched from the fourteenth century to the late nineteenth century, when Danby Fry published his book on *Lunacy Law*. That is why the Acts stipulate that the separation of the mad and their confinement in a secure place 'shall not extend, or be construed to extend to restrain or abridge the Prerogative of the King or the Power or Authority of the Lord chancellor, Lord Keeper or commissioners of the Great Seal of Great Britain for the Time being ...'. The prerogative of the king and the power of the Lord Chancellor referred to the royal and state powers related to a body of law that can be conveniently called *lunacy investigation law*. This body of law, shaped and qualified by commissions of lunacy (or lunacy trials), constituted a far older and long-standing understanding of, and response to, madness. It was a socio-legal framework for understanding and responding to mental incapacity that would eventually be situated in parallel with laws that signalled a growing emphasis on institutional confinement and inspection in England and, later, in parts of North America.

Furthermore, the last section of the Acts, which read, 'or to restrain or prevent any Friend or Relation of such Lunaticks from taking them under their own Care and Protection', speaks to a historical reality that spans both the earlier tradition of lunacy investigation law and the later trend towards institutional confinement. As Danby Fry acknowledged, it is likely that, until well into the nineteenth century, a great many people without means in England who were considered mad were kept at home and continued to live out their lives in the domestic and community spheres familiar to them. The role the law played in these cases, like the historical records we are left from which to reconstruct their lives and experiences, is limited or non-existent. Finally, the very last line in the two Acts which reads, 'any thing in this Act contained to the contrary notwithstanding', coming as it does just after the same Acts maintained that 'this Act, or any Thing therein contained, shall not extend, or be construed to extend to restrain or abridge' the powers of the Crown or of the Lord Chancellor, suggests the awkward juxtaposition of the impulse to confine certain forms of aberrant and threatening behaviour, the longer-standing legal traditions of lunacy investigation and the extra-legal traditions of family and community care for dependent relatives.

This chapter traces the history of lunacy investigation law – the legal tradition that was still being highlighted alongside other elements of the response to madness in the Acts of 1714 and 1744. It argues that the development of lunacy investigation law was central to the definition of and response to madness for those who were more economically privileged in English society.[9] This is not to say that *all* ideas of and responses to madness revolved around the laws of *non compos mentis*.[10] Nevertheless, as a body of law committed to the social organisation of madness that thrived for 500 years, lunacy investigation law needs to be considered as fundamental to the shaping of understandings of and responses to madness in English society. Madness was in large measure defined in this evolving body of law and in its practice, not according to specific medical symptoms or behaviours but, rather, according to the ability to govern one's property in a rational manner – in a way that preserved and/or expanded capital accumulation and that maintained the integrity of property inheritance. This law transitioned successfully, with modifications, from a feudal to a capitalist society in England, partly because it contributed to safeguarding the social relations of production and inheritance in both eras. The importance of lunacy investigation law is also apparent in the work of the Lord Chancellors during and after these trials. The laws relating to lunacy trials were refined and altered over the centuries. Equally important was an accumulation of perceived wisdom about madness, procedure and property that, by the nineteenth century, constituted a significant form of knowledge about madness and how to respond to it. Lord Chancellors' use of precedent, their intellectual opinions and their verdicts in cases of lunacy created an influential discourse on the nature of madness, its manifestations and its relationship to legal processes. Moreover, the content of the trials, including lay and medical testimony and the contributions of various legal authorities, linked lunacy investigation law with the everyday responses of English families to madness.

Origins and early history of lunacy investigation law

The law of lunacy investigation centred on three aspects of madness: the right of legal power over the person and estate of someone deemed a lunatic; the legal power to investigate if a rightful interest in a given property could be exercised; and the responsibility of guardianship over the person and property of the lunatic and his/her spouse and children. The Prerogativa Regis, a landmark document from the second half of the thirteenth century, vested authority over 'lunatics' and 'idiots' in the Crown. In a meticulously detailed PhD thesis on the subject, Richard Neugebauer explains that:

> As a result of its erroneous inclusion in collections of statutes, many legal authorities considered [the Prerogativa Regis] a genuine statute. Both [Anthony] Fitzherbert and [Edward] Coke viewed it as such, although the latter believed, too, that it declared the pre-existing common law. Prerogativa Regis was also the subject of numerous readings at the Inns of Court at the end of the fifteenth century.[11]

Neugebauer concludes that, 'As a consequence of these developments, its statements of the Crown's rights over the mentally disabled became the implicit legal framework within which much subsequent Court of Wards practice evolved.'[12] Crown representatives further developed this legal framework for the mad through to the mid-nineteenth century.

For 'idiots', the Prerogativa Regis read: 'The King shall have the Custody of the Lands of natural Fools, taking the Profits of them without Waste or Destruction, and shall find them their Necessaries, of whose Fee soever the Lands be holden. And after the Death of such Idiots he shall render it to the right Heirs, so that such Idiots shall not aliene, nor their Heirs shall be disinherited.'[13] For 'lunatics' the document stated:

> Also the King shall provide, when any (that beforetime hath had his Wit and Memory) happen to fail of his Wit, as there are many *per lucida intervalla*, that their Lands and Tenements shall be safely kept without Waste and Destruction, and that they and their Household shall live and be maintained competently with the Profits of the same, and the Residue besides their Sustentation shall be kept to their Use, to be delivered unto them when they come to right Mind; so that such Lands and Tenements shall in no wise be aliened; and the King shall take nothing to his own Use. And if the Party die in such Estate, then the Residue shall be distributed for his Soul by the Advice of the Ordinary.[14]

The Prerogativa Regis thus established the King's prerogative over the property of the mentally alienated, but it differentiated in important ways between those who were 'idiots' (alienated from birth and with no hope of mental recovery) and those who were 'lunatics' (alienated but with lucid intervals and thus capable of full mental recovery). According to Neugebauer, this differentiation was often, out of convenience, not recognised from the fourteenth to the sixteenth centuries, in order to increase the Crown's revenue.[15] However, with the creation of the Court of Wards in the 1540s, the separation between 'idiots' and 'lunatics' outlined in the Prerogativa Regis was more consistently followed.

At a broad remove, this differentiation can be seen as grounded in a feudal understanding of landownership. Those who were considered mentally incapacitated for life could not undertake their responsibilities to the king – responsibilities that, at whatever rank in society, were directly tied to the king's ownership of all lands and the feudal obligations of the king's subjects. In not being able to provide the king with services directly tied to his ownership of the kingdom's lands – be they rent or military service – the land was forfeited automatically to the Crown, the king thereby being responsible for the wellbeing of the subject in question. Prevailing wisdom also held that, as idiots did not have families and as there was thus no progeny to provide for, the King's rights over the idiot's land lasted for the lifespan of the individual. On the other hand, lunatics could recover, and so the king's hold over their property was more tenuous and potentially short term.[16]

Of course, whether the person in question was really an idiot or lunatic depended upon an evaluation based within the social context of the times. Jonathan Andrews offers an important extended discussion on the 'meaningfulness and coherence of the distinctions made between idiocy and insanity during early modern times',[17] which were at once cultural, legal and political. In order to more clearly ascertain the mental capacity of the individual in question, the Crown had the right to launch an inquisition. This power formed part of the Crown's authority to make an inquisition into property which it believed it had a right to in a variety of contexts, including inquisitions '*post mortem*, inquisitions as to escheat, … inquisitions as to treasure-trove [etc.]'.[18] Inquisitions in lunacy, then, were one expression among many of the Crown's powers to inquire into the extent of its authority over various forms of property. The feudal basis of the Crown's hold on land, including the land held by those who were mentally unsound, and the Crown's long-standing powers of investigation, marked the key general features of a lunacy investigation process that long outlived its feudal roots, remaining remarkably stable in England until the late nineteenth century.

This having been said, Neugebauer argues that 'the Crown's authority over lunatics and idiots was not tied directly to feudal principles'. Instead, this authority 'stemmed from the Crown's general right and duty, as *pater patriae*, to protect the person and property of individuals unable to care for themselves'.[19] Thus, Neugebauer observes, 'in theory' the Crown's authority in this regard applied to 'any and all mentally disabled persons in the realm', regardless of their property status.[20] This likely explains the numerous examples throughout this period of creative legal solutions to persons of more humble economic means where the resolution did not involve or require the full elaboration of lunacy investigation law.[21]

Despite the emergence of the Prerogativa Regis (which technically made the king solely responsible for the mentally incapacitated during the medieval period), the authorities in English boroughs with charters responded in two ways in order to preserve that authority for themselves. This was especially the case when chartered boroughs risked losing valuable economic resources to the prerogative of the Crown. Wendy Turner explains that 'in some areas such as Bristol, the idea of the "keeper" seems to have continued, with this guardian being in place, or at least chosen, prior to the death of the [mentally incapacitated] individual's parents'. Other cities 'updated their charters to include a similar claim as that of the king', thereby establishing themselves as the rightful guardians of the insane.[22] While this municipal authority over the insane was usually compatible with the charters granted by the Crown to English towns, it could sometimes result in major contests of authority when there was substantial property at stake. Turner's examples demonstrate the considerable lengths to which borough leaders were willing to go – for example, through arranged marriages and concealments – in order to avoid the interference of royal prerogative in matters regarding their mentally incompetent wealthy inhabitants.[23] In the fifteenth century this included a growth in families' use of wills in order to bypass mentally incompetent family heirs and thus avoid the interventions of the Crown.[24]

With the creation of the Court of Wards and Liveries, and the establishment of its jurisdiction over the mentally incompetent, the period from 1540 to 1646 saw a more systematised lunacy investigation law. Richard Neugebauer explains that this Court requested a formal petition to be sent to the Master of the Court identifying the petitioner, the individual suspected of insanity, an 'assertion' that the individual was mentally disabled and a request for a Court investigation.[25] This was referred to as 'suing for a lunatic'. The Master of the Court brought the petition to the Court Attorney, who 'drew up a warrant for a writ or a commission for a lunacy inquisition'.[26] Neugebauer argues that this process was expensive and also very public, thus drawing attention to the petition and raising the possibility of other petitioners competing for the privilege of profiting as guardian of the lunatic's estate. While concerned family members issued most petitions, several petitions arose from 'royal suitors' who were in it for profit, and from neighbours and friends with possibly mixed motives.

The next step in this process was for the chief county official of the Court of Wards, the 'feodary', to take charge of the investigation. The feodary called for a commission in the nature of a *writ de lunatic inquirendo* or *de idiota inquirendo*, depending on the case. These commissions included the involvement of a handful of commissioners who represented various interests in the investigation, and the establishment of a jury of at least twelve men. Both commissioners and jury members were required to live in the county of the alleged lunatic and to be propertied men of good standing. The trial was held in a public place and evidence was heard from family, friends, neighbours, local authorities and, occasionally, medical experts acquainted with the alleged lunatic.

If the individual was found *non compos mentis*, a committee was formed to establish guardianship of the lunatic and to issue a grant of responsibility over the lunatic's estate. While there could be more than one petitioner for guardianship and for the grant, the court preferred to select close family members who were not direct heirs and whose financial interests would not immediately benefit from the death of the mentally troubled individual. Guardianship and the establishment of the grant were accomplished through a set of covenants or obligations that the committee made to the Crown, and another set of covenants that the committee made to the mentally troubled individual and his/her family. These covenants were complicated; in theory, however, the main objective was to ensure the wellbeing of the lunatic and his/her family. While technically the Crown could profit in cases of idiocy, in which it had no obligations to an individual deemed mentally incompetent from birth, it could not profit in cases of lunacy, in which there was always the possibility that the lunatic might recover. As for the committee in charge of the grant and of the guardianship of the individual, profits were made largely through subtle manipulations in the accounts of the costs of maintenance of the person, estate and family of the mentally troubled. These accounts were calculated against the annual revenues brought in from the estate that the committee controlled. Most of the main features hammered out during the Court of Wards and Liveries' 100-year control over the process of lunacy investigation law became entrenched in England until the late nineteenth century, and in various British colonial jurisdictions (including New Jersey) from the eighteenth century to the end of the nineteenth century.

The case of Beverley v. Snow

For a number of reasons, what appeared to be a rather innocuous late sixteenth-century commission of lunacy turned out to be a reference point for hundreds of subsequent lunacy trials from the seventeenth to the nineteenth centuries. This was the 1598 case of Beverley v. Snow.[27] Part of the enduring influence of this case was no doubt the fact that it was Attorney-General Sir Edward Coke who compiled it. In his report of this case, Coke took the opportunity to convey lengthy explanations on several subjects relating to property, law and madness. The case itself examined the circumstances in which an individual who was considered *non compos mentis* could be held to account over a financial transaction. This led Coke to detail these varying circumstances, including *non compos mentis* caused by drunkenness, acts committed in a state of madness with lucid intervals and whether felony, murder or treason could be committed in a state of *non compos mentis*. However, the bulk of Coke's report was a treatise on the origins of, and differences between, the king's prerogatives over idiots and lunatics. Coke took great pains to argue that the king's prerogatives (and the limitations of his powers in cases of lunacy) were 'but a declaration of the common law' that preceded it.[28] This he did by linking the law as it stood in 1598 with the common law traditions as espoused by the renowned thirteenth-century English jurist Henry of Bracton with the work of Britton (likely an 'epitome' of Bracton's own work)[29] and with the work of the fifteenth-century judge Thomas Littleton.[30] Coke wanted to emphasise the spirit of the earlier common law that, he argued, had been embodied in the 1324 'statute' of prerogatives and that ensured that the 'King is bound to keep the said lunatic, his wife, children, and household, with the profits of the land, and without taking anything to his own use, but all to the use of [the] non compos mentis and his family, and all this to the intent that the King may provide, that he who wants reason shall not alien his lands, nor waste his goods.'[31] Coke insisted that 'if the King provides one to have care and charge, that he who is non compos mentis, and his family shall be maintained, and that nothing shall be wasted; or if one of his own head, takes so much upon himself, in this case he is but as bailiff of him who is non compos mentis, and shall be accountable as bailiff to him who is non compos mentis, or to his executors or administrators.'[32] Here we see the reaffirmation of the enduring tradition of guardianship in cases of *non compos mentis*.

Aspects of the structure of commission of lunacy law as envisioned by Edward Coke were, of course, subject to change over time. One change of major importance was the jurisdiction under which the control over the mad person's property and person was held. Originally, this royal prerogative fell under the jurisdiction of the Court of Exchequer; however, in 1540 it was vested in the new Court of Wards. The Court of Wards attempted to more effectively safeguard the property of the mad from profiteering by lords and courtiers who could, through their influence, obtain a grant of the profits made from the property of the mad that had been taken over by the Crown. Nevertheless, concern persisted as to possible abuses of royal prerogative; concern that was only partly resolved by the decision to entrust the person and property of idiots and lunatics to the Court of Chancery. According to H. R. Pope, this decision was a convenient one, as the Lord Chancellor embodied 'in himself many offices and jurisdictions relating or applicable to the insane'.[33] He controlled the Court of Chancery, from which 'the writs of attendance in matters of lunacy issued' from common law; he was 'keeper of the king's conscience, and therefore continued to direct and control the administration of the estate by the committee'; and he was 'a judge in equity, and could bring his ordinary jurisdiction to the help of his lunacy jurisdiction'.[34] As Akihito Suzuki notes, this by no means ended the corruption connected with the process of lunacy investigation.[35] Nevertheless, the control of lunacy investigation law by Chancery became permanent until 1890.

Just as the legal jurisdiction of lunacy investigation law changed over time, so too did the process of initiating an inquisition in lunacy. In the thirteenth and fourteenth centuries, the proceedings of an inquisition in lunacy investigation were initiated by a writ of petition. Escheators and sheriffs were usually responsible for making a preliminary inquiry into the property that might be controlled by a mad person or idiot, although commissions were sometimes formed for this purpose.[36] However, from the time of the Court of Wards and Liveries until the end of the nineteenth century, commissions became the predominant means of investigation, and petitions to initiate commissions were made by family and sometimes by acquaintances of suspected lunatics. If the commissioners deemed the petition worthy of further investigation, an inquisition was held in open court and the verdict of the inquisition was reached and sworn to by a jury of twelve propertied and respectable individuals. This process included witnesses' testimonies and, depending on his/her mental and physical state, an examination and questioning of the mad person. If a verdict of insanity was reached, it was then necessary to establish a committee of individuals to manage the mad person's estate and person. This included the appointment of one or more guardians who acted on behalf of the Lord Chancellor in the control of the estate, and the appointment of another guardian to ensure the wellbeing of the mad person. From the fourteenth century onwards, the committee was required to give security against a grant from the Crown. An account was established so that the committee could draw on the funds of the grant to pay for the maintenance of the mad individual, for the expenses of the inquisition and for other expenses related to the management of the mad person's property.[37] As several cases described in this book show, such a committee could abuse its relationship to the property of the mad individual. In other cases of seizure of property by the Crown, the right of *traverse* existed for those who wished to challenge the decision that had been made. The right of traverse was made legal in the mid-1500s, thus allowing challenges to verdicts of *non compos mentis*.[38]

By the time of the 1714 statute cited at the beginning of this chapter, a clear legal process had been built around the concept and practice of lunacy investigation. This entailed a petition and an investigation into the mental status of an individual by trial, with testimonials and, when possible, an examination of the alleged lunatic him/herself. In the case of a verdict of *non compos mentis*, a committee was established to appoint a guardian to maintain the property and person of the lunatic until such time as he/she was sufficiently recovered in mind to traverse the earlier decision. This required petitioning the Lord Chancellor and conducting another lunacy investigation to reverse the earlier decision.

Nineteenth-century changes to lunacy investigation law

By the early nineteenth century, although the essence of this process remained intact, it had become complicated by two factors. First, lunacy investigation law was increasingly influenced by other legal developments in the management of and response to madness. For example, the 1845 Act for the Regulation of the Care and Treatment of Lunatics, created 'a permanent national Lunacy Commission, with power to make detailed and frequent inspections of all types of asylums'.[39] The Asylums Act of 1845 'made the erection of county and borough asylums to house pauper lunatics compulsory'.[40] The legal statutes covering institutions and lunacy investigation also became very complex during this period, with the bureaucratisation of positions and functions related to the management of insanity. This began to alter significantly the process of lunacy investigation and its relationship to madness in England. For example, in 1833 the Lunatics' Visitors' Act was passed, giving the Lord Chancellor the power to appoint 'visitors' to visit at least once a year those found mad or idiotic by inquisition. The visitors made reports to the Lord Chancellor on the 'State of Mind and bodily Health, and of the general Condition, and also of the Care and Treatment of each such Person so found idiot, lunatic, or of unsound Mind who shall have been visited by him as aforesaid.'[41] The visitors consisted of two physicians, one lawyer and a secretary. All four were paid salaries out of the income from the estates of lunatics who had been found insane through lunacy inquisition. The accounts generated from all of these transactions were audited yearly in an effort to limit instances of financial abuse. The addition of a small army of clerks, officers and messengers working for the commissioners in lunacy increased the bureaucracy of lunacy inquisitions, and it elevated the costs (to the estates of the lunatics) required to salary the employees of this expanding government office. Further evidence of a more medical approach to the management of lunacy inquisitions can be seen in the fact that by 1844 it was general practice in England to have the initial petition for a commission in lunacy accompanied by affidavits from two or three physicians or surgeons, along with those from family and friends.[42]

The bureaucratisation of the laws governing lunacy investigation was (perhaps ironically) accompanied by efforts to make the process of the investigation itself faster. Under the 1853 Act for the Regulation of Proceedings Under Commissions of Lunacy, it was no longer necessary for a lunacy inquisition to include a full trial by a twelve-member jury if the Lord Chancellor deemed the case sufficiently obvious not to hold a trial. This resulted in a sharp reduction in expenses required for witnesses, juries and those hired to administer their work – savings that were largely countered by the appointment in the same Act of two full-time masters in lunacy who were each paid £2000 per year to take over the work formerly done by commissioners. The powers of the masters in lunacy (in the name of the Lord Chancellor) to make executive decisions in cases where they were certain about the mental state of the subject of lunacy inquisition also changed the nature of the legal process significantly. In such cases, witnesses' testimonials as to the mental state of an individual were no longer heard and evaluated in court. The public nature of such open court trials was also eliminated in those cases where the master felt that he could make the judgment himself.[43]

The process of lunacy investigation was further altered by the 1862 Amendment to the 1853 Act. This amendment made the commission of lunacy much more accessible by allowing petitioners of suspected lunatics whose property was valued at less than £1000 the option of applying to the Lord Chancellor directly, in order to avoid most of the costs of the process itself. This, of course, added to the power of the Lord Chancellor, while at the same time further reducing the public dimensions of the procedure. In a further Amendment in 1882, the required value of the property of the suspected lunatic to qualify for such a procedural 'short cut' was increased to £ 2000.[44]

The Act that altered the nature of lunacy investigation law the most was the Lunacy Act of 1890.[45] This Act, in effect, made the process of lunacy investigation through inquisition redundant by consolidating what had become overlapping legal jurisdictions in the determination of mental status in England. Prior to the 1890 Act, the legal procedure required to prove that a person was *non compos mentis* and thus not capable of governing him/herself or his/her property (the lunacy investigation), and the legal procedure required to prove that a person was insane and therefore requiring asylum committal, were completely separate. However, by 1890 it had become far more common to determine insanity through the legal process of asylum committal than through the legal process of lunacy inquisition. Moreover, it was possible for an individual to be committed to a private or public lunatic asylum because he/she was proven by law to be medically insane without actually depriving that individual of his/her right of control over his/her property. This inconsistency was addressed in the 1890 Act, by which an individual who was legally deemed mentally unsound through the process of asylum committal was also effectively deprived of control over his/her property when a judge granted the case 'an exemption from a commission of lunacy'. As Suzuki notes, 'commissions of lunacy were reduced to near extinction [in England] after the First World War'.[46] In effect, the legal process of asylum committal made lunacy investigation law largely redundant.

Conclusion

This chapter has explained the development of the law of lunacy inquisition, and it has indicated its importance, from a legal perspective, to the response to madness in England from the medieval period to the end of the nineteenth century. Although grounded in concepts of property and royal prerogative consistent with the fourteenth century, this legal process endured for several centuries, providing a basis for determining the mental capacity to manage person and property. This legal process also established a method of protecting property, and it provided some material stability for the individual found to be mad.

Crucial changes to this legal process reflected the desire to prevent its exploitation for financial gain by the public and by the Crown. More significantly, changes in the late eighteenth and the nineteenth centuries, involving an increasing emphasis on inspection, bureaucratisation and medicalisation, reflected the integration of a more institutional outlook on and response to madness in England. Throughout most of the nineteenth century, this legal process appeared flexible enough to accommodate these changes. However, by 1890 the weight of change in these respects was becoming too much for the structure of the law of lunacy investigation to bear.

As important as lunacy investigation law was in England, its significance in the colonial context of New Jersey was greater still. This was because, both in law and in practice, the lunacy investigation in New Jersey was used and adapted in ways that were not possible in England. This was partially the result of a relative paucity of institutional provision for the insane that endured from the colonial period in New Jersey until well into the nineteenth century. Lunacy investigation law also took on new meaning in New Jersey because of the very different social and economic circumstances that existed there. As we shall see later in this book, this relatively well-developed English legal procedure was adapted to colonial circumstances in ways that made lunacy investigation law even more powerful and influential. However, its introduction into the colonies made sense in the first place because it had already proved to be a reliable and long-standing response to madness in England. The following three chapters explore in greater detail how the development of lunacy investigation law shaped the response to madness in English society.

Notes

1 D. P. Fry, *Lunacy Law: The Statutes Relating to Private Lunatics: Pauper Lunatics: Criminal Lunatics: Commissions of Lunacy: Public and Private*

Asylums: And the Commissioners in Lunacy (London: Knight and Co., 1890), p. 2.
2 *Ibid.*
3 *Ibid.*
4 Some of the major works on these aspects of the history of madness include: J. Andrews and A. Scull, *Customers and Patrons of the Mad-Trade: The Management of Lunacy in Eighteenth-Century London: With the Complete Text of John Monro's 1766 Case Book* (Berkeley: University of California Press, 2003); P. Bartlett, *The Poor Law of Lunacy: The Administration of Pauper Lunatics in Mid-Nineteenth-Century England* (London: Leicester University Press, 1999); A. Digby, *Madness, Morality and Medicine: A Study of the York Retreat, 1792–1914* (Cambridge: Cambridge University Press, 1985); R. A. Houston, *Madness and Society in Eighteenth-Century Scotland* (Oxford: Oxford University Press, 2000); R. A. Hunt and I. McAlpine (eds), *Three Hundred Years of Psychiatry, 1535–1860: A History Presented in Selected English Texts* (London: Oxford University Press, 1963); W. Parry-Jones, *The Trade in Lunacy: A Study of Private Madhouses in England in the Eighteenth and Nineteenth Centuries* (London: Routledge and K. Paul, 1971); C. Philo, *A Geographical History of Institutional Provision for the Insane from Medieval Times to the 1860s in England and Wales: The Space Reserved for Insanity* (Lampeter: Edwin Mellen Press, 2004); R. Porter, *Mind-Forg'd Manacles: A History of Madness in England from the Restoration to the Regency* (Harvard: Harvard University Press, 1987); K. Jones, *Lunacy, Law, and Conscience, 1744–1845: The Social History of the Care of the Insane* (London: Routledge & K. Paul, 1955); Scull, *The Most Solitary of Afflictions*.
5 12 Anne c. 23, 1714.
6 Philo, *A Geographical History*, p. 177. It should be noted here that, according to the Act, this separation was restricted to those lunatics who were 'furiously mad and dangerous to be permitted to go abroad', a fact that Philo argues probably included 'any mentally disordered person found loose on the streets, dangerous or not'.
7 *Ibid.*, p. 179. Justices Commitment Act, 17 Geo. II, c. 5, 1744.
8 12 Anne, c. 23; 17 Geo. II, c. 5.
9 No attempt is being made here to write a comprehensive history of lunacy investigation law over the course of this extraordinarily long period. The subject begs further investigation that is beyond the parameters of this study. Rather, in this chapter I wish to establish that this body of law constituted a powerful force in shaping the history of madness in England

– a force that was no less influential but, in some ways, recast as it crossed the Atlantic and was established in North American colonial settings. For a history of how verdicts of *non compos mentis* were reached (rarely, from 1500 to 1700, and more frequently thereafter) in trials involving suicide, see M. MacDonald and T. Murphy, *Sleepless Souls: Suicide in Early Modern England* (Oxford: Clarendon Press; 1990), pp. 57–9 and 125–32.

10 The rich repertoire of religious, metaphysical and medical contexts of madness has been explored by many, including M. MacDonald, *Mystical Bedlam: Madness, Anxiety, and Healing in Seventeenth-Century England* (Cambridge: Cambridge University Press, 1981); J. Andrews, 'Begging the question of idiocy: The definition and socio-cultural meaning of idiocy in early modern Britain', *History of Psychiatry*, 9:33 (1998), 65–95, and his second article with the same title: J. Andrews, 'Begging the question of idiocy: The definition and socio-cultural meaning of idiocy in early modern Britain', *History of Psychiatry*, 9:34 (1998), 179–200; Porter, *Mind Forg'd Manacles*; Andrews and Scull, *Customers and Patrons of the Mad-Trade*; Houston, *Madness and Society in Eighteenth-Century Scotland*.

11 R. Neugebauer, 'Mental Illness and Government Policy in Sixteenth and Seventeenth Century England' (PhD dissertation, Columbia University, 1978), p. 12.

12 *Ibid.*, pp. 12–13.

13 *De Prerogativa Regis*, 17 Edward II, stat I (1324).

14 *Ibid.*

15 Neugebauer, 'Mental Illness and Government Policy', p. 17.

16 *Ibid.*, pp. 69–70.

17 J. Andrews, 'Begging the question of idiocy, Part I'. See also Andrews, 'Begging the question of idiocy, Part 2'.

18 G. Pitt-Lewis, R. Smith and J. A. Hawke, *The Insane and the Law: A Plain Guide for Medical Men, Solicitors and Others* (London: Sweet and Maxwell, 1895), p. 71.

19 Neugebauer, 'Mental Illness and Government Policy', p. 23.

20 *Ibid.*

21 Neugebauer notes that as early as the sixteenth century, 'An eschaetor might hold an inquisition on his own initiative without any Chancery writ, the resulting process being known as an inquisition *virtute officii*. Such inquisitions were extremely common in pre-1540 disability jurisdictions. At the end of Henry VIII's reign, however, a statutory effort was made to limit them to lands worth 5L or less per annum.' Neugebauer, 'Mental Illness and

Government Policy', p. 39. See also M. McGlynn, 'Idiots, lunatics and the royal prerogative in early Tudor England', *Journal of Legal History*, 26:1 (2005), 1–24. Efforts to find creative legal solutions to humble petitioners persisted into the nineteenth century.
22 W. J. Turner, 'Town and country: A comparison of the treatment of the mentally disabled in late medieval English common law and chartered boroughs', in W. Turner (ed.), *Madness in Medieval Law and Custom* (Boston: Brill, 2010), p. 22.
23 *Ibid.*, p. 35.
24 *Ibid.*, pp. 35–7.
25 The following description of the Court of Wards is based on Chapter 2, 'Court Procedure', of Neugebauer, 'Mental Illness and Government Policy', pp. 30–86.
26 *Ibid.*, p. 33.
27 76 E.R., Beverley's Case of Non Compos Mentis, 1598, pp. 1118–27.
28 *Ibid.*, p. 1124.
29 In Beverley's Case, Coke refers to Britton as if he is a distinct person.
30 See A. K. R. Kiralfy, *Potter's Historical Introduction to English Law and Its Institutions* (London: Sweet and Maxwell Limited, 4th edn, 1958), pp. 282–6.
31 76 E.R., Beverley's Case of Non Compos Mentis.
32 *Ibid.*, p. 1126.
33 H. M. R. Pope, *A Treatise on the Law and Practice of Lunacy* (London: Sweet and Maxwell, 1890), p. 29.
34 *Ibid.*
35 Suzuki, *Madness at Home*, p. 20.
36 Pope, *A Treatise on the Law and Practice of Lunacy*, pp. 47–8.
37 *Ibid.*, 117.
38 2 & 3 Edw. 6, c. 8; Pope, *A Treatise on the Law and Practice of Lunacy*, p. 76. See, for example, 22 E.R., Sir Geoffrey Palmer, the King's Attorney General, on the Behalf of Jerome Smith, a Lunatick, against Sir Robert, 1688, p. 719.
39 8 and 9 Vict. c. 100. A. Scull, *The Most Solitary of Afflictions*, p. 165.
40 8 and 9 Vict. c. 126. *Ibid.*, p. 165.
41 3 & 4 Wm. IV, c. 36. A long description can be found in J. Elmer, *An Outline of the Practice in Lunacy under Commissions in the Nature of Writs de Lunatico Inquirendo* (London: V. & R. Stevens and G. S. Norton Publishers, 1844), pp. 263–70.

42 Elmer, *An Outline of the Practice in Lunacy*, p. 1.
43 16 & 17 Vict. c. 70. The end of jury-based lunacy trials formed part of a broader 'decline of civil jury trial' in England. See C. Hanly, 'The decline of civil jury trial in nineteenth-century England', *Journal of Legal History*, 26:3 (2005), 253–78.
44 25 & 26. Vict. c. 86.
45 53 Vict. c. 5.
46 Suzuki, *Madness at Home*, p. 22.

3

Indefinite mental states: negotiating the legal definition of madness

An examination of English trials in lunacy between the early seventeenth and early nineteenth centuries demonstrates how the basic principles of lunacy investigation law were put into practice. Not surprisingly, as increasing numbers of lunacy trials took place there were significant nuances to the general outline of the process that had developed from the fourteenth to the eighteenth centuries. These were the products not only of the legislative changes described in the last chapter but also of the particular circumstances of the given trials, of the positions put forth by the claimants and defendants and of the reasoning of the Lord Chancellors in each case. Moreover, it is clear that Lord Chancellors (and other lawyers in the trials) drew increasingly on the precedent of past cases to create a storehouse of tradition upon which to make their arguments. This, of course, was much like the process for any other field of law. But, in the case of lunacy trials, this process contributed to the creation of a complex understanding of and response to madness. The trial process tied madness to specific mental states, to issues of legal guardianship, to the principles of property ownership and to perceptions of familial and state responsibility over the mad. Finally, in their sometimes lengthy explanations of how the process of lunacy law worked in relation to the official rule of law, Lord Chancellors helped to define madness and to shape the socio-legal response to it.

In order to explain more thoroughly how the historical development of the commission of lunacy contributed to the definition of and response to madness in England, the following chapters analyse lunacy trials in relation to central issues of contemporary concern. The current chapter assesses how the trials' claimants, defendants, lawyers and Lord Chancellors occasionally challenged the definitions of insanity embodied in lunacy investigation law. Several of these cases dealt with individuals who, during the course of the trial, were considered to be on the borderlands of madness – that is, they were considered mentally 'weak' and/or 'incapable', but not necessarily *non compos mentis* enough to fit neatly into the laws related to commissions of lunacy. Legal struggles among relations of the mentally troubled and, occasionally, between family members and opportunistic individuals who took advantage of mental weakness to exploit the lunacy investigation further shaped the definition of madness inside and outside the courts. Throughout the period under study, legal and social definitions of madness retained a flexibility that reflected the peculiarities of each case under consideration by lunacy investigation law. In several of these trials Lord Chancellors exercised their discretionary powers in order to influence the process and outcomes of the trial process.

Lunacy law on the borderlands of madness

The case of Sir John Leigh dramatically highlights the difficulties that the borderlands of madness could pose.[1] This trial pitted the heirs of John Leigh's estate (his two nieces, Mary Bennett and Ann Spencer) against William Vade, who had convinced Leigh to give him legal control over Leigh's very large estate – located in the counties of Surrey and Kent and worth £2500 annually. According to the case report, Vade, who was a surgeon and apothecary, attended to John Leigh and, realising that he was both physically and mentally infirm as well as very wealthy, hatched a complicated scheme to bring Leigh's property under his control.

Part of the plan was to arrange a marriage between Leigh and Vade's sixteen-year-old daughter. This Vade accomplished with the help of another surgeon, Mr Douglas. In 1733, on the pretext of taking Leigh to a christening, the two doctors took him to Mr Gheton, a 'colour-man's in Long-Acre', who proceeded to get Leigh drunk on 'punch'.[2] During Leigh's drinking session with Gheton, Vade and Douglas found a 'Fleet parson' who was willing to perform the marriage ceremony. At this point, one of Leigh's servants who 'used to attend constantly on Leigh's person' was 'sent away with other servants, to an alehouse'.[3] With no objecting witnesses, Leigh was married to Vade's daughter, after which they moved into Leigh's residence at Addington and Vade began to take over control of Leigh's business affairs.

As Vade worked to increase his control of Leigh's fortune, Leigh's two niece heirs fought back by petitioning for a commission of lunacy. Their aim was to prove that their uncle had been mad at the time of signing over his property to Vade. However, the trial that was held in 1733 did not work in their favour, as Leigh was not found to be incapable of managing his affairs. According to the Lord Chancellor of a subsequent trial, this was largely because, between the petition and the trial, Vade coached Leigh heavily on what questions to expect and how to answer them. During the 1733 trial witnesses also expressed confidence that Leigh was 'an excellent scholar who understood classical authors and figures' and that he was thus surely able to manage his property and person.[4] Shortly after 1733 another lunacy commission was brought forth, and the trial that ensued also failed to find Leigh *non compos mentis*. In the lead-up to this trial, the Lord Chancellor was of the opinion that Vade had spread rumours to Leigh's neighbours (and his servants who had a vested interest in the outcome of the trial) that the trial had been issued to deprive Leigh of his property at the hands of conniving relations. As a result, trial witnesses were only too willing to testify as to Leigh's mental competence, and this made Leigh increasingly sceptical of the intentions of his relatives.

During the same period that these trials were taking place, Vade was manoeuvring for a more complete consolidation of Leigh's wealth. On the domestic front, he intercepted mail addressed to Leigh from relations potentially hostile to Vade's interests, set up a 'watchman' upon 'Windmill Hill to see when any coach was coming ... to exclude any intercourse between the heirs at law and Sir John Leigh,'[5] and instructed the family servants not to admit relatives onto the premises. Vade also continued to take advantage of Leigh's fondness for alcohol, drinking with him late into the night while discussing how he might better manage his property. From a legal standpoint, Vade took great care to disinherit Leigh's relations. Vade became sole executor of Leigh's will, having the whole estate 'settled and conveyed' to three men and their heirs for life. Vade himself took over control of Leigh's estates in Kent and Middlesex. He signed over Leigh's estate in Surrey to Francis Leigh (apparently of no relation to Sir John) and Frances Jones. More ingeniously (and deviously, according to the Lord Chancellor), Vade constructed a complicated proviso enabling Leigh to revoke his will at any time, but only by having his proposed changes attested to by three men unknown to Leigh who lived in three different parts of England. According to the Lord Chancellor, this power of revocation was 'of the most extraordinary nature ever met with', and designed to 'pin' Leigh 'down' completely, while at the same time avoiding possible legal objections to the settlement. It was not until the third commission of lunacy, well over ten years after the original machinations, that Vade's legal workings were 'set aside and the estate conveyed to the heirs at law'.[6]

The case of John Leigh highlights the social and legal ambiguities of eighteenth-century madness. Clearly frustrated by the outcomes of the first two lunacy trials, in his report on the third trial the Lord Chancellor pointed out several examples that, to him, demonstrated Leigh's obvious mental incapacity. First, he argued that 'if he had been a man of any sense' Leigh would 'not have submitted to' the 'governance' of Vade and his compatriots. Another 'great sign' of Leigh's 'weakness and incapacity' was evidenced by the fact that Vade convinced him to amputate badly infected toes by telling him that they would grow back again. Leigh's marriage to Vade's daughter was, according to the Lord Chancellor, another 'proof of weakness'.[7] As for those witnesses who thought Leigh to be mentally competent because of his great learning, the Lord Chancellor cautioned:

> [It] often happens, that people *non compos*, or if not so yet very weak, may retain some things or pieces of learning which have been taught them in their youth, and yet the same people be incapable of remembering facts or new incidents; and you may go into Bedlam and meet with people who will talk Latin and impose upon some such witnesses as these.[8]

Finally, it was clear to the Lord Chancellor that Leigh had been mentally unstable for many years before his more recent round of troubles. In the preamble to Leigh's case, he noted that when Leigh had married years earlier, 'he and his affairs were under the entire governance of [his son in law] Sir Stephen [Leonard], and that after his decease he fell into the management of Sir Samuel Leonard[,] his son'.[9] When Sir John Leigh's son reached the age of twenty-one, he took over guardianship of his father for nine years. After the death of Leigh's son, 'Sir John's well-wishers were so sensible of his weakness, that several neighbouring gentlemen were solicited to take upon themselves a kind of voluntary trust and custody of his affairs'.[10] It was at this point that Leigh became vulnerable to William Vade's control.

Here was a set of actions that, in defying the rational behaviour of a man of Leigh's rank and station, made it clear to the Lord Chancellor that this was a case of madness, or at the very least a mental weakness so great as to require the careful guardianship by next of kin. The witnesses who argued sincerely against Leigh's mental weakness were simply 'mistaken in judgement'. Yet, as the Lord Chancellor pointed out, part of the problem in this case was that 'the boundaries between an *actual insanity* and *great mental weakness* are but very narrow'.[11] In his opinion, Leigh was, at the end of the day, not so much insane as physically and mentally compromised to the point that he required the sound judgement of others to properly maintain his person and property.

Despite the social and legal ambiguities in the definition and understanding of madness revealed in cases like that of John Leigh, Lord Chancellors attempted to manage commissions of lunacy in order to bring the definition of madness into line with the rational management of private property. In the report of the third trial, one can see the efforts of the Lord Chancellor to bring Leigh's ambiguous state of mind more clearly into conformity with legal procedure through deliberation and argument. Although reluctant to find Leigh outright mad, the Lord Chancellor went to great lengths to explain how a man as mentally unstable as Leigh was vulnerable to abuse. Towards the end of the report, the Lord Chancellor relied on precedent to more clearly situate Leigh's case at the centre of England's laws relating to commissions of lunacy. Vade's lawyers had tried to argue that Leigh's case was no different to that of the Duke of Albemarle who was sent off to be Governor of Jamaica. Before his departure, the Duke agreed to a power of revocation that seemed even more restrictive than the one pertaining to John Leigh. But, upon investigation, the Lord Chancellor argued 'in that case, that the deed was made between relations of the family, and that it was drawn up by Sir Thomas Stringer, the family counsel, by the direction of the Duke himself', whereas in the 'the present case, … the present settlement is not made to relations or people of the family, no counsel advised upon it, and no instructions given for it by Sir John Leigh'.[12] The Lord Chancellor then outlined two other cases where settlements seemed to have been obtained from mentally unstable individuals under questionable circumstances. But, in the one case (Standard v. Metcalfe), Barbara Standard appears to have made an almost identical will 'when she was in her senses'. It was therefore considered legitimate. In the other case (Topp v. Stanhope), 'where a mother got her son, Sir John Topp into her power', his will was 'set aside' in the Court of Chancery. In the Lord Chancellor's opinion, 'the evidence of the weakness of Sir John Topp, and the power and government of the mother and brother-in-law, was not one-tenth so strong as in the present case'.[13]

The power of Lord Chancellors in matters of lunacy law

Aside from exercising their powers of persuasion through deliberation and argument to reason their way through indefinite cases of madness, Lord Chancellors exploited the flexibility of lunacy investigation law, and their discretionary powers, in order to protect those individuals who they thought deserved it. One can see this flexibility in the case of Earl Ferrers, who, in May 1730, petitioned to supersede a commission of lunacy that had found him to be a lunatic.[14] In defence of this petition, his physician, Dr Monro (of Bethlem Hospital), testified that Ferrers had recovered and had been in a sane mental state for four or five months. The chances of a relapse, Dr Monro argued, were unlikely because Ferrers 'was greatly afraid of running into any excesses, which might bring on a return of his disorder', a self-awareness that 'physicians always looked upon as a very good symptom'.[15] Ferrers' sister, Lady Betty Shirley, also considered her brother to be once more in his right mind. But Lawrence Shirley, the Earl's brother and also the committee of his estate, was more dubious of Ferrers' mental state. Relying on the testimony of physicians who cared for Ferrers before the attendance of Monro, Lawrence Shirley noted that Ferrers was found to be a lunatic with lucid intervals and that he continued to be so. He pointed out that 'a surgeon and apothecary, who formerly attended [Ferrers] made affidavit, that after a salivation by Doctor Hale, he had enjoyed his senses for a longer period of time, and yet relapsed', becoming 'incurable'.[16] Some time later, Dr Lewis managed to pull Ferrers into a 'sanity of mind for several months after a violent fever, and yet his distemper returned'.[17] Under these circumstances Lawrence Shirley requested that the petition to supersede the commission of lunacy be suspended 'till after the fall of the leaf to see whether his recovery was perfect or not'. Drawing on the precedent of an earlier case (that of 'Mr Vincent'), the Lord Chancellor agreed that the petition of '*supersedeas*' should be suspended until the new round of petitions before '*Michaelmas* term', but that in the meantime the Earl 'should have his full liberty'.[18]

Cases like that of Earl Ferrers conjure interesting speculation. It is possible that Ferrers' sister was in conflict with her brother about Ferrers' state of mind and she was therefore willing to support his petition of *supersedeas* against the wishes of her other brother. As the committee of his brother's estate, Lawrence Shirley would not, by law, have been the committee of his brother's person. In England, such a dual role was seen by the courts as an obvious conflict of interest. Lady Betty Shirley might have been appointed guardian of her brother's person (the case report does not specify this), but even if she was not it is likely that as his closest female relative she was responsible for organising the care of her insane brother. In this capacity, she could easily have developed a different opinion of Ferrers' state of mind to that of her brother. This may account for the succession of physicians that were called into his attendance. Monro's contradictory testimony also suggests a divergence of medical opinion about Ferrers' mental state. Finally, this case may have been further complicated by conflict between Lawrence Shirley and Betty Shirley in securing their respective stakes in the property of their wealthy insane brother. In any case, the Lord Chancellor's decision suggests that the judges could adapt the law to fit the circumstances of the case as they saw it. Although Ferrers' quest for a clean bill of mental health was delayed, he was granted his freedom of action until that time. Although this decision does not fall neatly within the letter of the law, it was within the powers of the Lord Chancellor to establish such a compromise.

This kind of innovation in the decisions of the Lord Chancellors relating to those found on the borderlands of madness was in great measure the result of the interplay of the social dynamics of actual cases, of the laws that structured lunacy trials and of the use of precedent as a tool of interpretation. The result was a kind of legal dialogue on the ambiguities of insanity that was threaded through the reports on the trials. It is possible to trace this thread running through the cases of Lord Donegal, Ann Kendrick, Henry Cranmer, Kitty Sherwood and Ann Goodwin. In the case of Lord Donegal, the Lord Chancellor noted that a commission of lunacy had been issued against him in 1750 but that, after a personal examination by the Lord Chancellor, it did not appear that he was insane.[19] According to the Lord Chancellor, when Donegal was examined, 'he gave very rational answers' to questions about the financial prospects for his estates in England and Ireland, but 'not to any questions touching figures, as to which he could not answer the most common'.[20] Nevertheless, in the Lord Chancellor's opinion this did not justify a commission of lunacy. A second attempt at a commission of lunacy was made in June 1751, but this too was unsuccessful. What is important in this case for our purposes is how the Lord Chancellor interpreted the law in relationship to the specific mental state of Lord Donegal. 'In the present case', he noted, 'I allow, Lord Donegal is of very weak understanding and of no resolution of mind: but that is not sufficient for me whereon to ground a commission. If I was to grant any it must be that of idiocy: for no time is mentioned, when he was of better understanding.'[21] The Lord Chancellor then argued that lunacy trials were called for in cases of lunacy clearly defined as a 'distemper occasioned either by disorders or accident'. At one point, he continued, the definition of lunacy for the purposes of guardianship was 'enlarged and extended to one who is *non compos mentis*'. But that was the limit to which the definition extended and 'therefore though a jury finds, that one is incapable of managing his affairs, yet such a finding is not sufficient, but they must expressly find him to be of unsound mind'.[22] Although admitting that 'it may be very difficult to draw the line between such weakness, which is the proper object of relief in this court, and such as amounts to insanity',[23] the Lord Chancellor nevertheless argued that commissions of lunacy that do not bring out clear cases for the insanity of the accused must be rejected. Finally, he concluded that this strict definition for the issuing of commissions of lunacy did not 'exclude from relief' a will or deed that had been obtained through connivance.

Over the course of the next fifty years, prevailing legal wisdom changed considerably. In his attempt to explain his decision in the 1802 case of Ann Kendrick, Lord Chancellor Eldon took care to explain how attitudes towards the law had evolved. Much like Lord Donegal, Ann Kendrick had a commission of lunacy issued against her, but it was rejected by the jury, which 'proceeded on upon the notion, that this commission could only be applied to a case of actual insanity'.[24] This perception Eldon attributed to cases like that of Lord Donegal and William Barnsley, wherein juries had acted according to the strict letter of the law. However, Eldon noted:

> Of late the question has not been, whether the party is absolutely insane: but the Court has thought itself authorised (though certainly many difficult cases with regard to the liberty of the subject occur upon that), to issue the commission, provided it is made out, that the party is unable to act with any proper and provident management; liable to be robbed by any one; under that imbecility of mind, not strictly insanity, but as to the mischief calling for as much protection as actual insanity.[25]

Eldon had in mind cases of mental exhaustion from hard work over a long period of time, of mental incompetence brought on by epilepsy and of insanity brought on by alcoholic intoxication. In the case of Ann Kendrick, Eldon was convinced that, although she was not strictly insane, 'some care should be thrown around her'. Eldon's solution was to have two physicians who were not previously connected to her care, or involved in her previous lunacy trial, to gather evidence from friends and family and to interview Kendrick 'without alarming her; for the purpose of determining whether her state of mind is competent to the management of her affairs'.[26] He did not want to subject Kendrick to the rigours of another lunacy trial, but he was convinced that this less formal physicians' scrutiny would find her mentally incompetent, although not insane. Although acknowledging that 'Lord Hardwicke would not have gone so far', Eldon argued that this had been the trend in such cases for some time, and that he felt 'a strong inclination to maintain it' until legislative changes could clear up the situation.[27]

Five years later, the case of Henry Cranmer strongly indicated that much confusion remained about individuals on the borderlands of insanity. In this case, Cranmer himself contested the commission of lunacy that had been issued against him by his next of kin. Cranmer's legal counsel exploited the legal ambiguities that Lord Chancellors Eldon and Hardwicke admitted were in evidence in such cases, arguing that Cranmer's mental state did not fall neatly into definitions of lunacy that were fixed. They argued that 'Words denoting mere weakness of mind, upon which there may be different judgements, cannot be substituted for lunacy, or unsoundness of mind; which latter description has by usage obtained a legal, technical, import.'[28] In support of the commission of lunacy against Cranmer, the influential Solicitor General Romilly agreed that, since Lord Hardwicke's day, commissions of lunacy had been used in cases where the state of lunacy had been harder to define as a way of protecting individuals and their property from danger. Nevertheless, Romilly and his fellow lawyers argued that: 'The law is surely in a most inconvenient state if the party is entitled to protection under circumstances, that are not permitted to appear upon either the Commission or the Inquisition; and the Jury are placed under a necessity of saying upon their oaths that, which they cannot say consistently with truth.'[29]

In his report on Cranmer's case, Lord Chancellor Thomas Erskine argued that an Act of Parliament would help to resolve these legal difficulties by allowing cases like that of Cranmer to be decided outside of the jurisdiction of the commission of lunacy. Erskine noted: 'A man [like Cranmer] may have passed a great and illustrious life; and by the course of nature his faculties may decay; so that he may not be fit either to govern himself or his affairs.' 'It is unseemly', Erskine continued, 'that he should be put upon the footing of a lunatic: and that a Commission should issue in the ordinary course.'[30] Erskine, like some of his Lord Chancellor predecessors, seemed to be advocating for a kind of third tier in the legal repertoire of responses to madness. There already existed laws empowering justices of the peace to round up the vagrant insane for safe keeping, expenses chargeable to the appropriate parish. There were also commissions of lunacy for those more wealthy individuals who were mad or idiotic. In addition, Erskine and other Lord Chancellors seemed to be advocating a legal option that spared wealthy and intelligent men who had lost their mental faculties from the indignities of madness. This anxiety about putting these men through the regular legal process likely stemmed from the loss of male authority and power that men suffered from the trial process and from verdicts of *non compos mentis*. This 'emasculinisation' and its wider implications are discussed in detail in the following chapter.

For Erskine, the commission of lunacy also served as too blunt an instrument, not appreciating mental states that, although not completely insane, nevertheless were debilitating enough to warrant the protection of the court. In order to strengthen his own argument, Erskine drew from the wisdom of Sir Edward Coke, the early modern legal authority cited in Chapter 2. Quoting at length from Coke's commentary on fifteenth-century judge Thomas Littleton, Erskine noted that 'non compos mentis' was used by these early authorities to express 'the sure term' for one who had become 'of no sound memory'. This was someone 'not born without reason [like an idiot]; but, who has lost it from sickness, grief, or other accident'. It was not someone 'who has sometimes understanding, and sometimes not', as in the case of a lunatic with lucid intervals. Erskine thought that such individuals like Cranmer who had 'survived the period that Providence has assigned to the stability of his mind' were entitled to protection, but that they did not fit well into the existing laws. Evidently, for Erskine, the issue of precision was at the heart of the matter. Inquiry could certainly discover the existence of a disorganised mind, but, he stated, 'you cannot enter into the mind to know, by what means it is disorganised'.[31]

Expressing sympathy for Eldon's decision to avoid calling another commission of lunacy in the case of Ann Kendrick (cited above), Erskine ordered that a *Melius Inquirendum* (a writ commanding further inquiry) be issued to inquire further into Cranmer's ability to govern himself or his affairs. But, as this form of inquiry had never been used in cases of lunacy, and had in fact been denied in a previous case, Erskine was forced to issue a new commission of lunacy in order to protect Cranmer and his estate. In the second lunacy trial, Henry Cranmer was found by jury to be a lunatic, thus setting up the guardianship process. This outcome was not satisfying to the Lord Chancellor, as it drew the response to ambiguous cases in lunacy further away from the nuanced innovations that had been made by others, like Eldon in the case of Ann Kendrick.

The 1815 trial of Kitty Sherwood was remarkably similar to those of Kendrick and Cranmer, but the focus in this case was on who would pay the costs of the legal proceedings. Sherwood's relatives sent a petition to the court that she was of unsound mind and therefore unable to manage her 'concerns'. This resulted in a visit by two physicians, who concluded that she was in fact mentally incompetent. Lord Chancellor John Scott Eldon noted that physicians' reports of this nature were a common way to produce enough evidence to warrant a commission of lunacy. However, the ensuing commission of lunacy found that Sherwood 'was not a lunatic; but is of unsound mind (Ex parte Cranmer, 12 Ves. 445), so that she is not sufficient for the government of herself, her manors, messuages, lands, &c.'[32] Sherwood responded by petitioning to traverse this indeterminate verdict concerning her sanity and mental competence. At this point, both the petitioners in favour of the commission of lunacy and those representing Sherwood appealed to the courts to avoid bearing the expensive financial responsibilities of the legal proceedings.

Eldon's analysis of these claims underscores the complications in the relationship between court procedure and ambiguous mental states. The petitioners advocating for the findings of the original commission of lunacy argued that they should not pay the costs of the proceedings because they anticipated spending more money to fight the traverse proceedings, a fight which they deemed necessary in order to safeguard Sherwood's interests. For their part, Sherwood's legal counsel argued that because the recourse to traverse had been granted, but the trial of traverse had not yet been held or concluded, there was as yet no property 'in the hands of the crown' and therefore no jurisdiction of the court to use Sherwood's estate to pay down the costs of the legal proceedings. Eldon was sympathetic about the money that was at stake (the court proceedings were expensive even for wealthy families) and expressed regret that his court could not defray the costs for the original petitioners, as they were expenses 'incurred from very proper motives'.[33] But, he argued, it was beyond his jurisdiction to do so.

Family dynamics in lunacy law proceedings

As the foregoing examples suggest, not only could the borderlands of insanity challenge the laws surrounding commissions of lunacy, but they also reflected the competing concerns of the family members (and occasionally of neighbours and acquaintances) involved in the trials. In many of the cases described so far, Lord Chancellors guided insanity trials and their outcomes ostensibly to protect those considered to be on the edge of madness, and to preserve their property for themselves and their 'rightful' heirs. Yet, an examination of the trial of Ann Goodwin emphasises that these objectives could be greatly complicated by the realities of familial relationships. Goodwin had been living with her aunt, Ann Wragg, and other Wragg family members when, in October 1799, she married William Ferne. Within a few months of the marriage, the Wraggs launched proceedings against Ann Ferne in the form of a commission of lunacy. At the Derby county assizes the commission found that she had been a lunatic of unsound mind for about six years.

However, the jury also found that she was no longer a lunatic by the time the verdict of the trial had been read. Furthermore, out of a jury of seventeen people, twelve 'joined the verdict' while five did not, in a trial that, according to the Lord Chancellor, heard 'a great deal of contradictory evidence'.[34]

Soon after this trial, the Wragg family petitioned the Court of Chancery to confirm that Thomas Wragg, Ann Wragg's son, be appointed as the committee of Ann Ferne's estate. The newly married couple immediately counter petitioned, asking either for another commission of lunacy or to traverse the first trial. According to the couple's legal counsel, the original commission of lunacy was flawed in finding Ann Ferne to be a lunatic without specifying whether or not she had lucid intervals. The legal counsel in favour of the original return (and in favour of Thomas Wragg becoming Ann Ferne's committee) argued that 'lunacy is a partial insanity' that 'implies lucid intervals'.[35] The question remained whether or not Ann was lucid during the wedding to her husband. This debate over the issue of lucid intervals was enough for Lord Chancellor Loughborough to ask his staff to investigate how frequently the verdicts in previous lunacy trials had been specific in this regard. He concluded that there had not been any uniformity of procedure and thus decided that the best course of action was to let the previous decision stand and to acknowledge the right of the Fernes to pursue a traverse. However, in the meantime, as the original petition found Ann Ferne to be a lunatic, her marriage to William Ferne was nullified. In the Lord Chancellor's view, 'I cannot say, upon the evidence I am dissatisfied with the finding [of Ann Ferne's lunacy]: but the traverse is of right. All I can do, and think discreet to do, is to suspend the order; for, supposing, upon the traverse she is found *compos mentis*, I cannot take her property.'[36] At the end of the first trial, the solicitor general asked that the traverse be issued as quickly as possible. The Lord Chancellor responded that it could be done 'immediately', and set the wheels in motion the next day, with the assurance that 'the pleading of a traverse is exceedingly short'.[37]

The trial of traverse found Ann Ferne to be mentally sound. The report of this second trial of her mental state also more clearly accounted for the sense of urgency displayed by both parties in their battle over the legal status of Ann's mental state. Ann and William Ferne had been so insistent that the earlier commission of lunacy 'and the inquisition taken in pursuance thereof and all other and farther proceedings had under it ... be entirely set aside and vacated' because, in nullifying their marriage, they feared it would also 'bastardise' their first child, who had been born sometime between the wedding and the lunacy proceedings.[38] In another effort to avoid this fate for their child, Ann and William also remarried at some point in the interim. The chancery court concluded that 'the child' was in fact 'born since the second marriage, solemnised after the period, at which the sanity was established'.[39] While it is impossible to precisely reconstruct the timing of these extraordinary events, it is clear that the Fernes were left with their marriage, the legitimacy of their first child and Ann's property intact.

This no doubt displeased Ann Wragg, who had hoped that her son would be the guardian of the estate of her niece, who she considered to be insane. In this case it is hard not to conclude that Ann Wragg strongly disapproved of the marriage between her niece and William Ferne. Given the timing of the birth of their first child, it is also possible that her niece's pregnancy and/or the affections between her and William formed part of Ann Wragg's critical assessment of her niece's mental state. In a final affront to the Wragg family, their attempts to recover the costs of their legal efforts were denied by the Lord Chancellor, for, because the original lunacy commission was traversed so quickly, there was no property in the possession of the Crown from which the costs of the legal proceedings could be drawn.

Physical debility on the borderlands of madness

In several trials the borderlands of madness were blurred by the physical state of those whose mental state was in question. Physical incapacities that complicated the analysis of mental capacity included old age, disease, intoxication and injury. As the cases of Jane Stedman and others demonstrate, disputes about physical wellbeing were woven into lunacy trials in complicated ways. Stedman lived for many years with a 'paralytic disorder', and she clearly required the care of others as a result. During the last twenty years of her life she resided in the house of her nephew William Lewis and his wife, Penelope. Over the course of these twenty years great acrimony developed between the Lewis family and that of Mary Rodd, Stedman's niece, over the estate of Jane Stedman. In February 1746 the Rodds launched a successful commission of lunacy against Stedman, finding her a lunatic without lucid intervals since the previous March. Nevertheless, with Penelope Lewis as one of the executors, Stedman made a last will on 2 December 1746 in which Penelope benefited and Mary did not. Stedman died soon after, in the spring of 1747. This set the stage for a further court challenge, heard in 1755, by the Rodds to stop Stedman's last will from taking effect. They claimed that Stedman's paralytic disorder had made her mentally incapable of managing her affairs, as was evidenced in the commission of lunacy. So mentally incapable was Stedman, according to witnesses for the Rodds, that she frequently performed 'the offices of nature'[40] without realising it. Furthermore, a local minister refused to give her the sacrament during Easter in 1745 because she appeared mad to him. Finally, the Rodds accused the Lewis household of keeping Stedman in confinement in the last year of her life, not allowing Mary Rodd to speak to her aunt. The commission of lunacy, they claimed, along with the obstructionist behaviour of the Lewis household, proved Stedman's insanity and made her last will void. In previous wills Mary Rodd had figured more prominently.

Witnesses for the Lewis family told a very different story. They claimed that Stedman had indeed been suffering from a paralytic disorder, but that it had not impaired her mental judgement. The commission of lunacy, they argued, was launched against Stedman abruptly and without notice on 'the morning it was to be executed'.[41] A few witnesses explained that the Lewis household had decided to bar Mary Rodd from their house because 'Rodd used to persuade the deceased to drink spirituous liquors, and she was often fuddled thereby'.[42] Others accused Mary Rodd of robbing 'her of her money, plates, clothes, &c.' during her previous visits.[43]

The judge in this case, Sir George Lee, was convinced by 'all the subscribing witnesses, who give very minute accounts of what deceased said and did at the execution of the will; all of which shew capacity, and no material objection has been proved against any of those witnesses'.[44] As for the confinement of Stedman within the Lewis household, the judge did not 'think this a custody, because nobody was restrained from coming to deceased but Mrs. Rodd'.[45] Judge Lee concluded that 'there was nothing to encumber this evidence but the verdict [of non compos mentis from the commission of lunacy] which I could not think strong enough to set aside the positive evidence of sanity at the time of making the will'.[46] Thus, in this case, the verdict of the earlier commission of lunacy was revoked and Stedman's last will was upheld. The law thus cleared Stedman of being a lunatic, eight years after her death. Stedman's advanced age and physical difficulties, along with familial acrimony about the inheritance of her wealth, created uncertainty about her mental state. The application of lunacy investigation law first led to a verdict of *non compos* mentis, and later, upon retrial, concluded that Stedman had the mental capacity to determine the fate of her property.

In the case of Samuel Bird, it was Bird himself who, in 1792, petitioned to the courts that he was 'afflicted with a paralytic disorder [stroke in this case] which rendered [him] so weak in body and in mind as to be incapable of conducting or managing his affairs or executing proper discharges, or doing such acts as may be necessary to enable [him] to avail himself of the benefit' of profits that he had accrued in South Sea stock.[47] The Court concluded that Bird was 'in a state of mind which, though not amounting to lunacy was of too great imbecility in consequence of a paralytic stroke to do legal acts'.[48] Because Bird was considered in 'very narrow circumstances', the Lords Commissioners, Ashurst and Wilson, decided to arrange for the funds to be set up in trust for Bird's maintenance under the control of Bird's wife, Anna Maria Bird. In the commissioners' opinion, 'it appearing to be for the benefit of the family that the interest should be so paid, it was ordered to be paid to [Anna Maria] from time to time'.[49]

The commissioners cited a similar case in which 'a sum of stock was bequeathed to a married woman whose husband was of unsound mind, though no commission of lunacy had issued against him'.[50] In this case, Elizabeth Steed and her husband filed a bill of complaint against Richard Smith, who was the executor of a will that had bequeathed '£20 in the long annuities' to Elizabeth Steed. At the hearing in 1833, the 'Master of the Rolls, in consideration of the poverty of the parties, directed the £20 long annuities to be transferred to the Accountant-General, to be carried to an account, entitled "the husband and wife account"'.[51] He also suggested that Elizabeth Steed petition, with an affidavit testifying to the insanity of her husband, for the money to be 'paid to her during her life'.[52] In the report of this case, Steed's petition was summarised in the following way:

> [It] appeared the husband was of unsound mind and incapable of managing his affairs, and that he was in confinement in a lunatic asylum; that he had a large family of young children, who resided with their mother at

a distance of upwards of fifty miles from London, and that the family were in narrow and distressed circumstances. The petition suggested that as Mrs. Steed lived at a distance from town, and as, by reason of her being a married woman, she was incapable of executing a valid power of attorney, the Court might authorise her solicitor and next friend to receive the dividends on her behalf, on his producing a receipt for them signed by herself.[53]

Steed's mental difficulties were clearly considered more serious than a problem of mental judgement brought on by physical debility. His treatment in a lunatic asylum also likely put him beyond the borderlands of insanity. However, what is consistent with his case and others in this chapter is the flexibility in the legal response to madness. In the face of her husband's being committed to a lunatic asylum, Elizabeth Steed needed somehow to secure her family's economic survival. This had to be arranged creatively. Given the paternalist structure of property ownership and transfer in early nineteenth-century England, it was difficult for Steed to gain access to the money bequeathed to her in the above-mentioned will. The costs of a commission of lunacy were well beyond consideration for the Steeds, but, as with the Birds, filing a petition or bill was a cheaper and simpler means to a similar end.

Legal precedent

This use of precedent to manage more effectively the ambiguities of lunacy trials can be seen in the occasional grouping of cases, possibly by 'reporters' of the decisions of Lord Chancellors, into mini expositions on procedure in cases of lunacy. One example that grouped together twenty cases over the period 1789–1817, and that considered updates to the statutes pertaining to lunacy trials, zeroed in on the procedure of traverse and the powers of the Lord Chancellor. Drawing on statutes from the period of Henry VIII and George IV, the exposition noted that 'the custody of the estates of persons found *non compos mentis* is not to be granted till one month after the return of the inquisition … in order to give the party an opportunity of traversing the verdict.'[54] Moreover, the traverse could be 'tendered' up to three months after the inquisition. More importantly, the third section of the sixth statute under George IV authorised the Lord Chancellor 'to order a new trial if he shall be dissatisfied with any verdict returned upon a traverse.'[55] The reasons for this extension of the powers of the Lord Chancellor were explained this way:

> For it seems (though Lord Hardwicke once intimated a contrary opinion, see, *ante* the note to *Eyre v. Wake*, 5 V. 450), it is discretionary in the great officer who administers this branch of the prerogative to grant or to refuse a commission of lunacy, even when unsoundness of mind is clearly established; *Ex parte Atkinson*, Jacob's Rep. 335; and it will never issue when there is good ground for believing the measure would defeat the party's cure. *Ex parte Tomlinson*, 1 Ves. & Bea. 59. With the same consideration for the welfare of persons supposed to labour under mental visitations, the access of medical men, or other proper persons, may be directed, without issuing a commission, either for the purpose of ascertaining the real state of their minds, or for preventing any imposition being practised upon them. *Ridgway v. Darwin*, 8 ves. 65. *Rex v. Wright*, 2 Burr. 1099. But, as such visits, if not delicately conducted, might have the effect of irritating the mind of the supposed lunatic, access will only be granted upon strong reasons, and not upon the principle of *quia timet*. *Ex parte Littleton*, 6 Ves. 7.[56]

In this analysis we can see an attempt to more clearly define the parameters of the Lord Chancellors' decision making in commissions of lunacy, while at the same time upholding their discretionary powers. For, as A. K. R. Kiralfy notes, although 'the increased certainty of its practice [through precedent] combined with the gradual introduction of reports to make equity [the Court of Chancery] a more settled system', the Lord Chancellors still wielded great discretionary powers, which, in part, reflected the earlier traditions of the chancery court as the court of conscience.[57] This sense of 'conscience as a criterion of judgement in the court of Chancery' was still in evidence in the decisions of Lord Chancellors in uncertain cases of lunacy.[58]

Conclusion

As we have seen in this chapter, this space for judicial discretion, along with other peculiarities of the chancery court, also enabled the Lord Chancellors greater latitude for settling cases in lunacy that were on the boundaries of madness. He could, as in the case of Ferrers, err on the side of caution and extend the period before which an individual could apply to supersede a commission of lunacy. In cases like that of

Ann Kendrick, where the insanity of the accused was not proven in the first trial, the Lord Chancellor could order another assessment from impartial physicians, in the hopes of establishing mental incompetence without the potentially damaging mental strain of another commission of lunacy. More extraordinarily still, in the case of Jane Stedman, it allowed the judge to revoke a successful commission of lunacy that had been in effect for eight years, in order to make her will legally valid to her 'rightful' heirs. Finally, in cases like that of Samuel Bird, it allowed commissioners to seek creative alternatives to full commissions of lunacy in order to achieve their objectives and the objectives of their petitioners of limited means. Nevertheless, as cases like that of Sir John Leigh and Henry Cranmer indicate, the commission of lunacy could be a very imprecise instrument that did not always sit well with Lord Chancellors who wanted to invoke the protection of the court over those that they deemed mentally weak without resorting to the socially undesirable verdict of *non compos mentis*.

If the cases bordering on lunacy examined in this chapter constituted a challenge to the laws established around commissions of lunacy, they also reveal the flexibility of the trial process and the creativity of the Lord Chancellors in shaping a response that addressed the long-standing priorities emanating from trials in lunacy. One priority was the preservation of property, at first for the prerogative of the king, and, with the abolition of feudal land tenure during the Restoration period, for the families whose property was at stake.[59] Another priority was establishing guardianship for those suffering from mental weakness. Finally, the negotiation of law, states of mental incapacity and familial relations was a major consideration in the work of Lord Chancellors in their prosecution of commissions of lunacy.

As we have seen, this sometimes required considerable latitude in how the laws were understood and applied. First, the commissions of lunacy were not automatically successful, reflecting in part the uncertainties of the jurors and, sometimes, of the Lord Chancellors about the mental state of some of the individuals on trial. This suggests that the law did not, in some ambiguous cases at least, merely 'rubber stamp' the wishes of those filing the petition. Moreover, the examples in this chapter indicate that, when successful, commissions of lunacy did not always, in the eyes of the Lord Chancellors, meet the expectations of the law. In order to accommodate both the uncertainties of some cases of lunacy and the pecuniary circumstance of other cases, legal settlements around lunacy also occasionally happened outside the parameters of commissions of lunacy. Finally, as increasing numbers of cases were heard at the Court of Chancery, legal counsels and Lord Chancellors built up a body of legal practice that they drew upon to understand and respond to cases involving lunacy.

Notes

1. 88 E.R., Bennett and His Wife and Spencer and His Wife against Vade and Several Others, 1742, pp. 474–83.
2. Ibid., p. 477.
3. Ibid.
4. Ibid., p. 478.
5. Ibid.
6. Ibid., p. 483. John and Mary Bennett, and Henry and Anne Spencer, continued their authority over these estates, as tenants in common, until 1767. See S. Urban, *The Gentlemen's Magazine and Historical Chronicle for the Year 1797* (London: John Nichols, 1797), 612.
7. 88 E.R., Bennett and His Wife and Spencer and His Wife.
8. Ibid., p. 477.
9. Ibid.
10. Ibid.
11. Ibid., p. 476.
12. Ibid., p. 481.
13. Ibid., pp. 482–3.
14. Earl Ferrers is not to be confused with his more infamous nephew who was the subject of 'one of the most sensational trials of the eighteenth century'. See the excellent account in J. Andrews and A. Scull, *Undertaker of the Mind: John Monro and Mad-Doctoring in Eighteenth-Century England* (Berkeley: University of California Press, 2001), pp. 193–215.
15. 25 E.R., Ex parte Ferrars, 1730, p. 424.
16. Ibid.
17. Ibid.
18. Ibid.
19. Akihito Suzuki takes up a similar discussion of the cases of Lord Donegal, Ann Kendrick and Henry Cranmer, though with somewhat different analysis, in *Madness at Home*, pp. 155–7.

Indefinite mental states　　　　　　　　　　　　　　　　　　　　69

20　28 E.R., Lord Donegal's Case, 1751, p. 260. A similar case is that of Lord Barnsley, in which much debate occurred about what forms of insanity warranted a commission of lunacy. See 26 E.R., Ex parte Barnsley, 1744, pp. 899–902.
21　28 E.R., Lord Donegal's Case, p. 260.
22　*Ibid.*
23　*Ibid.*
24　32 E.R., Ridgeway v. Darwin, 1802, p. 276.
25　*Ibid.*
26　*Ibid.*
27　*Ibid.*
28　33 E.R., Cranmer, Ex parte, 1806, p. 169.
29　*Ibid.*
30　*Ibid.*, p. 170.
31　*Ibid.*
32　34 E.R., Sherwood v. Sanderson, 1815, p. 496.
33　*Ibid.*
34　31 E.R., Wragg, Ex parte. Ferne, Ex parte, 1800, p. 677.
35　*Ibid.*
36　*Ibid.*
37　*Ibid.*
38　31 E.R., Ferne, Ex Parte, 1801, p. 882.
39　*Ibid.*
40　161 E.R., Rodd against Lewis, 1755, p. 306.
41　*Ibid.*, p. 304.
42　*Ibid.*, p. 307.
43　*Ibid.*
44　*Ibid.*, p. 308.
45　*Ibid.*
46　*Ibid.*
47　47 E.R., Bird v. Lefevre, 1792, p. 1127.
48　*Ibid.*
49　*Ibid.*
50　Steed's case is mentioned in 47 E.R. Bird v. Lefevre 1792, p. 1127.
51　*Ibid.*
52　*Ibid.*
53　*Ibid.*
54　34 E.R., p. 902, 1789–1817.

55 *Ibid.*
56 *Ibid.*
57 Kiralfy, *Potter's Historical Introduction*, p. 595.
58 D. R. Klinck, 'Lord Nottingham and the conscience of equity', *Journal of the History of Ideas*, 67:1 (2006), 123.
59 As Vecliten Veeder notes, 'the abolition of the incidents of feudal tenure by the Restoration Parliament introduced a system of real property which continued almost to the reign of Victoria. Controversies arising out of these new methods of conveyancing and settlement naturally found their way into chancery, where alone trusts were recognised, mortgages redeemed, and contracts specifically enforced; and the contemporaneous abolition of the court of wards ultimately turned the guardianship of the estates of infants into chancery.' V. Veeder, 'The English Law Reports, 1292–1865', *Harvard Law Review*, 15:2 (1901), 113. The guardianship of the estates of lunatics was likewise turned over to the Court of Chancery. See Chapter 1 of the present study.

4

Trials of madness: family struggles over property in England

The previous chapter explored some of the complex combinations of legislative, legal, economic and social pressures that contributed to the development of lunacy investigation law. It suggested how this body of law, in turn, helped to frame understandings of and responses to madness. As befitted a process of this sort, the lens through which madness was brought into focus was largely legal and involved the participation of Lord Chancellors and lawyers, as well as the building of a body of legal precedent. It is also not surprising that the participation of families of the mad weighed heavily in a legal process that focused on mentally troubled and financially affluent individuals. In many trials, family members fought mightily to ensure that they, the heirs, would not be disappointed by the legal implications of their relatives' going mad. In other cases, the welfare of the mad individual lay at the centre of familial concern. In most cases, the good management of property, in the face of the disruptions brought on by madness, was considered by family to be essential.

Chapter 4 takes a closer look at the dynamics of power and property, family and folly in England. Many lunacy trials reveal intense debate among family members over the outcome of such trials. The emphasis in all cases was on keeping family property intact in the face of the disruptions from mad behaviour, in order to protect the economic interests of would-be inheritors. However, the complicated economics of middle- and upper-class eighteenth- and nineteenth-century families made it virtually impossible for there to be only one set of family interests at stake. In many trials this fact led to fierce struggles over the verdict of *non compos mentis*. An individual found to be legally mad greatly altered the economic situation in many families, and the implications of a finding of *non compos mentis* were not lost on families who stood to be affected by the results. Moreover, legal authorities, especially Lord Chancellors, attempted to impose clarity and rational solutions in the face of familial disputes – solutions that were not designed to please everyone who had a social and economic stake in the outcome. The decisions of the Lord Chancellors reflected the broader concerns of the role of civil law in arbitrating social and economic conflict brought on by the disruptions of an irrational mind. This role of legal referee sometimes included disciplining the aggressive efforts of family members, and outsiders, who sought to gain from their mad relations in ways that Lord Chancellors considered to be morally repugnant. These legal authorities thus attempted to shape the decisions of the court in favour of a rational outlook that protected the interests of those considered *non compos mentis* within the framework of family economic interests. As a result, sometimes Lord Chancellors openly chastised attempts to take advantage of the insane as they imposed solutions that they saw fit.

The detail of some English lunacy trials also allows for a gender analysis of lunacy investigation law in the broader context of the responses of family and legal authorities in lunacy trials. This analysis reveals interesting paradoxes within an otherwise familiar situation for women and men. These paradoxes add to the reinterpretation of the ways in which madness, gender and law intersected in understandings of the cultural experiences and expectations of men and women. In the case of women, their relative lack of power and the ways in which property law weakened their economic position led them to be particularly vulnerable as the subjects of lunacy investigations. This having been said, women participated in all aspects of lunacy investigation law; as witnesses, as guardians of their husbands' wealth, as stubborn resistors to the due process of lunacy investigations and, occasionally, even as opportunistic beneficiaries of the mental weaknesses of men. While not wanting to over-estimate the extent to which women benefited in the process of lunacy investigation law, it is nevertheless important to recognise their agency in the face of clear economic inequalities. In the case of men, it is obvious that on the one hand they controlled much of the decision making in their capacity as legal authorities, and as decision-making heads of households. On the other hand, as subjects of lunacy investigation law, men stood to lose that which lay at the core of middle- and upper-class masculinity in eighteenth- and nineteenth-century England – control over their property and control over their person. Once deemed *non compos mentis*, in the legal sense, men in English society ceased to be men. This rather paradoxical outcome of lunacy investigation law deserves some attention for what it reveals about masculinity and madness. Finally, as the following case of Anne Ashe demonstrates, in a few cases the participation and resistance of those at the centre of attention in lunacy trials highlights how men and women attempted to shape the outcome of legal and family expectations concerning their mental states.

The case of Anne Ashe

A spectacular family feud over the mental state and property of Anne Ashe puts many of these elements into relief. In 1702 Anne's mother, Dame Mary Ashe, issued a commission of lunacy against her daughter, by which Anne was found to be *non compos mentis*. Anne's sister, Katherine Windham, was made Anne's guardian. The Windhams and the Ashes were wealthy and influential families in Yorkshire. Dame Mary Ashe was at this point a widow and Anne already possessed considerable wealth through inheritance. She was 'entitled to the sum of £5500 secured to her by a mortgage for years on the estate of Sir Edmund Bacon, taken in the name of trustees', the sum of £3000 secured in a similar arrangement by a mortgage on the estate of Sir Humphrey Briggs 'taken in her own name', along with a 'bond debt' of money, jewels and other valuables.[1] In the same year, Dr Gibbons and Dr Sloan, physicians appointed by the Court of Chancery to attend to Ashe, recommended that she stay for a while at the popular Tunbridge Wells in Kent, where they claimed she would benefit from drinking its curative spring waters. Arrangements were made for Anne to stay close to the springs at the house of Mrs Packer.

Towards the beginning of her stay, in what appeared to be a striking heist-like event, Mrs Packer's son, Philip, conspired to take Ashe away from that property to a nearby chapel where he convinced a clerk, John Winteley, to marry them 'without license or publication of banns'.[2] In an ensuing trial in 1702, Mr Packer, the parson who conducted the marriage, and Anne Ashe were all committed to the Fleet prison for contempt of court, as provision for Ashe's person and property was, at the time of the marriage, still 'in the custody of the court'. The judge of this trial committed Anne Ashe and the others to prison because he thought that Mrs Ashe was 'mightily recovered *per consortium mariti*'.[3] If Anne Ashe was considered recovered from her insanity, the question for the courts became 'whether she should be discharged of the commitment and left to her husband; or if she were to be continued under commitment, if her husband Packer should be the committee?'[4] Lord Keeper, Sir Nathan Wright, settled this dilemma by concluding that:

> Though she is not out of order now, she may be again; the commitment is *regium munus*, not a prerogative but a duty; and the marriage, though good, is no *supersedeas* to it ... but I think she ought not to go back again to the same commitment, though I will not now discharge her from it; suppose she did contract when mad, and agreed and consummated when sober, it would be good.[5]

The marriage was also upheld in the 'Spiritual Court' and remained intact despite subsequent appeals.

Shortly thereafter, through the influence of Dame Mary Ashe, Anne Ashe's mother, 'An Act for making some Provision for, and settling the Fortune of, *Anne Packer*, in Trustees, for the Purposes therein mentioned' was passed in order to protect Anne's property from her new husband.[6] According to the case report of proceedings, 'all the deeds and securities relating to the lunatick's fortune' were thus 'brought before, and lodged with one of the Masters of this Court [of Chancery], in order to secure a Provision for the Wife in case she should survive her husband; and likewise for the children of that marriage in case there should be any'.[7]

Even at this stage of events, the surviving sources suggest a complex situation in which Ashe's mental state appeared to be mixed, and in which her wishes ran counter to those of her mother. In a document entitled 'Mrs. Packer's Answer to the Lady Ashe's reasons for Passing the bill sent from the House of Lords', Ashe offered a strong rebuttal to some of her mother's claims. First, she contested the claim that while 'under a commission of lunacy', she had been 'violently taken from her keepers' at the Packer household and forced to marry Philip Packer, a total stranger.[8] Ashe's version of the story was that after the marriage, 'proceedings' had found her to be sane and that she repeatedly requested that Lord Chancellor Somers interview her in order to demonstrate her sanity, but that these requests were rejected. Moreover, in Ashe's account, her keepers, who were overwhelmed by Philip and his assistants during Ashe's removal, were actually her real 'Goalers [*sic*]' and that it was her 'earnest request to be delivered from their cruelty'.[9] If she was forced into marriage, she argued, it was 'the only means to deliver me from a hard and miserable *confinement*'.[10] Ashe also challenged the claim that Philip was a total stranger to her, arguing that she had 'seen him more than once, and had often conversed with him by writing'. In what was clearly a barb for her sister (and possibly a more general commentary on options for wealthy women in early eighteenth-century England), Anne added: 'if not having seen him be any Argument against the validity of the marriage; another in the *Family* must for ever want a *Husband*, which it is humbly conceiv'd will be thought a *hardship*'.[11]

Anne next addressed claims that her husband was keeping her from communication with her family and friends, and that she was now in danger of losing her rather large fortune. In her quippy response to the first claim Anne noted:

> That I am not permitted to visit my *Friends* and *Relations is not true*, but I do not visit *Relations* because they are not *Friends*, and therefore conceive it more unreasonable that the *Bill* should provide that they may intrude on me against my *Will*; and yet in case the *Trustees* (as they are called) think fit to remove me from my *Husband*, there is no Provision that he be permitted to visit me. Let every Woman make this her own *Case*.[12]

As for the concerns about her wealth, Anne certainly acknowledged that her husband and his father had contracted debts on their own estates. But she made it quite clear that this was no more a problem for her than the loss of her wealth to her own family. In her view, 'that my *Fortune* is lost I know to be the Opinion of my Relations, and they are in the right of it, for they mean it, lost to themselves, but if the disposition of the Law in giving it to the Husband, be to lose it; Old as I am given out to be I should so lose it again ....'[13]

Philip Packer next applied, on behalf of his wife, to supersede the earlier commission of lunacy. Anne Ashe was found to be sane and, in its deliberations, the Court of Chancery devised a settlement that would help both to disencumber Philip Packer's estate and also to give Anne Packer some financial protection in the new arrangement. To that effect, the court arranged that Anne Packer's £5500, which had been secured to her by a mortgage on Sir Edmond Bacon's estate, would be used to disencumber Philip Packer's estate, 'and the residue [would] be laid out in a purchase of lands, which, together with so much of Mr Packer's estate as would make up 500lbs *per ann*, to be settled on Mr Packer for life, with remainder to his wife for life, for her jointure.'[14] With this settlement in place 'the residue of his lady's fortune was to be paid and delivered to [Philip]'.[15]

Although this arrangement would most likely have displeased Anne Packer's family, Philip's reaction to the *supersedeas* proceedings made things much worse. He ignored the court order completely and began to use his wife's fortune to make his own settlements on his debts, including debt that he owed to his sisters. At some point before 1715 Philip died, and Anne passed away two years later. This began a series of chancery court challenges for Anne's remaining fortune. In his deliberations, the Lord Chancellor made an interesting argument that encompassed much of the long and interesting mental and legal history of Anne Ashe, her property, the law and family contests. He noted that, although in theory the Court of Chancery still had legal power over Anne Ashe's fortune, because Philip had not complied with the terms of the chancery court's order during the *supersedeas* of Ashe's lunacy, 'it's now as if no such order had been made'.[16] Moreover, with Anne Ashe's death and the fact that she had no children, 'the Reason of the Court's interposing is at an End'.[17] To the Lord Chancellor, under these circumstances, the marriage of Philip and Anne Ashe made Ashe's fortune his and thus at the disposal of his family heirs.[18]

Women, gender and lunacy investigation law

On the one hand, this example reaffirms the obvious historical fact that the structure of property law strongly favoured the interests of men over women. However, as Amy Louise Erickson explains in *Women and Property in Early Modern England*, 'most marriage settlement cases in the Court of Chancery were extremely complex, both as to the parties' relation to one another and as to the terms of the settlement itself'. Moreover, 'the passage of time ... exacerbated the tangle of issues and interests'.[19] Arguably, the added dynamic of mental incapacity made these cases even more complicated. Erickson's analysis of property law evolution in relation to women's marriage adds insight to cases like that of Anne Ashe. As Erickson points out, the common law stipulated that 'the property a woman brought to marriage – her dowry or portion – all came under the immediate control of her husband'.[20] In the event of a husband's death, the surviving spouse was entitled 'to dower for her lifetime which amounted to a percentage of the real property of her husband'.[21] However, due to 'difficulties for apportioning and enforcement, both from the point of view of wives and in the interests of an efficient land market', jointure made more sense. Jointure was 'a joint tenancy of land by husband and wife, in which the survivor of the two enjoyed the income from the land so held'.[22] By the time of Anne Ashe's case, 'jointure generally took the form of an annuity arising from a rent charge on specified lands. The cash portion a woman brought into marriage was generally used to buy land to provide an annual income, first to support the new couple and subsequently to support the wife should she survive to become a widow'.[23] It was precisely this jointure arrangement that the Court of Chancery attempted to impose upon the marriage settlement of Philip Packer and Anne Packer, once the commission of lunacy against her had been superseded. Once she was no longer considered legally *non compos mentis*, the logic of the court was to create a situation that satisfied the debts of Anne Packer's husband's property, while protecting her economically through the purchase of lands. This would guarantee the couple a certain level of income – £500 per year in this case – through jointure. However, not only did Philip Packer ignore the chancery court order but, upon his death and the death of his wife, the same court no longer saw reason to exert control over what had become a more straightforward case of dealing with the inheritance of a man's fortunes by his family – fortunes which had been accrued from his wife through marriage.

The legal workings of married women's property as played out in individual cases were made more complicated still by what Erickson describes as the 'disjuncture' between the theory of the law, which was heavily weighted against women, and its practice, which offered them both opportunities and obvious restrictions. As Erickson notes: 'Despite the fact that women exercised considerably more power over property than has previously been allowed, both the legal system and individual men still kept women firmly subordinate.'[24] Erickson notes the ways in which 'ordinary women working within a massively restrictive system … registered their disagreement with the principle of inheritance and the marital property laws'.[25] To the extent that we can uncover them, Anne Ashe's decisions appear to fit within this general characterisation of women's resistance to the structure of the law as applied both to marriage and also to lunacy. In her case, marriage to Philip, despite its potential for exploitation, can be seen as a form of resistance to the conventions of courtship and marital practices for the early eighteenth-century English well-to-do. Without under-estimating the realities of the mental troubles that Anne Ashe may have experienced, her ability to skilfully invert the conventions of gender and legal authority in her written challenges to those whom she did not see as acting in her best interests is remarkable.[26]

As the case of Anne Ashe suggests, married women figured prominently in a wide range of lunacy commissions that probed the relationship between madness and contested marriage. Perceptions of madness played a key role in all of these trials, but married women's situations varied considerably from one trial to the next. In some cases, wealthy women who were weak of mind were the victims of opportunistic men. For example, sometime in the 1780s, at the age of twenty-one, Fanny Fust was spirited away by Mr Bowerman from her family home near Bristol to Flanders, where he married her. Fust was a wealthy woman entitled to real estate worth £1500 per year and she also had about £70,000 in other permanent assets. Fust's family issued a commission of lunacy that found Fanny to be a lunatic and they brought her back into the care of her mother in Bristol. Bowerman responded in 1787 by petitioning the chancery court to traverse the earlier decision and to issue a new one. Although acknowledging Bowerman's right to petition for a traverse, Lord Chancellor Thurlow emphasised the need for discretion in cases of madness, arguing that the protection of the lunatic must be kept in mind. He noted that 'the Court will never give any assistance or countenance to a man who has obtained [a] women in such a manner' and concluded that 'it is the duty of the mother to discuss this marriage most seriously, and to see whether she cannot in that manner get rid of this gentleman's pretentions'.[27] In this case, it appears that Bowerman did not get his way, but the matter is left tantalisingly unresolved for the historian. Lord Chancellor Thurlow, acting as a surrogate father in this case, felt compelled to explain the chancery court's responsibility to protect the mad and to direct Fanny Fust's mother to use her influence to dispose of the opportunistic Bowerman.

In the case of Mary White, a much clearer picture emerges of a woman whose mental difficulties were taken advantage of by a male opportunist. White lived in Bath and was the daughter of a baker. All of the neighbours who testified in this trial agreed with witness Mary Turner that White was a 'silly or foolish person, possessing a very weak understanding'.[28] She was frequently teased by youth in the neighbourhood and in local pubs. White's brother frequently paid others in the neighbourhood to accommodate and to look after her in exchange for her labours as a servant. At one point, she was apprenticed to a mantua-maker, and at another time she was sent to school. However, in both cases she was deemed unable to learn. White became wealthy through inheritance when her brother died and, at this point, was coerced into marriage to James Reane, who lured her away to Gloucester to marry him. Six months after the marriage, Mary Reane's family issued a *writ de lunatic inquirendo* that found her mentally 'incapable' and thus not able to conduct a marriage. Yet James Reane continued to take charge of her care until her death in 1810, possibly because, in the absence of her brother, there was no one else interested in the welfare of a woman whose behaviour was embarrassing and who was at times difficult to control. Shortly after her death, James Reane issued a court plea for Mary's remaining wealth, still claiming to be her rightful husband. At this point, one of Mary Reane's nephews, John Browning, issued a counter claim denying once more the validity of the marriage and contesting James Reane's right to Mary's property. Judge Sir John Nicholl agreed with Browning, summarising the situation in this way:

> Here then is a young man [Reane], in the middle of life, marrying an old woman of seventy, an habitual drunkard, and labouring under great infirmities, but possessed of a considerable property, which is to be acquired by this marriage, without the knowledge of any of her friends, or any settlement or security whatever. Upon uncontroverted facts the case has an unfavourable aspect, and has much the appearance of fraud and confederacy.[29]

Such was the concern about this sort of forced marriage that the subject was broached in other cases involving wealthy women who weren't married. In his summary of the lunacy trial of Kitty Sherwood, Lord Chancellor Eldon, emphasising the need to protect the mentally weak, pondered rhetorically:

> Suppose this lady, at the age of seventeen or eighteen, had been married by an adventurer for the sake of her fortune: it would be competent for

the Lord Chancellor in the Court of Chancery to direct an inquiry, whether she was of sound mind, when married; and whether it would be for her benefit, that a Commission of Lunacy should issue.'[30]

The case of contested control over the person and estate of Le Heup highlights how women sometimes battled each other for control of family wealth in the face of madness.[31] In this lunacy trial, Le Heup's wife and his uncle, Dr Waddington, were appointed to the committee of Le Heup's person, and a person outside of the family was appointed as committee of the lunatic's estate. Unhappy about this state of affairs, Le Heup's mother petitioned for Dr Waddington and herself to be the committee of the lunatic's person, excluding his wife, and for Dr Waddington and a family friend, Mr Halsted, to be put in charge of her son's estate. Part of the dispute here was about whether the affections of Le Heup's wife for her husband were getting in the way of proper medical treatment. Another strand of the dispute focused on the character of Dr Waddington, which some trial participants questioned. In his response to the issue of Le Heup's wife being guardian in this case, Lord Chancellor Eldon stated that he 'should have felt great pain in exposing this lady [Le Heup's wife] to the possible consequences of being the sole Committee of her husband', as the person 'who fills this office, in the exercise of which affection must be tempered with firmness, is often under the necessity of doing what is unacceptable to the object of his care; and a rooted, though unjust, aversion is the usual effect of a line of conduct, ungrateful perhaps to the feelings, but essential to the recovery.'[32] As for the intense family feuding attendant to this case (and to many others), Eldon added that: 'It is not a judicious mode of dealing with this calamity [of madness] by prying too minutely into family quarrels, perhaps founded in affection, and raking up every little bickering, to exclude different relations, until, as in this instance, I may be called upon to forget, that any of them are related.'[33] Noting that 'the governing principle has always been' that the appointment of committees for the person and estate of a lunatic is at the discretion of the 'holder of the great seal' or his representative, Eldon stated that a family relation was as qualified as anyone else, and in most cases preferable.[34]

Women's struggles with each other in the face of madness in the family could take unusual directions. Thomas Smith lived with his wife, Anne Smith, at their homes in Olmarch and Vailallt in Cardiganshire.

On 4 October 1817 Thomas was on his way to a 'bathing-place' in Carmarthenshire when he fell from his horse, injuring his head. During the next three days at the baths, and for a few days back in Olmarch, Thomas experienced 'many symptoms of lunacy',[35] which were attributed to his equestrian accident. On 10 October, Thomas and Anne took a return trip to the baths, hoping to relieve his persistent mental symptoms. Anne returned to Olmarch ahead of Thomas, at which point Smith's mother, Mary Smith, and one of his brothers, packed him off in a post-chaise to Swansea, placing him under the care of a physician who ran a private madhouse. Thomas's mother then applied to the courts for a commission of lunacy to be held in Swansea and not in Cardiganshire. She claimed, with medical support from the private mad-doctor, that her son's condition would only worsen, should he be subjected to the trip back home to Cardiganshire and exposed to trial witnesses who were too familiar to him.

Thomas's mother also claimed that the asylum doctors could prove that her son had been a lunatic since before his marriage to Anne Smith, thus rendering that marriage null and void. However, Anne fought this attempt to cut her out of her husband's marriage and, presumably, out of the financial benefits that went with it. In court, she argued that all of the relevant witnesses who could speak authoritatively about her husband resided in Cardiganshire. She also pointed out that none of them, including herself, could afford the trip to and stay in Swansea, where her mother-in-law had proposed that the trial be held. Lord Chancellor Eldon agreed with the logic of Anne's arguments, adding that 'the old and settled law' was that 'a commission of lunacy cannot be executed at any other place than the residence of the supposed lunatic'.[36] He further noted that it was common practice in such situations that one or two of the jury should travel to where the supposed lunatic was, make an examination and report their observations back to the rest of the jury. Eldon ordered that the trial should be held in Cardiganshire, at least giving Anne a fighting chance against the ministrations of her mother-in-law. In this case, the Lord Chancellor was enforcing the law in order to protect the interests of the mad and to help a married woman fight for her wealth in the absence of her husband and in the face of hostile in-laws.

An important outcome of lunacy trials was the guardianship of the person and property of those found to be *non compos mentis*. In many instances, married women were considered the most appropriate family members to handle funds of the family estate for the maintenance and care of their insane or mentally incompetent husbands. This was evident in the case of Joseph Gandy, whose wife, Eleanor Susanna Baptiste Gandy, petitioned the court successfully for funds to provide for her husband's wellbeing. In the words of the Lord Chancellor, 'notwithstanding her coverture', Mrs Gandy was given the power to 'apply the ... moneys for the benefit of the said Joseph Gandy', 'during such time as the said Joseph Gandy shall remain of incompetent mind and understanding'.[37] During his madness, Mr Bumpton's two sisters were appointed as the committees of his person and estate. In this case, Bumpton eventually recovered and was able to supersede his commission of lunacy.[38] In other cases, where the costs of the lunacy commission were too much for property and funds of the petitioners to bear, the chancery court was in the habit of providing arrangements for married women to receive funds for the care and maintenance of their husbands and, by extension, themselves and their families. This can be seen, for example, in the case of the Binfields. Mr Binfield died in 1754, leaving behind his wife and young child. The courts gave Mrs Binfield administration of her husband's modest estate. However, within a short period she became insane and was sent to Bedlam. The courts thus assigned guardianship of the infant and wife to the child's aunt, 'for the use and benefit of the widow and infant during the incapacity of the widow and minority of the infant'.[39]

Occasionally married women worked hard at defying the law of lunacy commissions, despite the harsh consequences that could result. One of the more spectacular examples was that of Lady Wenman, who, upon learning that a commission of lunacy had been issued against her husband, refused to produce him for the trial and then hid him for several weeks so that he could not be subjected to the trial process. For this legal indiscretion, Lord Chancellor Parker had her committed to the Fleet prison in 1721. His justification indicates his incredulity with her defiance of the law:

> it was a great imprudence, as well as obstinacy in her, not to do what she could for the producing of her husband, who upon the affidavits that had been made, could not but be thought a lunatic; for if he were found so, his wife must have the commitment of his person, and also an allowance made her suitable to the estate and greatness of his quality.[40]

Parker further stated that 'it would be a scandal to the Court if this ... contempt of not producing the Lord Wenman, were not punished after so long time given for that purpose ... not to mention the reflection it would bring on the justice of the Court'.[41] Lady Wenman was sent to the Fleet, but shortly afterwards the jury found Lord Wenman to be *non compos mentis*. The courts gave Lady Wenman custody of his person, and she was discharged from her jail commitment. There is no indication in the trial evidence at hand as to why Lady Wenman hid her husband from the law. Perhaps he wished her to do so. It could also have been an aversion on her part to concede that he was mentally unwell. Finally, it is possible that sheltering her husband formed part of a much more complicated family dynamic. In any case, she was clearly willing to defy the law and to suffer its consequences in her efforts to do so.

In perhaps an even more spectacular act of defiance, the wife of Mr Jones wrote a pamphlet criticising the court proceedings that led to her husband's verdict of *non compos mentis* and implicating the master's office in the mismanagement of her husband's affairs. Lord Chancellor Erskine found this to be a case of 'very high contempt' that deserved imprisonment as a result of 'defaming the proceeding of the Court, standing upon its Rules and Orders, and interesting the public, prejudiced in favour of the author by her own partial representation, to procure a different species of judgement from that, which would be administered in the ordinary course'.[42] Erskine ordered Mrs Jones and the printer of the pamphlet to be sent to the Fleet prison and dismissed Mr Jones' committee, replacing it with another. As in the case of Lady Wenman, it is hard to glean exactly what motivated Mrs Jones to react in this way, although there was no shortage of eighteenth- and nineteenth-century pamphlets, written by those considered to be insane, about the injustices of their treatment.[43] As the court findings demonstrated, activities like these were very risky.

In other cases, strategically minded women seemed to gain advantage from their decisions to marry those who were subsequently found by trial to be mad. For example, in 1787 the uncle of Mr Bennet brought the marriage and last will of his nephew into question in a trial. In this case, the fact that a commission of lunacy had not been issued made it difficult to argue that Mr Bennet was outright insane. Bennet's uncle posited that Mrs Hartford, a widow, hatched a plot with Mr Parry wherein she seduced Mr Bennet, knowing that he would live for only another few months. Once married, she then convinced Mr Bennet to sign over much of his estate to her, whereupon, after his death, she married Mr Parry. According to Bennet's uncle, it was Mr Bennet's bouts of mental incapacity that allowed Mrs Hartford to perform these many deceptions, which, among other things, deprived the uncle of his rightful inheritance. In his deliberations after an eleven-hour trial, the judge, Lord Chief Baron, noted that 'it does not appear … that this woman originally threw herself in the way of Mr Bennet; he was naturally a debauched man and fond of women; in that state he took a fancy to this woman, and in fact he sought her out more than she sought him.'[44] The judge concluded that if the marriage was a conspiracy, it was one of Bennet's own making, and that, although a drunkard, he was in his right mind when he made out his will. In this case, Hartford gained much in her brief marriage to Bennet, although how much of it she controlled after marrying Mr Parry is unclear.[45]

Another marriage that may have involved the deliberations of a strategically minded woman highlighted the consequences of not pursuing a commission of lunacy for families who fought over their insane relatives' wealth. In the last few years of his life, Virgil Parker became very fond of one of his servants, Mary Mills – so much so that he proposed to marry her. Unlike the previous examples (and much to the chagrin of his relatives), Parker's marriage was in many ways respectable and official. Parker paid for a marriage licence, announced the marriage, had the local parish curate of Minty in Wiltshire conduct it and 'went through the ceremony with as much propriety as any man could do.'[46] The marriage took place on 23 June 1752. On 3 August, Parker's two brothers had him confined to a 'madhouse'. He remained at the asylum until he died, intestate, on 24 May 1753. At this point, Parker's brothers and sister claimed his estate and attempted to deny his wife her share. Their argument against Mary Mills inheriting her dead husband's wealth was that 'he was a lunatic incapable of consenting to marriage.'[47] However, assessing the evidence from the trial, the Lord Chancellor concluded that: 'It did appear that he had a very weak understanding from his infancy, and by hard drinking was at times lunatic, and did many mad and frantic acts, but no commission of lunacy was taken out, nor was he constantly mad, but only by fits.'[48] The Lord Chancellor concluded that Parker conducted his marriage in between his fits of madness and that the ceremony was therefore valid. In the absence of a commission of lunacy that said otherwise, and despite his time in the madhouse at the end of his life, Parker was deemed sane in marriage and his wife thus entitled to her 'interest' of his wealth.

Given the evidence, it is not hard to imagine that Parker himself would have wanted a share of his wealth to be used for the maintenance of his wife after his death. In this and other cases, the lack of a commission of lunacy made it difficult for family members, eager to claim their share, to prove legally that their relative's madness rendered them mentally incompetent in the legal sense.[49] As we saw in the case of Sir John Leigh at the beginning of Chapter 2, even when lunacy trials were issued, they could sometimes give very ambiguous verdicts that did not accord with the attempts of relations to protect the insane relative or to keep the wealth of their insane relative within the family. In this chapter it has been demonstrated that the madness of a family member could also be considered as an opportunity for next of kin to dispossess those not related 'by blood' of their share of the family fortune. In all cases, the structure of the law gave men considerable power in determining the outcome of lunacy trials, in marshalling the evidence and in controlling the wealth brought into marriages by women. However, it is also clear that women were active in these struggles over the person and property of mad individuals, and that sometimes their efforts were successful.

Legal protection of the mad

Trials revolving around power, property, family and folly clearly 'exacerbated the tangle of issues and interests' involved.[50] Nevertheless, lunacy investigation law was, by design, established to protect the interests of the person deemed to be insane. In several trials it is clear that the protection of the lunatic lay at the heart of the Lord Chancellors' verdicts, despite the machinations of family members. For example, when a lunacy trial found a young Sir William Dormer to be insane in 1693, his estate was put into the care of his uncle, Mr Justice Robert Dormer. Sir Robert Jenkinson was given guardianship of the insane Dormer's person. However, in practice, Justice Dormer also took over the guardianship of his nephew, a practice not officially sanctioned in the lunacy proceedings but which resulted in Justice Dormer taking care of his nephew in his nephew's own house. This arrangement lasted for many years until, in 1724, Mr Sheldon, a nephew of William Dormer, petitioned that the financial arrangement established for the care and management of his insane uncle was 'excessive and to the prejudice of the next of kin to whom would belong what the lunatic should leave at his death'.[51] Clearly worried about what might be left to inherit from his insane uncle, Sheldon highlighted the irregularities of Dormer's maintenance by the same relative that was also in charge of his estate, and tried to plant a seed of doubt about how the 'excessive' maintenance money was being spent. The Lord Chancellor was unimpressed, noting that for thirty-two years Mr Justice Dormer had 'maintained his nephew in the most tender and careful manner',[52] and had not been inclined to hasten his nephew's demise in order to take advantage of his property. Moreover, according to the Lord Chancellor, Sheldon's petition indicated that he was more interested in his own welfare than that of his uncle.

The Lord Chancellor's extended view of the matter made clear the close relationship between the long traditions of legal thinking about lunacy and the responsibilities of the guardian. He applauded improvements that Justice Dormer had made to his nephew's estate, explaining that 'the lunatic may recover, and then to see his estate in good condition … may be greatly to his comfort; and though he has been so long in this unhappy condition yet a lunatic in the eye of the law is never looked upon to be desperate, but always at least in a possibility of recovering'.[53] This view, the legacy of the fourteenth-century Prerogativa Regis, held that, in cases of lunacy, the fact that an individual could in theory become mentally reasonable again made it mandatory for the law to protect his/her person and property. The Lord Chancellor ordered no change to the financial arrangements made for William Dormer, concluding that 'it is his benefit and comfort I am to take care of … and not to heap up wealth for the benefit of his administrators, or next of kin'.[54]

Although the Lord Chancellor looked favourably on the maintenance that Justice Dormer had provided for his nephew, including the improvements made to William Dormer's estate, the use of lunatics' wealth by guardians was frequently a touchy issue that butted up against the financial interests of family and non-family alike. This can be seen in the case of Thomas Audley, who, upon being found insane at a lunacy trial, was put under the guardianship of Sir George Audley, his father, and Lord Cornwallis, among others. Thomas Audley's father died in 1666, leaving Thomas with estates valued at £2000 per year. Over time, Thomas's committee banked considerable savings from this yearly income, even 'after paying for the lunatic's maintenance'.[55] The committee decided to spend £9700 of the money they had saved to purchase lands adjacent to Thomas's estate in his name in order to increase his wealth. This decision was challenged by Thomas' half-brother, who, as a next of kin, was concerned that in turning Thomas's 'personal estate into a real estate' the committee was 'defeating the next of kin in favour of the heirs at law'.[56] The plaintiff's legal counsel argued that it was 'not in the power of a committee to alter the nature of a lunatic's estate'.[57] The court concluded that a lunatic's committee did not have 'the power to alter the nature of a lunatic's property', but that 'the laying out of the lunatic's money in the purchase of lands did not in any manner alter the property thereof'.[58] Thomas's half-brother would be entitled to the same percentage of the new lands purchased as he would to other parts of his insane relative's estate. Despite these reassurances to the concerned half-brother, the court reiterated that its first duty was to safeguard, through committee, the interests of the lunatic – 'that the surplus shall be safely kept and delivered to him, if he recover'.[59] In a similar case involving the estate of Bridget Grimstone, who was declared insane in 1748, concerns about what could and could not be done by the committee were also raised. Here, the Lord Chancellor stated that 'in the management of the lunatic's estate, the ruling principle is, do what is for the benefit of the lunatic'.[60] This, he argued, sometimes required savings from rents to be 'laid out in repairs', to 'discharge encumbrances on the real estate' and to augment the value of the lunatic's property.[61] The consequences to those hoping to benefit through inheritance were, in principle, secondary.

The protection of a lunatic, which was built into the laws of lunacy investigation, could become more complicated when creditors' attempts to recoup their money ran into the funds allotted for the maintenance of those found *non compos mentis*. Lord Chancellor Eldon expressed his views on such a situation in the case of a clergyman who had become mad, and whose committee petitioned for the release of some of his maintenance funds of £5000 to be given to angry creditors who threatened to arrest him. Eldon responded that he had:

> no authority to pay the debts of the lunatic; unless I see that it is for the accommodation of his estate. I cannot pay his debts, and leave him destitute of any provision ... There is no instance of paying the debts of a lunatic without reserving a sufficient maintenance for him; as the

creditors cannot touch these funds. They may put him in gaol; where I can maintain him; and they may sequester his Living. These Orders are made for the accommodation, not of the creditors, but of the lunatic.[62]

Sometimes family interests proved the most difficult threat to the protection of the interests of the insane. John Niell was a plumber who, in 1796, seemed to be afflicted with an 'inflammatory fever'.[63] Whether this condition precipitated insanity was a question that was hotly contested in the chancery court. Niell had behaved erratically at an auction at Gunnersbury House in May 1800, at which he bought £3923 worth of lots and goods from owner John Morley. By August 1800, Niell's family launched a commission of lunacy in which he was found to be a lunatic from 1 May 1797, without lucid intervals. This finding emboldened Niell's committee to file a bill to the chancery court asking John Morley to pay to the committee the money that had been spent by Niell at the auction. As noted in the court case, 'a great deal of contradictory evidence was produced as to the state of mind of the lunatic, and his conduct at the sale', with some witnesses testifying to Niell's rational bidding at the auction and others describing his actions as 'extravagant'.[64] Complicating matters was the fact that, on the last day of the auction, someone openly suggested that Niell was 'out of his mind'.[65]

In his deliberations, the Master of the Rolls for the Lord Chancellor, Sir W. Grant, noted that 'it would have been more satisfactory' if the lunacy trial in 1800 had stated more clearly 'that [Niell] was a lunatic at the day of the contract', rather (presumably) than just stating that he had had no lucid intervals since 1797.[66] Nevertheless, Grant reasoned, if Niell was insane at the time of the auction, the main question was 'how far, under all the circumstances, this Court will interfere to set aside the whole of the lunatic's transactions: supposing them void at law'.[67] The problem was that Niell had made many transactions since 1797, including selling lots and goods that he had purchased at the auction at Gunnersbury House. In this case, the inconvenience of undoing the complex chain of sales and purchases was evidently not worth the effort. Besides, concluded Grant rather cynically, if Niell's transactions had 'sold to advantage, he or his family would have kept the profit [and] … the objection would not have been made: but now that it has turned out otherwise, not by circumstances to be imputed to the Defendant [Morley] (for there is nothing upon the evidence to shew, the loss was occasioned by an exorbitant price paid to him), a Court of Equity is called upon to make the Defendant pay'.[68] In this case, with a committee for the maintenance of Niell's person and property already in place, the court considered his family's bid to recover the costs of his mad auctioneering more a case of self-interest than of concern for an insane relative.

Men, masculinity and lunacy investigation law

While the wellbeing of the person and estate of a mad individual was clearly a priority in the lunacy trial process, in declaring a person *non compos mentis* the chancery court was effectively depriving an individual of control over his or her person and property. This result had repercussions that were profound for both men and women, but, given the gendered nature of power in English society, the results were radically different for each. Men who were the focus of lunacy trials were often left in peculiarly vulnerable situations. In his reflections on *Manliness and Masculinities in Nineteenth-Century Britain,* John Tosh notes that, 'masculinity is insecure in two senses: its social recognition depends on material accomplishments which may not be attainable; and its hegemonic form is exposed to resistance from both women and subordinated masculinities'.[69] If the structure of English law in general, and that of lunacy investigation law in particular, was designed (among other things) to reinforce a patriarchal set of social relations, this chapter has pointed out many instances in which women responded outside of the strict conventions of hegemonic masculinity and femininity as they were drawn into the play of lunacy investigation law in specific situations.

In most lunacy trials, the problem for men wasn't the struggle for social recognition of material accomplishments beyond reach but, rather, the loss of material accomplishments already obtained. Trials in lunacy compromised male identity by questioning men's ability to govern themselves and their property. If they were found to be *non compos mentis* in a lunacy commission, the guardianship process made men dependent upon others for the provision of their everyday needs and for the management of their property. As we have seen so far in the book, there were many reasons why men found themselves on the wrong side of the rational/irrational divide, but the outcome for all of those subjected to a lunacy trial was a severe loss of masculine identity. During lunacy trials, men had their property and their ability to control it scrutinised and questioned. Most lunacy trials resulted in men's property and the control of their personal lives being governed by others. In suggesting that masculinity may have been historically more resilient to change than other key elements of English society, John Tosh points out that for long periods of time 'it remained deeply wedded to the exercise of private patriarchy' and to 'the sexual rite of passage of young men on the threshold of manhood'.[70] If, as Tosh puts it, 'sexual mastery and household authority' were 'at the very heart of face-to-face patriarchy',[71] lunacy investigation trials marked instances in which men stood to lose complete control over the household.

In some trials, what was at stake was not so much the loss of male domestic authority, which had already been diminished or lost among mentally disordered men who were not likely to reach the kind of mature masculinity characterised by a rational marriage choice, the control and management of economic resources and the establishment of household authority. These men, having been cared for by family members for months or years, had to deal with the consequences of not being recognised as fully fledged males. Nevertheless, lunacy trials marked the beginning of a public investigation into, among other things, the extent of masculine inadequacy in the private and public sphere, and into the attempts of family members to shore up the economic assets that had been bestowed upon men who were found to be incapable of performing their duties.

The case of Turner offers a compelling example of how anxious families could become about men whose mental faculties faltered as they approached 'the threshold of manhood'. In about 1794 Turner, who was living with his father, began to experience bouts of insanity in the 'spring and autumn', during which he was consumed with a 'passion for a military life'.[72] In 1803, on the pretence of going to see a cattle show, Turner set off for Newark and then to London, where he 'accidentally' met Sarah Myers 'in the street, somewhere near one of the Theatres Royal'.[73] Myers' servant, Susannah Squire, stated that 'on Friday, the 9th of September, [Turner] came with her mistress, who lived in Ann Street East, and that almost immediately she heard him say to her mistress – "he could not live without her"'.[74] The couple then went to church on Sunday: Turner obtained a marriage licence on Monday; and they married on the following Wednesday.

It is difficult to trace events during the year following this marriage, but by 16 November 1804, Turner's father, Samuel Turner, clearly unhappy with his son's marital choice, decided to file a suit to have his son's marriage annulled. However, the courts could not pursue this course of action, as there had been no prior lunacy commission proving Turner the son to be *non compos mentis*. The marriage lasted for another four years, at which point Turner the son decided to file for an annulment on the grounds that, at the time of his marriage, he was mentally incapable of making a rational choice. This was clearly a difficult case to make, for he also insisted that at other times he was mentally capable of managing himself and his affairs. The trial was made more difficult for Turner by the accounts of Myers and Myers' sister, in which Turner was said to be perfectly rational, although perhaps eccentric, in his short courtship with and marriage to Myers.

The trial judge, Sir William Scott, worked hard to explain how an expert understanding of madness was the key to getting Turner out of what had become an awkward situation. 'Persons in [a state of madness]', he explained, 'nevertheless often pursue a favourite purpose [like marriage] with the composure and regularity of apparently sound minds. It is in the extravagance of the act itself rather than in the manner of pursuing it that the proof of madness is to be discovered.'[75] In case his point had not been made explicitly enough, Judge Scott stated that Turner's marriage to Myers was 'an act of a man connecting himself, in marriage, with a common prostitute, without any rational prospect of happiness.'[76] This annulment hinged on a form of madness that was defined culturally in relation to differences in expectations of rank. The best that witnesses and the judge could do in this trial was to argue that Turner's behaviour was very eccentric, especially in the spring and the autumn – a pattern that synchronised with theories linking the seasons and the onset of madness. Turner's military flights of fancy further suggested to his father and the judge that his mental judgement was suspect. However, not wanting to find him *non compos mentis*, yet mentally unsound at the time of his marriage, the focus became the profound lapse of mental judgement attendant to marriage to the likes of Sarah Myers. In this case, Turner's father, with the help of the trial judge, shored up the reckless behaviour of a young man on the verge of full male adulthood. It was not so much his sexual encounters with a female Londoner of lesser rank that was the problem but, rather, his insistence on true love and marriage with one of them. At his father's insistence, he apparently saw the light.

Conclusion

This chapter has emphasised the benefits of keeping an analysis of gender in mind in assessing the relations of power, property, family and folly. The study of lunacy trials offers an excellent opportunity to consider how family interests intersected with problems resulting from madness. Lunacy trials capture for the historian examples of the complex 'field of power'[77] generated by the gendered structures of property law, the resistance of women to their legal subordination, the unusually weak position of men found to be *non compos mentis* and the exceptional circumstances created by instances of madness. The law allowed scope for individuals to play out their familial struggles in ways that could frustrate Lord Chancellors. This is exemplified by those who successfully superseded their verdicts of lunacy, despite the concerns of Lord Chancellors that such results would lead to the exploitation of the mentally weak. Examples like that of Anne Ashe highlight how such episodes are not so easily evaluated. The families of the mentally troubled no doubt felt as wide a range of sympathies, frustrations and fears in the seventeenth, eighteenth and nineteenth centuries as in any other era. Their responses were as much about mitigating the mad behaviour and its implications as they were about a concern for the mad individual. In the rare cache of primary sources on the life of Anne Ashe, we also catch a glimpse of how one individual struggling with mental trouble evaluated and responded to the machinations of her family.

At a broad remove, lunacy trials were designed to impose order onto these chaotic situations. Although the efforts of Lord Chancellors to realign the relationships of gender and rank in the face of the many struggles precipitated by cases of mad behaviour were only partially successful, they did wield tremendous influence. The trial process over which they presided determined the mental state of an individual and, if required, organised guardianship of the lunatic and his/her property. An examination of Lord Chancellors' opinions in these cases demonstrates their efforts to impose rational solutions that consolidated and protected the property of the mad while setting aright what they considered to be transgressions of behaviour, be they malicious marriages of convenience, avaricious behaviour towards the mad or obstructions of the trial process itself.

As constrained as Lord Chancellors could be in trials that also included the participation of legal experts, a jury and a host of witnesses, their position of power in the trial process allowed them to make decisions on behalf of the mad that could trump the intentions of family members. The long legal tradition of protecting the interests of the lunatic through the guardianship process allowed Lord Chancellors to make decisions that, as they saw it, privileged the mad over the interests of their relatives. Although institutional confinement certainly could form part of family strategies around madness, a likelier resort from the fifteenth to the nineteenth centuries was the commission of lunacy. As we have seen in Chapter 2, although lunacy investigation law evolved from one era to the next, it remained a remarkably stable legal process through which families attempted to settle unsettled circumstances created by the mad behaviour of a relative. This included the management of the mad and of their property and also the safeguarding of inheritance. Lunacy trials could impinge upon a range of familial concerns including marriage, control of family assets and unacceptable male and female behaviour. Lunacy trials thus served as a powerful and enduring filter through which families of the mad attempted to reorganise in the face of madness. As a resource for families of the mad, and, as an instrument by which legal authorities oversaw madness, this body of law was instrumental in shaping family dynamics in relation to madness. By the eighteenth century, the process of assigning one or more person to the care of the mad and one or more person to the management of the mad person's estate had helped to structure family responses to madness. The precedent in lunacy trials upon which Lord Chancellors drew heavily in their deliberations and decisions further contributed to a set of traditions and expectations that families of the mad would come to know and understand.

Notes

1 25 E.R., Packer against Windham and others, 1715, p. 68.
2 *Ibid.*
3 22 E.R., Mrs. Ash's Case, 1702, p. 1196.
4 67 E.R., Mrs. Ash's Case, 1702, p. 99.
5 *Ibid.* p. 100.

6   See 'House of Lords Journal Volume 17, 5 February 1704', in *Journal of the House of Lords: volume 17, 1701–1705* (1767–1830), pp. 396–98, British History Online, www.british-history.ac.uk/report.aspx?compid=14727 (accessed 15 September 2012).
7   24 E.R., Case of Anne Ashe, 1715, p. 185.
8   Norfolk Record Office, WKC 7/17, in folder of notes by Ketton Cremer and others about the Ashe family, 'Mrs. Packers Answer to the Lady Ashe's reasons for Passing the bill sent from the House of Lords'. I would like to thank Professor Barbara Todd for sharing her primary source sleuthing about Anne Ashe with me.
9   *Ibid.*
10 *Ibid.*
11 *Ibid.*
12 *Ibid.*
13 Norfolk Record Office, WKC 7/17, 'Mrs. Packer's Answer', .
14 25 E.R., Parker against Windham and others, 1715, p. 69.
15 *Ibid.*
16 *Ibid.*, p. 71.
17 *Ibid.*
18 The only exception was a bond of £400 that was a 'Chose in Action' and thus the property of Anne's family. See *ibid.*
19 A. L. Erickson, *Women and Property in Early Modern England* (London: Routledge, 1993), p. 117.
20 *Ibid.*, p. 24.
21 *Ibid.*, p. 25.
22 *Ibid.*
23 *Ibid.* See also S. Staves, *Married Women's Separate Property in England, 1660–1833* (Cambridge, MA: Harvard University Press, 1990).
24 Erickson, *Women and Property*, p. 19.
25 *Ibid.*, p. 20.
26 Judith Walkowitz describes a much more successful attempt of a woman to create an alternative narrative to that of her scheming husband who depicted her as insane. See, J. Walkowitz, 'Science and the séance: Transgressions of gender and genre in late Victorian London', *Representations*, 22 (1988), 3–29.
27 29 E.R., In Matter of Fust, 1787, p. 1230.
28 161 E.R. Browning v. Reane, 1812, p. 1081.
29 *Ibid.*, p. 1085.

30 34 E.R., Sherwood v. Sanderson, 1815, p. 522.
31 34 E.R., Le Heup, Ex parte, 1811, pp. 300–3 (first name missing).
32 Ibid., p. 302.
33 Ibid.
34 Ibid.
35 36 E.R., Ex parte Smith, 1818, p. 274.
36 Ibid., p. 275.
37 This case is described in 47 E.R., Bird v. Lefevre, 1792, p. 1128.
38 25 E.R., Ex parte Bumpton, 1728, p. 281.
39 161 E.R., Plunket, Formerly Sharpe against Sharpe, 1754, p. 228.
40 24 E.R., Lord Wenman's Case, 1721, p. 571.
41 Ibid.
42 33 E.R., Ex parte Jones, 1806, p. 284.
43 See, for example, J. Edmonds, *The Apology, or Vindication of Sir Cleave More, Bart. Upon the Suing forth a Commission of Lunacy against Joseph Edmonds, Esquire* ... (London: George Croom, 1711).
44 29 E.R., Mountain v. Bennet, 1787, p. 1201.
45 Ibid. See also 35 E.R., Turing Ex parte, 1912, pp. 55–6.
46 161 E.R., Parker v. Parker, 1757, p. 378.
47 Ibid., p. 377.
48 Ibid.
49 Although not launching a commission of lunacy could be problematic for families trying to sort out the wealth of their insane relatives, as we will see in the next chapter, Lord Chancellors sometimes regarded these same legal investigations as hazardous to the mental health of those considered to be mad.
50 See, Erickson, *Women and Property*, p. 117.
51 24 E.R., Mr. Justice Dormer's Case, 1724, p. 724.
52 Ibid., p. 724.
53 Ibid.
54 Ibid.
55 21 E.R., Audley v. Audley, 1690, p. 172.
56 Ibid.
57 Ibid.
58 Ibid.
59 Ibid.
60 27 E.R., Ex parte Grimstone, 1772, p. 459.
61 Ibid.

62 33 E.R., Hastings Ex parte, 1807, pp. 490–1. See also 34 E.R., Ex parte Phillips, p. 1123: 'the consideration of the personal comfort of a lunatic being the leading object in the administration of that branch of the prerogative, and order for payment, even of a lunatic's just debts, out of the funds in court, or by sale of part of his estate, will not be made, unless a sufficient maintenance for the lunatic will remain.' As of the statute of 43 Geo. 3, 75, the freehold and leasehold estates of those deemed made by commission of lunacy could be sold to pay off their debts.
63 32 E.R., Niell v. Morley, 1804, p. 687.
64 Ibid., p. 688.
65 Ibid.
66 Ibid.
67 Ibid.
68 Ibid., p. 689.
69 J. Tosh, *Manliness and Masculinities in Nineteenth-Century Britain* (Harlow: Pearson), 2005, p. 44.
70 Ibid., p. 67.
71 Ibid.
72 161 E.R., 1808, Turner v. Myers, p. 602. See also Porter, *Mind-Forg'd Manacles*, p. 23 for another case of madness expressing itself in part in military delusions.
73 Ibid.
74 Ibid.
75 Ibid., p. 603.
76 Ibid., p. 601.
77 Tosh, *Manliness and Masculinities*, p. 29.

5

Care and protection: managing madness in England

Chapters 3 and 4 have hinted at how, over a considerable period in English society, lunacy investigation law served, in principle, as a way to protect the interests of the mad. This despite the ambiguities of the law, the uncertain nature of the madness of individuals who came under the auspices of the law and the unsettling family dynamics that often accompanied the law's use. This chapter focuses on how the law acted in a caring capacity for those put on trial for *non compos mentis*. As Roy Porter has noted, in the late seventeenth and eighteenth centuries there were a rather eclectic range of understandings and responses to madness. Moreover, even by the end of the eighteenth century, 'talking about madness – even talking *authoritatively* about it – was not traditionally the preserve of any profession'.[1] Arguably, the meanings of madness, and the response to it, were not primarily medical until well into the nineteenth century. In this context, lunacy investigation law constituted a significant response to madness – one that included the considerable capacity to care for and protect the mad. Specifically, the structure of the law of lunacy investigation was, in principle, designed to arrange for proper care and protection. Despite these 'built-in' protections for the care and welfare of the mad, in some cases, Lord Chancellors also gauged whether, in the first instance, the use of commissions of lunacy would be detrimental or not to the mental state of those under consideration. In other words, the value of using lunacy investigation law was weighed against its potential impact on the mental condition of the individual. Court of Chancery officials and Lord Chancellors also exercised their discretionary powers to inquire about the wellbeing of the mad in order to evaluate the best means of care. This they did, for example, in cases of *supercedeas*, in the guardianship arrangements after the verdict of *non compos mentis* was reached, and in cases in which families could not afford to pay for the process of a full commission of lunacy. Occasionally, lunacy investigation law was used beyond England's borders to bring mad people under the protection and care of English law. Finally, the deliberations of legal experts during and after lunacy trials were sometimes occasions for discussion and debate about the nature of the condition of madness and how best to respond to it legally. Families sometimes initiated lunacy investigation law at least partially because they were concerned for the proper care and welfare of their mad relations. However, as this chapter demonstrates, Lord Chancellors played an instrumental role in keeping the care and protection of the mad in focus during and after trial processes that were frequently complicated and acrimonious.

Prevailing views of madness

From the late seventeenth to the early nineteenth centuries, doctors, along with English people of varying ranks, shared remarkably similar views about the origins of madness and its treatment. The prevailing view, founded upon humoral understandings, and nuanced by the end of the eighteenth century by competing ideas about the nervous system, considered a balance between mind and body to be essential. As Roy Porter puts it, 'everyday medicine ... remained as routinely psychosomatic as ever, presuming – as common experience suggested – a two-way traffic between mind and body within the whole person as integral to both the cause and cure of afflictions'.[2] This was a shared understanding of illness in general and of madness in particular, that rested on what Charles Rosenberg has described as a shared set of expectations about illness and its treatment, or 'a conspiracy to believe'[3] in a predictable armamentarium of therapeutic responses to specific symptoms reflecting imbalances of the body and mind. This shared understanding was, in turn, rooted in the literature, art, politics and experiences of everyday life in English society.

Essential to keeping this healthy balance of mind was the exercise of the 'rational soul' over the passions and instincts that were sources of mental disarray. As mad-doctor William Pargeter put it:

> a fellow creature destitute of the guidance of that governing principle, reason – which chiefly distinguishes us from the inferior animals around

us ... retains indeed the outward figure of the human species, but like the ruins of a once magnificent edifice, it only serves to remind us of his former dignity, and fills us with gloomy reflections for the loss of it. Within, all is confused and deranged, every look and expression testifies internal anarchy and disorder.[4]

Cultivating the art of mental discipline was considered essential to ensuring good mental health. When reason failed to keep the lid on love, anger, pride, jealousy or fear, a slide into various manifestations of madness was more likely. Over the course of the eighteenth century, this general understanding of madness was overlaid by what George Cheyne coined as 'the English malady' – mental troubles in the form of nervous disorders that were more the product of England's rapidly advancing society than the result of reason's subjugation by the baser passions.[5] This form of mental illness, located by physicians in the spleen, was the prerogative of the wealthy. The excesses of food and drink, along with the preoccupations of modern society and the mental quickness of the more privileged, led to particular mental conditions characterised as 'vapours', 'melancholy' and 'nerves'.[6]

Jonathan Andrews and Andrew Scull explain how this view of madness created opportunities for an emerging group of mad-doctors to diagnose and manage the mental incapacities of the wealthy. Though intimately connected to England's infamous Bethlem Hospital as visiting physician, the bulk of mad-doctor John Monro's clientele were upper-crust patients whose families employed his expert services to treat their relatives at home. Over the course of the eighteenth century, Monro, along with William Battie and a small group of others, were taking advantage of 'England's growing affluence and the advent of a thoroughgoing reorganisation of society along market principles'[7] to suggest to their clients that their expert care was worth paying for. As Andrews and Scull put it:

> Over time, it simply became increasingly common ... for one of the more celebrated mad-doctors to be brought in on the consultation [of cases of lunacy] and asked for his advice. As the most prominent amongst such specialists in Georgian London, John Monro and William Battie derived much of their income from their involvement in cases of this sort. Of course, if the lunatic proved unusually troublesome, recalcitrant, or dangerous, even the very wealthy might be tempted to avail themselves of the services of one of the new madhouses ... In these circumstances

Monro and Battie profited by referring the patient to the madhouse with which they had established connections. More usually, however, ministering to affluent patients in their own homes provided the mad-doctors with highly lucrative opportunities to peddle their wares, sometimes attending individual cases for months or even years at a time.[8]

Although this fledgling profession was on the rise in eighteenth-century England, institutionalisation clearly was not. Private madhouses were 'a temporary resort in this period ... Families were generally unwilling to support it for long, either financially or emotionally.'[9]

It is in the context of these prevailing views of madness that the role of the law of lunacy investigation in the care and protection of the mad needs to be considered. Building on a legal history in England that stretched back for centuries, by the 1700s lunacy investigation law developed into a significant and particular mode of caring for those whose mental troubles brought them into the orbit of the civil law. This was partly the result of the two enduring principles upon which the spirit of the law rested. First, the law of lunacy investigation viewed the wellbeing of the person and property of the lunatic as a priority. This point was reiterated and acted upon constantly by Lord Chancellors in lunacy trials throughout the period under study. As stated in one trial report: 'One general principle, admitting, perhaps, some possible, but rare, deviations pervades all orders made in cases of lunacy; namely, that the great object in view of the administrator of this jurisdiction is, solely and exclusively, the interest and comfort of the lunatic himself.'[10] Second, the possibility of recovery of those found to be *non compos mentis* was built into the structure of lunacy investigation law, and led Lord Chancellors and other legal authorities to pay considerable attention to the manner of caring for the insane.

Gauging the effects of lunacy investigation on the mad

Despite their convictions about the benefits of the civil law in this regard, Lord Chancellors frequently weighed the likely effects of commissions of lunacy on the mental health of those considered by family to be mad before they allowed the process to continue. For example, a first cousin of a lunatic who had for years been cared for by his brother and sister applied for a commission of lunacy, presumably to confirm his deranged cousin's mental state and to determine the terms of guardianship. The brother and sister opposed this move, and their legal representatives, Sir Samuel Romilly and Mr Wetherell, argued that the commission of lunacy was 'unnecessary for any purpose, with reference either to the person or property [and] likely to produce the most fatal consequences.'[11] More specifically, they asserted that the rigours of a lunacy trial would likely 'occasion a relapse' of their clients' charge into a worse state of lunacy. They then pleaded that, if the Lord Chancellor insisted on a lunacy trial, the proceedings should be delayed for six months and they, not their cousin, should 'have the carriage' of the petitioning process. In his deliberations, Lord Chancellor Eldon noted that the main point for the chancery court in such cases 'was whether it is really necessary for the benefit of the lunatic, with reference to his mental health and his property, that a commission should issue.'[12] Eldon agreed with Romilly and Wetherell's argument, concluding that in this, as in many previous cases, 'by granting' a commission of lunacy now 'I might for ever prevent the cure'. Eldon ordered that a physician should be tasked to determine the mental state of the 'patient', thus assuring a certain level of legal (and medical) probing into the case but not, he hoped, to the patient's therapeutic detriment.[13]

The decisions of the Lord Chancellor about the pros and cons of lunacy trials were sometimes rendered very complicated by circumstance. In 1762 Dr Monro gave advice to Mrs Threlkeld, whose daughter, Anne Hunt, was demonstrating symptoms of madness. He suggested that Hunt be sent off to William Clarke who ran a private madhouse in Clapton.[14] About nine months after Hunt's confinement, Monro, who apparently monitored this case closely, learned that Hunt's family intended to launch a commission of lunacy against her. Monro strongly urged the court that the lunacy trial should be deferred as 'Hunt was not in a condition fit to be taken out of the care and custody of those to whom her person was entrusted.'[15] Although a commission of lunacy could put Hunt's person and property on a more secure footing, her state of lunacy, according to the medical experts, needed more immediate treatment at the private asylum. In this case, the court agreed, deferring an application for a lunacy commission 'till the next term'.[16]

The courts were motivated by a similar concern in the case of Thomas Southcot. In about 1733 Southcot's father sent him across the English Channel to a 'religious house' which cared for the insane in Ghent. In 1741, unhappy with the state of his care, Southcot's father had him relocated to an institution in St Venant. In 1751 a commission of lunacy was issued against Southcot (the record is unclear about who issued it) which prompted two related debates – one about the consequences of bringing Southcot out of institutional care to stand trial, and the other about the English court's jurisdiction in lunacy law abroad. The physician attending to Thomas Southcot at St Venant argued that 'it would be very dangerous to his health' to move him out of institutional care for the purposes of putting him on trial for lunacy.[17] In response to these debates, Lord Chancellor Hardwicke noted that the identity of Thomas Southcot was itself in some doubt. '[I]t appeared only', he stated, 'that two persons had been sent over who never saw Thomas Southcot before, had gone to St. Venant, where a person was produced to them as such, of whom they could know nothing but by reputation.'[18] Noting that the chancery court had the right to demand that the alleged lunatic be produced for inspection at a lunacy trial, Hardwicke recommended that Southcot be sent for, despite the words of warning from the attending physician at St Venant.

Hardwicke observed that there were one or two previous cases in which those suspected of lunacy were removed from England in order to avoid its legal jurisdiction. Although careful not to imply that this was the motivation for removing Southcot, the Lord Chancellor did note that in every case: 'A subject cannot transfer his allegiance: the crown has a right to its subject, wherever he is; can send for him over; and then the committee of the crown may take his person. That is the proper method, by giving authority in an amicable way to bring the person over, though it cannot be done by force.'[19] Hardwicke's last consideration was about where to hold the commission of lunacy in the case of a man who had for seventeen years been cared for 'oversees'. Technically, he acknowledged, 'the jury must be summoned by the sheriff of the county in which the person resides.'[20] As we have seen in previous cases, this rule was designed to allow the jury to hear testimony from family and neighbours who had a more intimate knowledge of those alleged to be insane. In this case, Hardwicke directed the trial to be held in Essex County, where the 'mansion-house' in which Southcot used to reside was located. Presumably there were people there who could both recognise Southcot and still say something about him.

Lord Chancellor Hardwicke made the connections between the deliberations about the legal reach of the chancery court of England overseas and the health and wellbeing of the insane quite clear. As he explained:

> [It] would be unreasonable, that the King's subject, being abroad, and a lunatic, should lose his protection. The commissioners cannot execute the commission beyond sea, as in case of a commission to appoint a guardian, because the authority is not in them alone, but in the jury too. But if a commission were not to be granted, what situation would the subject be in with respect to his safety and protection from the King? ... It would be in the power of any body to defeat the prerogative, by conveying the party beyond sea. No mischief can follow from the granting [of] a commission; for if the jury are satisfied without inspection, they will find so; if not, they will not make a return, or will return that it does not appear to them that he is an idiot or lunatic. If he has notice of it, he may oppose the commission; or if he has not, yet any body may apply for him to traverse or supersede the commission: in either of those cases he must appear to be examined *coram rege in concilio*, which words have been considered to mean, this Court; of opinion, there is reasonable ground to issue a commission in this case.[21]

Here the law, as a manifestation of the Crown's authority over its subjects, was seen as the best form of protection for those made vulnerable through mental incapacity.

Considering madness through the lens of civil law

In some lunacy trials, concern over the care, protection and provision of the mad evolved into more abstract considerations about the nature of lunacy as a disease and how it was best understood and responded to in a legal context. This can be seen, for example, in the opinions of Lord Chancellor Thurlow over what was a common-enough type of trial about whether an individual who was generally considered to be mad had conducted a legal transaction during a lucid interval. In this case, in 1780 Frances Barker had given over to her husband a considerable inheritance from her father – one that had been intended for 'her separate use'. Some time later, after the death of her husband, a lunacy commission was launched against Frances Barker, finding her to have been insane since 1783. Alexander Aubert, Arnold Mello, Dorothy Olympia and Henrietta Aubert were appointed guardians of Barker's committee and estate. But Alexander Aubert and Arnold Mello had also facilitated the legal transaction in which Barker had signed away her inheritance to her husband. Although they admitted that Barker was, at times, not in her right mind, by 1791 her mental state elicited enough concern among family members for them to launch an inquiry to determine whether or not 'Frances Barker was a lunatic at the time she executed the letter of attorney'.[22] At this trial, Lord Kenyon 'and a full special jury'[23] decided that she was in fact sane at the crucial signing. Unhappy with this verdict, in 1792 Barker's family applied to Lord Chancellor Thurlow for a new trial.

Thurlow disagreed with the earlier verdict and, in so doing, articulated views of madness, disease, medicine and law that went far beyond the parameters of this particular trial. First, the Lord Chancellor explained how difficult it was to fit the peculiar circumstances of any given case involving madness into 'general rules' or 'abstract propositions' about the subject. Thurlow noted that 'though it be true, that a mind, in ... possession of itself, ought, when acting, to act efficiently, yet it is extremely difficult to lay down, with tolerable precision, the rules by which such state of mind can be tried'.[24] In cases where madness was alleged, Thurlow stated that it was 'incumbent on the party alleging it, to prove such derangement'.[25] In cases where a lucid interval was alleged to have occurred in one generally deranged, then it was up to those alleging this to prove it. Thus, in cases like that of Frances Barker:

> The evidence ... applying to stated intervals, ought to go to the state and habit of the person, and not to the accidental interview of any individual, or to the degree of self-possession in any particular act; for from an act with reference to certain circumstances, and which does not, of itself, mark the restriction of that mind which is deemed necessary, in general, to the disposition and management of affairs, it were certainly extremely dangerous to draw a conclusion so general, as, that the party, who had confessedly before laboured under a mental derangement, was capable of doing acts binding on himself and others.[26]

According to Thurlow, in order to get at the 'state and habit' of those alleged to be mad, it was necessary to consider evidence from those who had spent enough time with them to judge properly. In this case, these more reliable testimonials came from 'the woman who attended her ... as an insane person [and] the medical man who attended [and] prescribed for' what he diagnosed as 'furor uterinus'.[27] Not wanting to condemn those who claimed that Barker was sane at the time that she signed her property over to her husband, the Lord Chancellor pointed out that they 'did not mean to circumvent a weak mind: but I think they scarcely watched the means with sufficient attention.'[28] This, along with the fact that all witnesses agreed that 'she was once undoubtedly insane' made it clear to the Lord Chancellor that the burden of evidence militated against a lucid interval. In a retrial, Barker was found *non compos mentis* at the time of her financial transaction. Other Lord Chancellors shared Thurlow's opinion that the most reliable testimony was from those who had been in close contact with the suspected lunatic for a longer period of time. Although the weight of medical testimony was duly considered, it was especially valuable when the medical professional also had a long-standing relationship with the alleged lunatic. In England, until the early nineteenth century, medical expertise based upon limited contact was usually seen as less valuable in the process of lunacy investigation law.

Exercising the legal power of inquiry

Another way in which the chancery court used its powers in lunacy to protect the wellbeing of the mad was to exercise its authority of inquiry. When, in 1813, a dispute arose about who should be paying for the care of Margaret M'Niven, who had been considered 'of unsound mind for many years preceding' the year 1810, Lord Chancellor Eldon expressed his concern for her welfare.[29] M'Niven lived with her brother in Scotland but was 'maintained' by her husband, who lived in England. At the heart of the pecuniary dispute was whether a part of her inheritance from her uncle could be used by the husband to pay for her care, in spite of the fact that the uncle had not wanted Mr M'Niven (the husband) to get his hands on it. This dispute was further complicated by the fact that a commission of lunacy had never been issued for Margaret M'Niven, meaning that the guardianship arrangement was not legally binding. Eldon was sufficiently worried by the testimony of this case to order an inquiry into 'how she has been maintained, and at whose expense ... whether her husband is of ability to maintain her, due regard being had to her comfort; and whether any of this separate maintenance should be applied for her use, to whom, and upon what securities.'[30] Presumably this inquiry helped to ensure M'Niven a decent standard of maintenance and care.

Sir Lloyd Kenyon, Master of the Rolls in Chancery, directed the same powers of inquiry into the mental health of John Bennet. Bennet first worked for Robert Sayer, a 'print and mapseller', as a servant, eventually becoming an apprentice in Sayer's business. In 1733, Sayer proposed to his young apprentice that, should he be willing to work for him as a journeyman for four more years, he would invite Bennet to join him in partnership. In 1777 the partnership was created. This seems to have worked out well until 1781, when Bennet 'grew very violent in his temper, and frequently quarrelled with the workmen, so that they would not work any longer for the shop; and at other times was very extravagant in payment of the workmen'.[31] By 1783, Bennet's behaviour was considered full-blown insanity and he was treated by Dr Monro for nine months at Brook House Asylum, then 'removed to private lodgings'.[32] In 1784 a debate arose between the two men about whether the partnership should be dissolved as a result of Bennet's insanity and consequent inability to fulfil his business responsibilities. In the absence of a commission of lunacy and of evidence by potentially key witnesses like Dr Monro, Kenyon ordered the Master of the Rolls to inquire 'whether Bennet is now in such a state of mind as to be able to conduct this business in partnership with Mr Sayer according to the articles of copartnership; for if he has merely a ray of intellect, I ought not to reingraft him in his partnership, and that in mercy to both, for the property of both is concerned, and he who cannot dispose of his property by law, must be restrained here'.[33] In this subsequent inquiry, the Master examined Bennet as well as 'several witnesses', concluding that Bennet had been in his right mind and able to conduct his business since November 1783. Sayer countered by demanding proof that Bennet was sane on 9 December 1783 and, if so, for how long he remained so. Although the final verdict seems to have escaped the historical record, the 'Sayer v. Bennet' case became a reference point for subsequent cases seeking the dissolution of business partnerships on the grounds of insanity.[34] This case determined that all courts of equity had the power to inquire further into the mental state of individuals in order to assess their ability to continue on as business partners. The intent was to safeguard the integrity of businesses and to 'see that the property of the [lunatic] unable to take care of himself, should be taken care of for him'.[35]

Cases of *supersedeas*, or the elimination of an earlier decision of *non compos mentis* after mental recovery, also highlight how the Court of

Chancery used its powers in consideration of the health and welfare of the mentally troubled. In 1730 Earl Ferrers (described in Chapter 4), armed with testimony from his sister, Lady Betty Shirley (who had been appointed as guardian of his person), and from Monro, his physician, petitioned the court to supersede his previous commission of lunacy verdict. Monro's affidavit claimed that Ferrers was 'restored to his senses, for four of five months last past'.[36] He further testified in court that 'there was not danger of a relapse because he was greatly afraid of running into any excesses, which might bring on a return of his disorder' – a clear sign of recovery in the doctor's opinion.[37] However, Ferrers' brother, Lawrence Shirley, who had been made the committee of the Earl's estate, was unconvinced, marshalling evidence from Dr Hale, who had attended Ferrers before Dr Monro and who still found him to be a 'lunatic with lucid intervals'.[38] As proof of this, Dr Hale and Dr Lewis, another attending physician, both highlighted Ferrers' tendency to recover for a few months after treatment by 'salivation', only to relapse into his former insane state. Weighing the medical and non-medical evidence, the Lord Chancellor decided to give Earl Ferrers 'his full liberty' but to suspend his bid for a *supersedeas* so that his mental progress could be further observed at a later date. Here we see a Lord Chancellor using his authority to nuance the legal process of lunacy investigation law in order to be sure that mental recovery was complete.

The complications of care and protection through lunacy investigation law

Although it is clear that the commission of lunacy was designed to promote the good management and care of those considered mad, chancery court officials did not always have control over how it was used. As we saw at the beginning of Chapter 3, the first two commissions of lunacy that tried Sir John Leigh did not find him *non compos mentis*. It was not until a third 'successful' trial that the Lord Chancellor felt that he could exercise the influence of the court to protect Leigh from pernicious property pilferers. Sometimes the verdict of *non compos mentis* in a lunacy trial could in itself be used in ways not consistent with the spirit of the chancery court. This was amply demonstrated in the rather complicated legal provisions arranged for Edward Brown, the son of Joseph and Jane Brown. In making his will, Joseph Brown directed that

£2000 along with his fee simple estate be committed to Mr How, 'in trust for Jane for life'.[39] Another £1700 was to be given to Edward, but only if he was to 'continue in his right mind'.[40] The will also stated that, as Edward had 'some times committed acts of lunacy ... he should be allowed but £50' per year along with one of the family estates, should he be mad at the time of inheritance.[41] Before his death in 1732, Joseph Brown placed Edward under the custody of Mr Crossly. Meanwhile, Joseph Brown's daughters both married, one to Zachary Baily and the other to Edward Baily. After Joseph Brown's death, his wife, Jane, made her will, leaving 'pretty large legacies'[42] to her two sons-in-law. When she died in 1733, her son, Edward, was still in the custody of Crossly.

This scenario set the context for a harrowing period during which Edward was treated very poorly. Mr How took over the fee simple estate and extended the term of Crossly's custody over Edward. When Crossly asked How for money to continue maintaining Edward, How responded that there was none. They settled on an agreement whereby Crossly could earn his pay by keeping Edward's allowance for clothing. This state of affairs continued for six months, after which time Edward managed to escape Crossly's custody by *Honine replegiando*, a form of habeas corpus. At this stage, the court described him as 'in a manner naked' but not mad.[43] Edward tried to acquire money from How, but How informed him that the tenants of the property would not pay any rent. Zachary Baily then told the tenants that they were to deal exclusively with How, and not Edward. How then threatened Edward, indicating that if he did not agree to hand over 'costs' for the management of Edward's trust and other forms of payment, he would 'take out a commission of lunacy against him'.[44] Edward balked, and How took out the commission, threatening to have him put under guardianship if he tried to fight the pecuniary disadvantage that How, along with the two Baily brothers (and possibly Edward's sisters), had conspired to force him into.

But Edward was clearly emboldened by his successful flight from custody. In a series of stabs and parries, Edward applied successfully to supersede the commission of lunacy that had been launched against him, only to have How successfully initiate a new one. Finally, in 1740 Edward brought a bill against How to quash the last commission of lunacy and to reclaim his rights to his family property. The Lord Chancellor roundly condemned the behaviour of How and the four Bailys, concluding that 'there was a contrivance between How and Zachary to keep the possession of the estate for the benefit of the children of the Bailys. Here is a commission of lunacy taken out, and never executed; the tenants forbid to pay to the proper person [Edward]; and all this was for the benefit of the children of the Bailys, in case it could appear that the plaintiff was a lunatick.'[45] In this instance, the chancery court was able to restore Edward's property to him, as the Lord Chancellor ended his deliberations by forcing How and Zachary to pay for the legal costs of Edward's suit against them. However, it is clear from this case that the threat of a lunacy trial could be used as a weapon in family feuds, just as families sometimes used the threat of asylum committal in a later period.[46]

Just as lunacy investigation law could sometimes be used in ways that ran counter to the principles of protection and care that it was supposed to provide for the mad, in other cases the initial arrangement of guardianship was contested and sometimes ignored by the families of the mad or other acquaintances with different interests at stake. The case of Thomas Blood offers a spectacular example of this uneven impact of chancery court arrangements. In 1732 the Archbishop of Tuam leased lands worth £100 per year for a term of twenty-one years in county Clare, Ireland to Thomas Blood. One year later, Blood began manifesting serious signs of madness that plagued him until his death in 1741. By 1735, his family had hired physicians to care for him and he was frequently 'confined and bound' out of fear for his violent behaviour. His mother and other relatives vacated the family home at Bohersallagh, moving to Carosin 'to avoid his fury'.[47] During the winter of 1735 he twice escaped from the house of a neighbour who had been hired to confine him, running barefoot in his 'nightcap and breeches', in a distracted state, to other neighbours' homes. According to witnesses, Thomas was at times 'melancholy' and at others 'outrageous' during the same bouts of 'phrenzy'. In the midst of one of his mad episodes in 1735, he ventured to the house of Richard Evans, who, according to Blood's family, 'took advantage of this disorder of mind',[48] offering £400 for Blood's land, despite the fact that it was worth closer to £800. Evans apparently did not actually pay the £400, but instead convinced Blood that smaller sums of money would suffice.

These events precipitated Blood's family to launch a commission of lunacy that found Blood to have been a lunatic since December 1733

– in other words, since well before his financial arrangement with Richard Evans. William Adams was appointed as Blood's committee (presumably of his person and estate, although the historical record is not clear). With the verdict of the commission of lunacy in hand, Blood's relations went after Evans to put an end to his 'unjust and fraudulent bargain'[49] by appeal to the exchequer of Ireland. But Evans resisted this legal action, putting in his own counter claim that Blood was in fact sane at the time of their business transaction. This case was tied up in the court for eleven years, three years past the life of Thomas Blood. However, in 1744 Blood's heirs retook possession of his property. In this case it is conceivable that Blood's guardian was able to offer him some modicum of care. But the decisions of the chancery court, although integral to family strategies in the response to Blood's madness, need to be considered alongside the complexities of his mental condition, his behaviour and the familial disputes over his property. In Blood's case it is not clear how much protection and care the law was able to provide.

Lunacy law for those of lesser means

In several cases the chancery court intervened in the welfare of the mad, despite a family's inability to afford the costs of a full commission of lunacy. Here, the same impulse of the law to protect, and to provide the circumstances for adequate care of the mad, was extended beyond the ordinary legal parameters of an actual lunacy trial process. For example, Elizabeth Price was insane at the time of her husband's death and continued in this state for some years. Although she was insane and 'totally incapable of managing herself and her affairs', no commission of lunacy was issued, 'on account of the small amount of her estate and fortune.'[50] Nevertheless, Price's daughter Catherine Price successfully petitioned the chancery court for control of the money that accrued from her mother's wealth in order to provide her with care and maintenance. When Catherine died in July 1783, in her will she left 'her reversionary right' in her mother's wealth to a friend, Elizabeth Priaulx, with whom she had 'a very great intimacy and friendship', and who in the meantime had taken over the care of Elizabeth Price.[51] The court approved this arrangement in 1784, thus providing consistency in care over the course of the long madness of Elizabeth Price.

Financing the care and maintenance of George Turberville [sic] was not so straightforward. Tuberville, who had been insane for several years before 1784, had signed over power of attorney of the dividends of his wealth to John Farrell, who paid for Tuberville's 'maintenance and support'.[52] However, in May 1784 Farrell went bankrupt at which point Tuberville's family intervened. In order to break the arrangement with Farrell and to secure Tuberville's care, the only next of kin, Anna Maria Auger and her husband, agreed to pay Farrell £12 for Tuberville's board and maintenance. Soon after, Farrell was sent to debtor's prison and, at this stage, the Augers petitioned the court to officially take over Tuberville's care. However, as Tuberville's yearly income was 'not more than £80 a year' there was 'no fund for defraying the great expense of suing out a commission of lunacy, and the proceedings consequential thereto'.[53] According to the Augers, Tuberville had already cost them plenty. They had, since taking over his care 'at their own expense not only maintained him, but also provided with linen and apparel of every kind fitting for him to wear'.[54] Moreover, they wanted to 'fit up and appropriate a sufficient part of their house at Streatham for his reception, with a proper person to attend on him, and to provide him with every requisite suitable for his situation'.[55] Under the circumstances, the Lord Chancellor ordered that Ferrell should be released from his financial hold on Tuberville, and that a master of the court should inspect Tuberville to 'inquire ... what is the state of mind, and age, and condition in point of health, of ... George Gleane Tuberville, and whether he is in a capacity to take care of himself and his own affairs'.[56] This, Court Master Mr Pepys did, concluding that he was insane and in need of care. With this information in hand, the Lord Chancellor ordered that the dividends of Tuberville's wealth should be delivered to the Augers, who, he agreed, were the most likely of guardians in this case.

As his response to the Augers implies, Lord Chancellors did not hesitate to appoint those whom they thought most fit to manage the person and property of the mad. Sometimes a decision came down to a choice between guardian contenders, and the justifications for those chosen could be revealing. Such was the case of Elizabeth Ludlow, in which three parties fought for her guardianship. Her father had willed for her to inherit real estate worth about £500 and 'personal estate' valued at £600, should she be in a sane state of mind at his death, but 'in case his daughter should not recover from her lunacy [she was] ... to remain under the care of Mrs. Bathurst', his sister.[57] Ludlow was still insane at her father's death. Soon thereafter, Mrs Bathurst made her own will in which she appointed a lawyer, Robert Bog, to be her 'executor and residuary legatee'.[58] At the same time Bathurst handed over the custody of her niece to Bog, who, through legal deception, 'got the lunatic under his care' and 'petitioned ... for the custody of [her] person'.[59] However, Henry Strangeways and Rachel Masters, both second cousins to Elizabeth Ludlow, petitioned that they were better choices as guardians than Bog.

In the chancery hearings, the Lord Chancellor certainly agreed that Bog was out of the running, despite the lawyer's contention that he had been chosen by Ludlow's closest living relative. The two cousins' testimonials amounted to a battle about who elicited the worst behaviour in their mad cousin during her 'raving fits'. Witnesses for Strangeways argued that he had a calming effect on her, and that Rachel Masters had the opposite effect. These contentions were strategically worded in the language of concern for the health of the ailing Ludlow. According to the case report, 'several affidavits were read, proving, that whenever Mr Strangeways appeared, the lunatic, though before in her furious fits, would ... grow calm; wherefore, as committing her to the care of Strangeways might facilitate her cure, or make her more easy under the continuance of her distemper, so the placing her with one for whom she had an aversion [read Rachel Masters], might ... prevent her cure, or retard it'.[60] Affidavits on behalf of Mrs Masters countered that, in her raving fits, Ludlow 'would use all her relations alike ill'.[61] The Lord Chancellor acknowledged that as they were both second cousins to Ludlow, they both appeared to have equal claim to guardianship over her person and property. However, appointing them both was out of the question, as he found that in past cases such arrangements had resulted in 'inconveniences' that compromised the estate of the mad. The solution, in the Lord Chancellor's view, was to select Mrs Masters, who, 'being of the same sex, may probably better know how to take care of the lunatic, and in this respect be more tender of her'.[62]

This decision was, of course, grounded in traditional gendered views that women were not only the more obvious providers of care in the domestic setting, but also likelier to be more understanding of maladies afflicting those of their own sex. In some respects, this contrasted markedly with the medical expertise thought to be the prerogative of specialists in the field of madness (the mad-doctors), who were exclusively male. Yet, this was not so much a contradiction as it was a division of labour in lunacy, which became more pronounced over the course of the eighteenth century. By this division of labour, male experts diagnosed and prescribed for lunatics while women continued to be viewed as their natural front-line caregivers at home. Yet, as noted at the beginning of this chapter, the number of medical experts in the diagnosis and treatment of madness was limited until the start of the nineteenth century.

Conclusion

As part of the wider English legal system, lunacy investigation law aimed to restore order and good management in the face of individual cases of mental disorder and to calm the chaos in familial relationships that frequently ensued. If madness was considered in part as rational thought's losing battle against the baser passions and instincts, lunacy commissions, in investigating the circumstances of mad behaviour, determining the timing and extent of mental decline and arranging for the good management and care of the lunatic's person and property, constituted a legal corrective to worlds that had been turned upside down. By arresting the destructive course of madness through the judicious appointment of committees for the care of the mad person and the good management of his/her property, commissions of lunacy were a powerful force in the care of the insane.

As we have seen, in practice the relationship between lunacy investigation law and the care of the insane was quite complex. Commissions of lunacy could be manipulated by families in ways that were detrimental to those deemed mentally unwell. Lord Chancellors sometimes withheld the use of commissions of lunacy in cases in which they thought that the mental health of the individual in question might suffer. Nevertheless, the principle upon which the commissions of lunacy rested was, in great measure, geared to safeguarding the wellbeing of those deemed mad. This principle, reiterated by Lord Chancellors throughout the eighteenth and nineteenth centuries, reflected the long-standing understanding of lunatics in English civil law as existing in a temporary state of madness, with the potential for regaining their sanity. As a mechanism for responding to madness in an era during which there was no dominant therapeutic or institutional response, the commission of lunacy was used by families to safeguard the property of their mad relations – property over which families often had complex vested interests. But Lord Chancellors also saw the protection of property as essential to the protection and care of the mad. Guardianship offered a measure of security for the mad in the event of their recovery, and also ensured the best possible direct care of the mad under the circumstances. Thus, Lord Chancellors were frequently happy to appoint those whom they considered to be the best guardians in individual cases. Moreover, they would use their legal authority to control the timing of cases in which individuals desired to supersede their legal status as *non compos mentis*. They were also frequently in the habit of expressing approbation towards those found to be abusing the mad, and were equally inclined to think more theoretically about the intersections between definitions of madness and civil law. Finally, a concern for improving unfortunate situations that had been created in part by the onset of madness led chancery court officials to extend and adapt the structure of commissions of lunacy to those who could not afford full court proceedings.

Notes

1 Porter, *Mind Forg'd Manacles*, p. 18. See also pp. 31–2.
2 *Ibid.*, p. 45.
3 C. E. Rosenberg, 'The therapeutic revolution: Medicine, meaning and social change in nineteenth-century America', *Perspectives in Biology and Medicine*, 20:4 (1977), 489.
4 William Pargeter, *Observations on Maniacal Disorders*, quoted in Porter, *Mind Forg'd Manacles*, p. 43.
5 G. Cheyne, *The English Malady, or, a Treatise of Nervous Diseases of All Kinds* (London: 1733), reprinted with an Introduction by R. Porter (London: Routledge, 1991).
6 See, Porter, *Mind Forg'd Manacles*, pp. 81–104.
7 Andrews and Scull, *Undertaker of the Mind*, p. 120.
8 *Ibid.*
9 *Ibid.*, p. 166. Andrews and Scull note that more than 75 per cent of Monro's patients were not sent to private madhouses.
10 34 E.R., Ex parte Chumley, 1789–1817, p. 721.

11 35 E.R., Tomlinson, Broadhurst Ex. parte, 1812, p. 23. The name of the person deemed *non compos mentis* is not given in this report.
12 *Ibid.*
13 *Ibid.*
14 This was probably Brooke House. See Andrews and Scull, *Customers and Patrons of the Mad-Trade*, pp. 43 and 106.
15 97 E.R., Rex v. William Clarke, 1762, p. 876. In the case of Deborah D'Vebre, who had been confined by her husband at Mr Turlington's private asylum, Monro was of the opinion that she had never been insane in the first place. This finding led to the court's protection of Mrs D'Vebre and an eventual separation from her husband. See 97 E.R., Rex v. Turlington, 1761, p. 741.
16 E.R., Rex v. William Clarke, 1762, p. 876.
17 27 E.R., Ex parte Southcote, 1751, p. 257.
18 *Ibid.*, p. 258.
19 *Ibid.*
20 *Ibid.*
21 *Ibid.*
22 29 E.R., Attorney general against Parnther, 1792, p. 633.
23 *Ibid.*
24 *Ibid.*
25 *Ibid.*
26 *Ibid.*, p. 634.
27 *Ibid.*
28 *Ibid.*
29 35 E.R., Brodie v. Barry, 1813, p. 233.
30 *Ibid.*
31 29 E.R., Sayer v. Bennet, 1784, p. 1084.
32 This case, along with a description of Brooke House, can be found in Andrews and Scull, *Undertaker of the Mind*, pp. 179–89.
33 29 E.R., Sayer v. Bennet, 1784, p. 1084.
34 See the discussion of other cases in *ibid.*, pp. 1084–86
35 *Ibid.*, p. 1084..
36 25 E.R., Ex parte Ferrars, 1730, p. 423.
37 *Ibid.*
38 *Ibid.*, p. 424.
39 27 E.R., Brown and How, 1740, p. 676.
40 *Ibid.*
41 *Ibid.*

42 *Ibid.*, p. 677.
43 *Ibid.*
44 *Ibid.*
45 *Ibid.*, p. 678.
46 For examples in a different context, see Warsh, *Moments of Unreason*, chapter 5, passim.
47 1 E.R., Richard Evans – Appellant William Blood, and others – Respondents, 1746, p. 1544.
48 *Ibid.*, p. 1543.
49 *Ibid.*
50 47 E.R., Price v. Bedford, 1784, p. 1125.
51 *Ibid.*
52 47 E.R., Machin v. Salkeld, 1784, p. 1124.
53 *Ibid.*
54 *Ibid.*, p. 1123.
55 *Ibid.*
56 *Ibid.*, p. 1124.
57 24 E.R., Ex parte Ludlow, 1731, p. 893.
58 *Ibid.*
59 *Ibid.*
60 *Ibid.*, p. 894.
61 *Ibid.*
62 *Ibid.*

6

Atlantic crossing: lunacy law as colonial inheritance

In Chapters 1 through 5 of this book, I argued that, over the course of a very long period in English society, the law of lunacy investigation was an important means of rendering rational the irrationalities of madness. In its application to specific cases, this legal process was subject to myriad nuances stemming from the concerns and actions of the families who initiated commissions of lunacy, from the disagreements between legal representatives, family members, Lord Chancellors and, occasionally, those suspected of being mad.[1] In the eyes of the legal authorities who adjudicated this law from the top (the Lord Chancellors) commissions of lunacy were the principal mechanisms by which to protect those mad people who had financial or economic means; to re-establish a sense of order upon the property and person of the mad; and to encourage, if not force, those whose interests were affected by the disruptions of madness to be rational in their responses. This was the broader regulatory agenda onto which legal authorities attempted to impress the law.

The effectiveness and longevity of lunacy investigation law in England at many levels largely explains why it was considered to be equally useful as a means for managing madness in the new colonial settings of England's empire. Lunacy investigation law was brought into colonial settings like New Jersey as part of a broader process of colonial rule through legal imposition. This chapter examines how the commission of lunacy was resettled and developed in one such colonial and post-colonial setting – New Jersey. Subsequent chapters explore how, in practice, the law of lunacy investigation came to hold an even more important place in this 'new world' society which, until the mid to late nineteenth century, had not developed the same scale of institutional provision for madness as was available in England by that time. But, before laying out the evidence for the effective resettling of lunacy law in North America, this chapter begins with a broader consideration of how lunacy law fits into more general assessments of the role of law in the exercise of imperial power.

Lunacy investigation law and empire

In his essay on the role of law in legitimising imperial rule in the Americas, Peter Fitzpatrick assesses the impact of Francisco de Vitoria's early sixteenth-century work, *De Indis*, on perceptions of governance and control in the 'new world'.[2] In part of his wide-ranging assessment, Fitzpatrick argues that European concepts of international law in the age of imperial expansion were designed to justify the subjugation of the peoples encountered in new-found lands while, at the same time, 'accommodating' them 'within the fold of [European] civilization'.[3] As Fitzpatrick put it: 'Law had responsively to extend towards new found worlds but, having done so, it sought their subjugation also in a determined order. The supreme justification of imperial rule was that it brought order to chaos, reined in "archaic instincts", and all this aptly enough through subjection to "laws".'[4] It is no stretch to consider that the 'archaic instincts' of indigenous peoples in lands of interest to England and other empires included their mental incapacity to understand key concepts of Western law – i.e. property ownership and inheritance – and thus their inability to govern them rationally. Although Fitzpatrick's principal concern was how Francisco de Vitoria justified the violence of imperial domination of indigenous peoples and newly encountered territory through the application of international law, it is clear that de Vitoria was one of many thinkers who *also* considered how these same legal concepts might establish order among the European colonists in the settler societies they were trying to create.[5] These men, including de Vitoria, Hugo Grotius[6] and Alberico Gentili,[7] also borrowed heavily from earlier Roman ideas about law and governance in their considerations of the rule of law and of the global domination of European powers.

The ideas circulating in Europe that connected law, imperial rule and their relationship to property ownership and rational thought were not lost on John Brydall, barrister of Lincoln's Inn and publisher of several authoritative tracts on a wide range of jurisprudence.[8] In 1700, Brydall published one of the earliest collections of English laws relating to those considered *non compos mentis*. One of the more extraordinary things about Brydall's work, *Non Compos Mentis: Or, the Law Relating to Natural Fools, Mad-Folks, and Lunatick Persons, Inquisited, and Explained, for Common Benefit*, is its introductory remarks explaining 'upon what Right the Dominion of Infants, Idiots and Mad-men is grounded.'[9] Brydall made his argument based largely on Roman jurist Hugo Grotius' work, *De Jure Belli et Pacis* (*On the Law of War and Peace*),[10] but also supplemented his study with words of wisdom from Roman statesman Cassiodorus, from the early seventeenth-century bishop of Exeter, Ralph Brownrig, and from the early modern English Protestant savant, William Ames.[11]

Using his own translation of Grotius' treatise *On the Law of War and Peace*, Brydall concurred with this father of international law that

> If we respect ... the Laws of Nature only, no Right of Property can be admitted to those, who have not the Use of Reason: But *Jus Gentium*, the Law of Nations, for the Common Good, doth indulge this Favour unto *Infants, Idiots and Mad-Men* that they may lawfully receive and retain the propriety of things. All Mankind in the mean time sustaining their Persons.[12]

Summarising Grotius and Cassiodorus, Brydall noted that if the 'right of Dominion' consisted both of 'the right to have and to hold things in Propriety', and 'freely and voluntarily to dispose of them without a Guardian', the latter could not be the prerogative of the mad. In effect, the 'right of Alienation'[13] was not a possibility for the mentally alienated. Brydall noted that civilised societies, from the Roman period forward, recognised that the law would exercise these rights on behalf of those who were *non compos mentis*.

Having established the legal foundations for the care and protection of those considered to be *non compos mentis*, Brydall then rhetorically asked the reader: 'If there be found a People that have no use of Natural Reason at all, Whether all Right and Dominion may be taken from them?'[14] Again his answer was heavily indebted to his translation of Grotius' *On the Law of War and Peace*. Brydall acknowledged Grotius' caution that in order to 'entitle ourselves to be the first founders, 'tis necessary, that the Land so found should belong to none.'[15] Thus, even if the land in question was inhabited by 'Pagans and Infidels, or by Men of dull Apprehension', these people could still have prior claim to the land. However, 'in case there can be found a People that have no use of natural Reason at all, there all Right and Dominion may be taken from them.'[16] Making the connections between states of *non compos mentis* and the dominion over new-found lands quite clear, Brydall concluded, once more with Grotius:

> Yet ought we in Charity to make them such an Allowance as is necessary for their support and maintenance, as well as to other Ideots and Madmen. For as to what has been already said concerning the Care which the Law of Nations take to preserve the Property of Infants and Lunatics, it appertains to such People with whom we have any commerce, or make any contract with, which we cannot have with such a People, as are wholly and altogether destitute of Reason; and therefore of these it may be very well doubted, whether they have any Property at all.[17]

Using this introduction as the background for his collection of English laws of *non compos mentis* is significant in many respects. Brydall was drawing a line from the earliest legal sages that he knew, from the Roman period, to his own English legal traditions in order to add integrity and significance to his arguments about madness. He wanted to emphasise the fundamental and long-standing relationship between mental alienation and the inability to control property. This applied equally to those found to be mentally unsound in England and to those peoples, newly encountered, who were found to be incapable of recognising the essence of the value of property or the property relationship. In both cases it was the duty of civilised society to provide for 'those wholly and altogether destitute of Reason.'[18]

The connections forged by Brydall between the origins of the English law of *non compos mentis* and the consideration of this legal tradition in terms of imperial rule, created a line of argument that was ready made for English colonial control in North America and elsewhere. Christopher Tomlins argues that 'geography and law' were mobilised as much as pure force was, to 'explain and justify' English colonial rule. In this respect, he notes: 'Colonization ... has an epistemology of its own – a theory of knowing that enables the processes of "discovery" and ordering (or more accurately reordering) inherent in appropriation to take place.'[19] In the English colonies, the legal inheritance of the law of *non compos mentis* would safeguard both immediate economic and social concerns of settlers whose relatives had gone mad, while at the same time preserving the integrity of property ownership.

Pundits of the colonial project claimed that the ownership and improvement of land as a Western inheritance differentiated European colonisers and colonists from aboriginal peoples. A legal mechanism that protected this claim in the face of awkward examples of mad colonists who had lost their mental capacity to govern their property rationally would be useful.[20] The utility of lunacy investigation law, as an English import that developed a life of its own in New Jersey, is thus bound up with English colonialism and legal concepts of landownership. As G. Edward White points out in *Law in American History*:

> At the opening of the seventeenth century the Spanish, French, and Dutch had established outposts in North America and were actively engaged in commercial trade with the Native tribes. The English presence was insignificant. A hundred years later, former residents of England were the dominant European group on the continent, and by the 1770s the influence of the Dutch and Spanish could have been described as negligible, although the French remained a significant presence.[21]

Moreover, the effects of 'English approaches to land use in North American on its Amerindian inhabitants', along with the displacement and death of thousands of indigenous peoples from 'microbe epidemics', heavily marked the English domination of New Jersey in the hundred years preceding the American Revolution.[22] A crucial part of this imperial unfolding connected landownership and law directly. As White puts it:

> When Amerindians first encountered English settlers in the early years of the seventeenth century, the two groups held dramatically different conceptions of landownership and use. The idea that land could be 'owned' exclusively by humans, who could then exclude other humans from it, was incompatible with Amerindian beliefs and practices. The Amerindian tribes practiced territoriality, returning to particular areas to hunt or to plant and harvest agricultural crops. They resented the invasion of other tribes into preferred areas, sometimes engaging in wars with the invaders ... Amerindians did not, however enclose the areas they used for agriculture, nor seek to change the shape of those areas.[23]

White explains that, despite these vast differences in land conceptualisation, early 'colonial courts had recognised that their procedures and outcomes needed to acknowledge the cultural traditions and practice of Amerindian tribes'.[24] However, this situation was to change during the course of the eighteenth century as the power of England over the region grew, as the population disparities between English colonists and indigenous peoples increased and as English migrants and their children increasingly dominated the landscape with their farms. The construction of fences, of enclosures and of farm buildings, and the production of grain crops and livestock, reflected their legal and cultural understandings of property ownership.

Indeed, as John Weaver explains in *The Great Land Rush and the Making of the Modern World: 1650–1900*, concepts of landownership were key to the unfolding domination of 'Neo-European settlement' in North America and elsewhere. In Weaver's view, 'as an outcome of democratic aspirations and manhood suffrage, the United States and subsequently British settlement colonies institutionalised access to land ownership by people of modest means'.[25] Furthermore:

> Improvement and its synonyms and antonyms – terms such as betterment and advancement; negligence and waste – were intrinsic to formal and informal practices of taking and allocating land. The rationalizations and rhetoric of legislators and administrators incorporated these almighty words when they justified formal schemes to take land from indigenous peoples or drafted regulations for distributing land to settlers.[26]

In this environment, the law of lunacy investigation helped, in New Jersey at least, to justify the imperial assertions of legal right to land occupation in North America. The laws of lunacy investigation also reinforced the right of property ownership and its improvement to a wider range of individuals in New Jersey than in England – including those 'of modest means'. At the same time, it protected this inherited legal right in the face of irrational decisions about property in Britain's colonies.

The practical reach of lunacy investigation law

Despite the obvious theoretical and practical advantages of transplanting a version of lunacy investigation law into the colonies, the question of this law's jurisdiction outside of England was frequently debated in the English courts from the eighteenth to the twentieth centuries.[27] The deliberations in several cases indicate concern and discussion about how to extend the law effectively into new territories whose social, political and economic circumstances did not easily fit the English context from which the law had emerged. In one case, John Houstoun in Jamaica was found to be insane by a commission of lunacy taken out in the colony, with three individuals appointed as the committee of the lunatic and his property. In 1826 the committee thought that he should be taken to England 'for the sake of his health'.[28] However, upon his arrival his 'illegitimate sister' and her husband petitioned for a commission of lunacy in England. The committee from Jamaica saw no reason for this duplication of legal services, but Lord Chancellor Eldon disagreed. In Eldon's view, 'the commission now existing in *Jamaica* is no reason why a commission should not issue here. On the contrary, it is evidence of the absolute necessity that there should be somebody authorised to deal with the person and estate of this lunatic. While the lunatic is here, no Court will have any authority over him or his property, unless a commission is taken out.'[29]

A more spectacular case of jurisdictional jostling over the legal control of lunacy involved Princess Bariatinski, whose father was a Russian nobleman and whose mother was English. Bariatinski's mother died giving birth to her in 1807 in Russia and, at some point, she was sent by her father to England to be cared for by her maternal grandmother and aunt. Her father died in 1826, and a year later, at the age of twenty-one, the Princess 'exhibited symptoms of mental derangement, and soon afterwards became a confirmed lunatic, in which state, however, she continued to live under the care of her mother's family, without any application being made for a commission of lunacy'.[30] The Lord Chancellor involved in this case clearly regretted the absence of an earlier lunacy trial by which Bariatinski's property and person could have been more securely protected – especially since the Princess's fortunes in England amounted to about £30,000, not counting the value of her property in Russia. In 1843, Prince Bariatinski, half-brother to the Princess, arrived in England to claim the 'custody and management of her person and property, insisting that by the laws of Russia, as the head of his family, he was entitled to them'.[31] This threat led Bariatinski's maternal aunt to file the petition for a commission of lunacy. The prince countered by arguing that the lunacy trial was unnecessary; but, covering his bases, he also wished to be in charge of the petition, if the courts insisted on this course of action.

This set the stage for remarkable legal wrangling between the two parties. Part of the issue was the fact that the Princess had been born in Russia, giving rise to the question of whether the English courts had jurisdiction to act in her case. Legal experts working on behalf of Princess Bariatinski's aunt could not find 'any reported case in which an alien has been the subject of a commission of lunacy'.[32] The Prince's counsel argued not only that he had a right to his sister and her property, according to the laws of Russia, but also that international law prohibited one country meddling in the affairs of another. Quoting Vattel's *Law of Nations*, the right of the Prince was laid out clearly: '[The] State, which ought to respect the rights of other nations, and in general those of all mankind, cannot arrogate to herself any power over the person of a foreigner, who, although he has entered her territory, has not become her subject.'[33] This evidence did not impress Lord Chancellor Lyndhurst, who countered that Vattel's proclamations on international law 'supposes that the proceeding is directed *against* the party'.[34] In this instance, Lyndhurst argued, 'this is all for [the Princess's] benefit'. Reiterating the English Crown's role of protecting the property and person of those found insane, in the hopes that they would at some point regain their sanity, Lyndhurst concluded that 'unless some authority [presumably more convincing than Vattel] can be cited to the contrary ... the Court has jurisdiction, and that it is its duty to throw protection around the person and property of an individual in this situation'.[35] In fact, Lyndhurst could not imagine what could 'be more proper, what more humane, what more consistent with the general character of the law of England, than such a course?'[36] Lyndhurst gave control of the commission of lunacy to the mad Bariatinski's 'aunt who has hitherto had the care of the lunatic'. His only concession to the Prince was to grant him permission to attend the proceedings, and to give him access to his sister 'in company, of course, with the medical gentleman' who attended her.[37]

The cases of Houstoun and Bariatinski reveal much about the English courts' thinking about the jurisdictional powers of the law of lunacy investigation. On the one hand, granting colonies the powers to hold commissions of lunacy and to appoint guardians through the auspices of their governors was no substitute for doing the same in England, should Lord Chancellors deemed it expedient. In some respects, this confirmed that the colonies, although empowered to deal with madness according to English civil legal traditions, were still junior players in their handling of the law. When an English subject came back to England, colonial law lost power. On the other hand, the English courts appeared quite willing to extend what they considered to be the generosity of their lunacy laws to those not technically considered to be English subjects. The 'generous' spirit of lunacy investigation law and its practical benefits could even outweigh considerations of citizenship.

The 1751 case of Thomas Southcot (previously discussed in Chapter 5), who had been institutionalised in France and whose inability to attend a lunacy trial was problematic for Lord Chancellor Hardwicke, gave rise to a much broader set of considerations about the jurisdiction of lunacy laws for those living outside of England – especially in the colonies. The case report of this trial noted that: 'In the *Plantations* indeed the governors will have a power to take care of the person and estate there by virtue of the king's commission appointing them governors: but no farther. They cannot take care of a lunatic's estate in *England*; for to that there must be a commission under the great seal of *England* appointing a committee of the estate.'[38] Further elaborating the point, the report of this case noted that:

> the king is to defend all his subjects if not capable of defending or governing themselves, or ordering their rights, goods, and chattels; which if from the necessity, extending to the person and the property; and the only way to do it is prescribed by the law by commission of inquiry, first to ascertain that he is a lunatic, after which being found, it is immaterial to the care of the estate, whether he is or is not in the kingdom ... The law gives this enquiry with two distinct views; for sake of the lunatic or idiot himself, and for the sake of the crown's right. The first is, that the party may not do himself a mischief, may be taken proper care of, and put into proper hands; which inquisition, when the person is beyond seas, would be fruitless, as it could not have effect: but in the other view it is absolutely necessary to have such inquiry relating to the prerogative of the crown as to these lands in *England*: of which right by the common law, and declared by the statute *de Prerog. Regis*, the crown cannot be deprived by the person's being beyond sea.[39]

Here, we can see the logic of the law trying to include cases of lunacy that lie beyond England's geographical jurisdiction. In the case of those going mad in the 'plantations' it was sometimes necessary to launch two lunacy law investigations – one sanctioned by the governor of the colony, securing the guardianship of the lunatic and his/her property in the colony, and the other sanctioned by the Lord Chancellor to secure the integrity of his/her property in England. As Hardwicke put it:

> there can be no good reason why, if any subject having an estate in *England*, happens to be an idiot or lunatic, but is out of the kingdom, there can be no inquiry here. No inquiry can be made beyond sea; for it is not to be executed by the commissioners only, as in taking an answer or assigning a guardian, which may be executed beyond sea, but there must be a jury to inquire of the fact; which must be of a county of *England:* then if no inquiry can be here, both the person and his estate would be in a very unfortunate case, and also the King as to his prerogative.[40]

Acknowledging that it was impossible for the English courts to secure a suspected lunatic's wellbeing in the colonies, Hardwicke nevertheless noted that by virtue of powers that England vested in the colonies' governors, the same process of lunacy investigation and guardianship would be guaranteed. Nevertheless, the result was still a complex overlapping of 'legal coverage' in cases of English lunatics abroad.

The cases of Houstoun, Bariatinski and Southcot (along with others) helped legal authorities to refine the use of lunacy investigation law in jurisdictions beyond England's borders, including colonial jurisdictions.[41] In the white settler colony of New Jersey, it is clear that the implementation and development of this law was more carefully considered. In New Jersey, the theoretical justifications for the implementation of this law, along with the practical rationales as described at the beginning of this chapter, were built into the fabric of colonial development from the start. The result was that lunacy investigation law was the first formal state response to madness in the colony of New Jersey, as it likely was in other English colonies in which more permanent white settlement was expected.

Settling lunacy investigation law in New Jersey

In New Jersey the integration of lunacy investigation law began relatively early in the colony's English history. In 1664 England took the colony over by force from the Dutch, who had established a colonial presence there in 1624.[42] England created two proprietary colonies: East Jersey, owned by Sir George Carteret, and West Jersey, owned by Lord John

Berkeley.[43] As early as 1692, there is evidence that Andrew Hamilton, the governor of both East and West Jersey for five years, was exercising his authority to provide guardianship for the insane. For example, he appointed the wife of Samuel H., of Shrewsburry, Samuel H.'s daughter and her husband as Samuel H.'s guardians, as he was 'rendered uncapable [sic] to act through a distemper of lunacy'.[44]

The paper trail documenting the New Jersey governor's exercise of this authority in lunacy is hard to trace in the first half of the eighteenth century, but by 1762 a recorded case indicates that a more fully elaborated version of the commission of lunacy process was in place. This case involved the application by Abraham Abrahams for a committee to be appointed to look after the property and person of Jacob L., his brother-in-law. Abrahams expressed concern that Jacob L. 'had for several years been a lunatic', a fact which became more problematic in the face of Jacob L.'s inheritance of estates in the New Jersey state counties of Somerset and Middlesex after the death of his father.[45] Abrahams proposed that he be appointed guardian of Jacob L.'s person and that he, along with Robert Sproull and David Goslins, 'go on a bond' to protect Jacob L.'s property 'while he is of unsound mind'.[46] This the governor granted. But, two years later, in 1764, Jacob L. successfully appealed to 'revoke' this earlier decision, based on the following challenge:

> Whereas Abraham Abrahams, brother-in-law of Jacob L., son and heir at law of Moses L., was appointed guardian of said Jacob, which letters were granted without inquisition taken, and not in due manner, and Jacob, who is now of age, has applied that the letters may be made void, and that he may take possession of his own property, therefore, the letters are made void.[47]

This was an early example of a New Jersey colonist who recognised the inconsistencies in the practice of lunacy investigation law and who was able to successfully challenge a wrongful process. Three years later, another case read more like a petition than a trial process. In 1767 petitioners on behalf of Benjamin B. of Middlesex County asked the colonial government to grant a 'Letter of Guardianship' to one of Benjamin B.'s sons, Ezekiel to take charge of another of his sons, William. The 'subscribers' were neighbours of Benjamin B. who testified that William had 'been a lunatic for some time, and is not able to provide for himself or family, and he must be confined with chains'.[48] Moreover, William's father, they said, had become too old and feeble to look after his son. In this case, William's custody was quickly given over to Ezekiel, with the latter and George Herriot serving as bondsmen.

These semblances of the law of lunacy investigation in practice in colonial New Jersey were made more official on 29 July 1772 with the circulation of a draft clause 'to be inserted in the instructions to Governors in America giving them, as Chancellors, the power to issue commissions for the care and custody of idiots and lunatics'.[49] This rather wordy draft document, which actually addressed the colony of Nova Scotia but circulated among all of England's North American possessions, reiterated the 'Royal Prerogative' in matters of idiocy and lunacy in England and in 'our Provinces in America', but it also noted that 'great trouble and charges may arise' for colonial officials who 'shall have occasion to resort unto Us for directions'.[50] With this in mind, the colonial governors were informed that they had 'full Power and Authority without expecting any further special Warrant from Us … to give Order and Warrant for the preparing of Grants of the Custodies of such Ideots and Lunaticks and their estates as are or shall be found by Inquisitions'.[51] The governors were further encouraged to follow the legal process of lunacy investigation law 'as nearly as may be as hath been heretofore used and accustomed in making the same under the Great Seal of Great Britain'.[52]

New Jersey governor William Franklin responded on 12 October that he saw no objection to the proposed clause, adding that 'it may be of Advantage to the King's Subjects in the Colonies'.[53] Franklin further noted that while 'the laws of this Province have made no Provision that I can find respecting either Ideots or Lunatics … I believe there have been Instances where the Governors, as Chancellors, have undertaken to act in the Manner which it is intended by the proposed Clause'.[54] The circulation and acceptance of this clause may have been prompted by colonial officials' concerns about obtaining for themselves this official authority over the legal process of those considered to be mad. In New Hampshire, for instance, as early as 1718 Richard West was appealing to the Council of Trade and Plantations that since 'ye Governors of ye Provinces in ye West Indies have alsoe ye power of a Chancellour likewise granted to them perhaps your Lordpps. may think it adviseable that ye like Commissions should issue from the Government there'.[55] Given that this clause was circulated to all of England's North American colonies, it is likely that several or all of them were in the practice of following this kind of procedure in cases of madness in which property was involved. While this book focuses on New Jersey, there is strong evidence indicating that the law of lunacy investigation was developed elsewhere in colonial and post-colonial North America – most notably in Massachusetts, New York, New Jersey, Upper Canada (present day Ontario), New Brunswick and Prince Edward Island.[56]

Within a few years of this correspondence, the relationship between England and her North American colonies changed permanently with the great upheavals of the American Revolutionary War. The secession of the thirteen colonies from England's political and economic grasp did not convince colonies further north to follow suit.[57] Thus, by 1776 there was still a British North America consisting of a handful of colonies situated geographically above an independent, expansionist United States of America. Yet, in former colonies like New Jersey, as strong as the impulse to sever ties with England might have been, this did not appear to include the wholesale rejection of English law.[58] In fact, section XXII of the 1776 Constitution of New Jersey explicitly states that 'the common law of England, as well as so much of the statute law, as have been heretofore practiced in this Colony, shall still remain in force, until they shall be altered by a future law of the Legislature; such parts only excepted, as are repugnant to the rights and privileges contained in this Charter; and that the inestimable right of trial by jury shall remain confirmed as a part of the law of this Colony, without repeal, forever'.[59]

When in 1794 it came time for the new State of New Jersey's Council and General Assembly to consider which aspects of the English civil law of lunacy were 'repugnant to the rights and privileges' laid out in New Jersey's constitution, the answer, it seemed, was very few. In fact, the 1794 New Jersey Act for Supporting Idiots and Lunatics, and Preserving their Estates left the intent of the English law largely intact. The chancellor (not the king or his representative) was vested with the power and authority to provide for the 'care' and 'safe keeping' of idiots and lunatics, along with their 'lands and tenements, goods and chattels'. For both categories of *non compos mentis*, provision was to be made through the profits from the lands and tenements of the alienated, and through the use of their own goods and chattels. It was explicitly stated that no 'waste or destruction' of the property was to be permitted. Much like in English law, it was understood that idiots had no likelihood of recovery and thus, after death, their property descended to their heirs, and the 'residue of their goods, chattels and profits' descended to their next of kin. The same applied to lunatics, with the exception that, also following English law, in the event of recovery from madness they were to have 'the residue of the goods, chattels and profits' restored to them.[60]

Six cases were presented to the New Jersey courts between the passing of this first legislation relating to idiots and lunatics in 1794 and a more detailed supplement to that Act in 1804. What is striking about these cases is that they suggest a much more sophisticated legal process of lunacy investigation law than that which is contained in the 1794 Act itself. In the first case, in 1797, Ahab S. is described in a petition made by his brother-in-law, Michael Asay as an idiot who is incapable of managing a 200-acre plot of 'well forested' land that had been passed down to him by his father. Worse, Ahab S.'s mother had been able to convince her son to agree to the cutting down of timber on his inherited property whenever she wanted money. According to Asay: 'She easily persuades him to consent to any bargain she proposes by which means the timber is destroyed.'[61] Asay made it clear in his petition that although 'not insensible to the unhappy state to which his brother in law is reduced', he was worried about the likelihood of his own two sons inheriting any of his brother-in-law's land at the rate that Ahab S. was wasting it.[62] With these circumstances described, and with the supporting petitions of several relatives and neighbours, Asay pleaded to the court for help. The court's response was to hold a commission on 2 December 'at the House of Joseph Hatkinson Inn Keeper, Mount Holly by ten of the clock' to inquire whether Ahab S. late of the township of Nothampton in the said County yeoman be a fool or ideot or not'.[63] The commission found Ahab S. to be an idiot, and his property was placed under the care of his brother-in-law.[64]

This process of an initial petition (usually from a family member, endorsed by family and neighbours) followed by an arrangement for a public trial (usually at the house of a local inn keeper, and which resulted in a decision and a guardianship arrangement if necessary) was put into legal form in the 1804 General Assembly of the New Jersey legislature. The 1804 supplement to the 1794 Act merely codified prior practice, making the law an even closer approximation to its English counterpart, with some necessary changes to accommodate the realities of the fledgling American state. There were three significant aspects of the 1804 Act. First, it explicitly stated: 'That all cases of Ideocy and Lunacy, shall be determined by an inquest on a commission of Ideocy or Lunacy issued by the Chancellor, and the proceedings thereon shall in all respects be conducted, the manner heretofore practised.' Second, the 'Orphans Court of the county in which the ideot or lunatic' resided was the legal authority in charge of the proceedings in lunacy. This included, among other things, the appointment of guardians 'who shall have the care and provide for the safe keeping of such Ideot or Lunatic, his or her lands, tenements, goods and chattles' according to the provisions of the 1794 Act. Finally, the 1804 Act outlined procedures for the Orphans Court to allow guardians to judiciously sell off the property and goods of the alienated under their charge if it was deemed necessary in order to settle their debts or provide for their continued maintenance.[65]

The Act passed in 1818 was the last, and in some respects most comprehensive, major legislative consideration about madness in New Jersey until the mid-nineteenth century. It consisted of two sections, both of which spelled out the conditions under which those considered to be mad could be imprisoned. The first section made it clear that 'no ideot or lunatic during the time of his or her lunacy, shall be, or stand committed, or detained in prison for want of bail, or in execution, in any civil action, or in any action for a penalty'. In the event that those considered *non compos mentis* were put into custody, they would be discharged by court motions or by writs of *habeas corpus*. However, section two of the Act explained that 'any lunatic furiously mad or dangerous to be permitted to go at large' could , by warrant of two justices of the peace, be 'apprehended, and kept safely locked up and chained if necessary, in some secure place'. The costs of this process were to be taken from the goods and chattels of the lunatic. However, if he/she was too poor, the costs were to be borne by the overseers of the poor of the county in which the lunatic resided.

In a proviso borrowed directly from early and mid-eighteenth-century English legislation, the Act concluded with the following: 'this act or any thing therein contained shall not extend, or be construed to restrain or abridge the power or authority of the chancellor, touching or concerning such lunatics or mad persons, or to prevent any of the friends or relations of such persons from taking them under their own care and protection'.[66] In many respects, New Jersey's 1818 Act was a replica of England's 1714 Act for the More Effectual Punishing of Rogues, Vagabonds, Sturdy Beggars and Vagrants and the subsequent 1743 Justices

Commitment Act, discussed in Chapter 2 of this book. The wording is in places so similar that it is clear that American legal experts in New Jersey were highly aware of the old English lunacy laws and how they worked. It also suggests that legal authorities in the American state were confident that they could respond adequately to the challenges of madness by adopting English law, despite the clear differences between the social and economic realities of New Jersey and those of England.

In 1820, the New Jersey Act Concerning Idiots and Lunatics consolidated and extended the three previous Acts. The Act required guardians to make careful accounts of their 'administration of the estate' of their charges.[67] Further supplements passed by New Jersey's general assembly in 1823, 1840, 1842, 1852 and 1854 were designed to tighten up the regulations provided in the 1820 Act. The 1823 supplement offered a more detailed explanation of the rules governing the apprehension of those considered to be 'furiously mad, or dangerous to be permitted to go at large', and payment for their confinement.[68] In an 1840 amendment, reminiscent of jurisdictional discussions in English lunacy trials, New Jersey legislators decided that a guardian could be 'appointed for an idiot or lunatic residing out of the state, if owning property within the state'.[69] The 1842 amendment detailed how a new guardian was to be selected through the Orphans Court in the event that the originally appointed guardian died.[70] Ever cognisant of the important relationship between madness and property, the 1852 and 1854 amendments added detail to the procedures by which an insane person's property could be sold for his/her maintenance, with all expenditures carefully accounted for.[71]

Although New Jersey's early legislators clearly viewed the somewhat modified replication of England's laws of lunacy investigation as advantageous to the determination of madness and its management, they were also well aware of the advantages of confinement in certain cases. As the legislative concerns expressed about those considered 'furiously mad' and thus 'dangerous to be at large' suggest, the confinement of some of those exhibiting signs of madness was certainly among the responses in New Jersey in both its colonial and post-colonial eras. There were different forms of confinement resorted to by overseers of the poor and local constables, including having an individual 'locked up and chained if necessary, in some secure place', or 'kept in the gaol' of the county in which the lunatic resided. Moreover, by 1839, a resolution at the sixty-third sitting of the Council and General Assembly authorised New Jersey's governor to 'appoint one or more competent person or persons to ascertain as accurately as practicable, the number, age, sex and condition of the lunatics of this state: also to ascertain the best and most effectual means for their relief: and if in their opinion the erection of a state asylum be the best remedy'.[72]

By 1843, there was enough momentum for the institutionalisation of New Jersey's mad for an Act mandating the overseers of the poor of the state's counties to examine 'the condition and circumstance of ... idiots and lunatics: and if it shall appear to them that there is reasonable ground to believe that any of such persons can be restored to their right mind, it shall be their duty to cause such persons, under a warrant ... be taken to a lunatic asylum in one of the adjoining states of New York or Pennsylvania, and there supported at the expense' of their respective counties of residence.[73] Completing the course towards institutional confinement, New Jersey's first State Lunatic Asylum was opened in 1848, receiving eighty-six patients by the end of the year.[74]

Conclusion

Lunacy law, borrowed directly from England, appeared incongruous, in some respects, within a context for which it was not created. As we have seen, in England this evolving body of law was serviceable over a remarkably long period of time, despite significant changes in the understanding of madness. For example, in *Madness at Home* Akahito Suzuki notes that the numbers of commissions of lunacy in England did not decline but, rather, increased as the asylum option became more readily available.[75] Nevertheless, from the mid to the late nineteenth century, the proliferation of private and public asylums in England, along with the bureaucratisation of legal certification of the insane at the point of asylum entry, made the long legal tradition of lunacy law investigation largely obsolete by the turn of the century. In North American settings like New Jersey, commissions of lunacy were both in theory and in practice a product of the broader British imperial impetus. They were introduced as an aspect of colonial governance when they were still in full use in England. Despite the tumultuous changes experienced as New Jersey transitioned from British colony to fledgling American state, the law of lunacy investigation was a very successful legal transplant, taking root in ways that could not have been anticipated by those who had shaped the law in England. In New Jersey, the law applied to a much broader socio-economic group – those controlling large and small land holdings, and those whose wealth ranged from fortunes in the bank, to different-sized properties, to a few household chattels. As we shall see in subsequent chapters, this democratisation of the application of lunacy investigation law enabled it to play a major role in the determination of madness, its management and treatment in nineteenth-century New Jersey.

By the time that the New Jersey asylum had opened its doors, the law of lunacy investigation and practice had been developing in New Jersey for well over a century. As in England, this body of law in New Jersey strongly influenced how madness was understood and how it was responded to. It served as a formidable regulatory, managerial and caring mechanism for madness well after the New Jersey State Lunatic Asylum opened its doors. In fact, there is strong evidence to indicate that the patterns of behaviour towards madness to which lunacy investigation law had greatly contributed were not readily abandoned during the early asylum period. The final chapters of this book explain how this law became so influential, how its practice influenced responses to madness at the familial and community levels, and how it was gradually affected by the introduction of the asylum alternative.

Notes

1 In this respect, the theory and practice of lunacy investigation law was very much like the theory and practice of asylum medicine. Whatever the intentions were of each method of managing madness, the realities were far more complex.
2 P. Fitzpatrick, 'Terminal legality: Imperialism and the (de)composition of law', in D. Kirby and C. Coleborne (eds), *Law, History, Colonialism: The Reach of Empire* (Manchester: Manchester University Press, 2001), pp. 9–25.
3 Ibid., p. 19.
4 Ibid.
5 Ibid. See also, O. P. Dickason, 'The sixteenth-century French version of empire: The other side of self-determination', in G. Warkentin and C. Podruchny (eds), *Decentering the Renaissance: Canada and Europe in*

Atlantic crossing

   Multidisciplinary Perspective, 1500–1700 (Toronto: University of Toronto Press, 2001), pp. 87–109.
6 P. Borschberg, *Hugo Grotius, the Portuguese and Free Trade in the East Indies* (Singapore: National University of Singapore Press, 2010).
7 B. Kingsbury and B. Straumann (eds), *Roman Foundations of the Law of Nations: Alberico Gentili and the Justice of Empire* (New York: Oxford University Press, 2010).
8 See F. Freemon, 'The origin of the medical expert witness: The insanity of Edward Oxford', *Journal of Legal Medicine*, 22:3 (2001), 349–73, at 350–1. Brydall's many legal publications included: John Brydall, *Jura coronae. His Majesties royal rights and prerogatives asserted, against papal usurpations, and other anti-monarchical attempts and practices. Collected out of the body of the municipal laws of England* (London: G. Dawes, 1680); Brydall, *Speculum juris anglicani, or, A view of the laws of England as they are divided into statutes, common-law and customs: incidently, of the customs appertaining to the famous city of London, never before printed; together with resolutions on several of them, given by the reverend judges at Westminster* (London: John Streater, Eliz. Flesher and H. Twyford, assignes of Rich. Atkyns and Edward Atkyns, for Thomas Dring, 1673).
9 J. Brydall, *Non compos mentis: Or, the Law Relating to Natural Fools, Mad-Folks and Lunatick Persons, Inquisited, and Explained, for Common Benefit* (London: Richard and Edward Atkins, 1700), p. 1.
10 Hugo Grotius, *On the Law of War and Peace*, ed. Stephen Neff (New York: Cambridge University Press, 2012).
11 M. S. Bjornlie, *Politics and Tradition Between Rome, Ravenna and Constantinople: A Study of Cassiodorus and the Variae, 527–554* (Cambridge: Cambridge University Press, 2012); K. L. Sprunger, *The Learned Doctor William Ames* (Urbana: University of Illinois Press, 1972).
12 Brydall, *Non compos mentis*, pp. 1–2.
13 *Ibid.*, p. 2.
14 *Ibid.*
15 *Ibid.*
16 *Ibid.*
17 *Ibid.*, p. 3.
18 *Ibid.*
19 C. Tomlins, 'Law's empire: Chartering English colonies on the American mainland in the seventeenth century', in D. Kirby and C. Coleborne (eds),

Law, History, Colonialism: The Reach of Empire (Manchester: Manchester University Press, 2001), pp. 28 and 27.
20 This could be as much an exercise in self-justification as it was an overt show to indigenous groups. It is unlikely that many indigenous people participated in or learned from the lunacy trials conducted in local colonial communities. I have found no cases about indigenous people in my search of New Jersey lunacy trials.
21 G. E. White, *Law in American History, Volume I* (Oxford: Oxford University Press, 2012), p. 21.
22 Ibid., p. 21.
23 Ibid., pp. 28–9.
24 Ibid., p. 41.
25 J. Weaver, *The Great Land Rush and the Making of the Modern World: 1650–1900* (Montreal: McGill Queen's University Press, 2003), p. 12.
26 Ibid., p. 5.
27 For an extended discussion of the jurisdiction of English lunacy investigation law outside of England see J. Moran and L. Chilton, 'Mad migrants and the reach of English civil law', in M. Harper (ed.), *Migration and Mental Health: Past and Present* (Basingstoke: Palgrave Macmillan, 2016), pp. 149–70.
28 38 E.R., In the Matter of John Houstoun, 1826, p. 121.
29 Ibid.
30 41 E.R., In the Matter of The Princess Bariatinski, 1843, p. 674.
31 Ibid.
32 Ibid., p. 675.
33 Ibid.
34 Ibid.
35 Ibid.
36 Ibid.
37 Ibid.
38 27 E.R., Ex parte Southcote, 1751, p. 257.
39 Ibid.
40 Ibid.
41 Moran and Chilton, 'Mad migrants and the reach of English civil law'.
42 New Sweden was also a colonial presence from 1638 to 1655 on lands along the Delaware river.
43 C. A. Stansfield, *A Geography of New Jersey: The City in the Garden* (New Brunswick: Rutgers University Press, 1998), pp. 73–6.

44 'Calendar of the records in the office of the Secretary of State, 1664–1703', in W. Nelson (ed.), *Documents Relating to the Colonial History of the State of New Jersey* (Patterson: The Press Printing and Publishing Company, Vol. 21, 1899), pp. 193–4.
45 'Calendar of New Jersey wills, administrations, etc.', in A. Honeyman (ed.), *Documents Relating to the Colonial, Revolutionary and Post Revolutionary History of the State of New Jersey, Volume IV 1761–1770* (Somerville: Unionist-Gazette Association Printers, 1928), p. 7.
46 Ibid.
47 Ibid.
48 Honeyman, *Documents Relating to the Colonial, Revolutionary and Post Revolutionary History of the State of New Jersey*, p. 47.
49 'Draft of a clause to be inserted in the instructions to Governors in America, 29 July 1772', in F. Richard and W. Nelson (eds), *Archives of the State of New Jersey, First Series, vol. X, Documents Relating to the Colonial History of the State of New Jersey, Administration of Governor William Franklin, 1767–1776* (Newark: Daily Advertiser Printing House, 1886), pp. 382–3. It is worth noting that two decades earlier, in the case of Thomas Southcot in 1751, legal authorities were already of the opinion that 'in the *Plantations* indeed the governors will have the power to take care of the person and the estate there by virtue of the king's commission appointing them governors ....'. 27 E.R., Ex parte Southcote, 1751, p. 257.
50 'Draft of a clause', in Richard and Nelson (eds), *Documents*, pp. 382–3.
51 Ibid.
52 Ibid.
53 'Letter from Governor Franklin to the Lords of Trade, relative to the care and custody of Idiots and Lunatics', in Richard and Nelson (eds), *Documents*.
54 Ibid.
55 Richard West to the Council of Trade and Plantations, vol. 30, 11 July 1718, *Calendar of State Papers, Colonial: North America and the West Indies 1574–1739*, https://search.proquest.com/docview/1845199536?accountid=14670, (accessed 20 May 2018).
56 Lunacy trials are used as evidence in the following works: M. A. Jiminez, *Changing Faces of Madness: Early American Attitudes and Treatment of the Insane* (Hanover: University Press of New England, 1987); P. McCandless, *Moonlight, Magnolias and Madness: Insanity in North Carolina from the Colonial Period to the Progressive Era* (Chapel Hill: University of North Carolina Press, 1996); Cellard, *Histoire de la folie au québec*; T. Nootens,

Fous, prodigues et ivrognes. How many colonies followed suit, in what form and for how long awaits further historical investigation.
57 See M. Anderson, *The Battle for the Fourteenth Colony: America's War of Liberation in Canada, 1774–1776* (Hanover: University Press of New England, 2013); G. Rawlyk, *Revolution Rejected, 1775–1776* (Scarborough: Prentice-Hall, 1968); G. Stanley, *Canada Invaded, 1775–1776* (Toronto: Hakkert, 1973).
58 D. Kirby and C. Coleborne (eds), *Law, History, Colonialism: The Reach of Empire*, (Manchester: Manchester University Press, 2001).
59 Constitution of New Jersey, 1775, Section XXII, http://www.nj.gov/state/archives/docconst76.html (accessed 15 August 2013).
60 NJSA, 'An Act for Supporting Idiots and Lunatics, and Preserving their Estates', Chap. CCCCXCI, 21 November 1794.
61 NJSA, CC, LCF, Case of Ahab S., 1797.
62 *Ibid.*
63 *Ibid.*
64 The lunacy trials were found unprocessed at the NJSA, in boxes referred to by their nineteenth-century cataloguer as 'Lunacy Bundles'. They have since been flat filed and catalogued. Many thanks to Betty Epstein and Joseph Klett of the NJSA, without whose help these documents would not have been made accessible for researchers.
65 NJSA, A Supplement to the Act Entitled, 'An Act for Supporting Ideots and Lunatics and Preserving their Estates', CXXIV, Sec. 1, Twenty-Eighth General Assembly of the State of New Jersey, Trenton, 1 March 1804.
66 NJSA, 'An Act Respecting the Persons of Ideots and Lunatics, 1818, Forty Second General Assembly of the State of New Jersey'.
67 NJSA, 'An Act Concerning Idiots and Lunatics, Acts of the 44th Council and General Assembly of the State of New Jersey', Trenton, 28 February 1820.
68 NJSA, 'A Supplement to an Act, Entitled, An Act Concerning Idiots and Lunatics, Acts of the 48th Council and General Assembly of the State of New Jersey', Trenton, 2 December 1823.
69 NJSA, 'A Further Supplement to An Act Entitled, An Act Concerning Idiots and Lunatics', Acts of the 64th Council and General Assembly of the State of New Jersey, Trenton', 7 February 1840.
70 NJSA, 'A Further Supplement to An Act Entitled, An Act Concerning Idiots and Lunatics', Acts of the 66th Council and General Assembly of the State of New Jersey, Trenton, 10 March 1842.

71 NJSA, 'A Supplement to an Act, Entitled, An Act Concerning Idiots and Lunatics', Acts of the 76th Council and General Assembly of the State of New Jersey, Trenton, 26 February 1852; NJSA, 'A Further Supplement to An Act Entitled, An Act Concerning Idiots and Lunatics', Acts of the 78th Council and General Assembly of the State of New Jersey, Trenton, 17 March 1854.

72 NJSA, 'Resolution at the 63rd Session of the Council and General Assembly of the State of New Jersey, Trenton', 6 March 1839.

73 NJSA, 'An Act Respecting Poor Lunatics and Idiots, Acts of the 67th Council and General Assembly of the State of New Jersey, Trenton', 22 February 1843.

74 NJSA, *First Annual Report of the New Jersey Asylum for the Insane*, Trenton, 31 December 1848.

75 Suzuki notes that the use of lunacy investigation law was conditioned by several developments: 'Some of the rises and falls [in the number of lunacy trials] ... were obviously related to legislative changes. The 1853 Act and its Amendment in 1862 increased the number of commissions by making a commission easier and cheaper to obtain. The Lunacy Act of 1890 prompted a precipitous decline, for it enabled people to seek a simpler form of the protection of the property of lunatics and to bypass a commission. For the first half of the nineteenth century, however, no such obvious correlation can be discerned. Without stimulus of new legislation, more people started to seek a commission' Suzuki, *Madness at Home*, p. 22.

7

Family, friends and neighbours: localising madness in New Jersey

From the British colonial period of the late 1600s to the late nineteenth century, lunacy investigation law was firmly entrenched in New Jersey. The surviving lunacy trials at the disposal of the historian from which to reconstruct this response vary in quality in terms of the fullness of witnesses' testimonies and the presence or absence of relevant documents. Overall, however, the extent of documentation for New Jersey is remarkable. In some cases, the records permit the historian to track more than one trial in which the concern about the mental health of an individual spanned the course of many years. Also included are the deliberations of the court, witnesses' testimonies, records relating to the guardian arrangements of the mad and, in some cases, the process of traverse of the earlier court's decision. The survival of a continuous run of documents relating to lunacy investigation law in New Jersey allows for a closer analysis of the dynamics of family members seeking redress by lunacy trial, as well as a more in-depth consideration of how concepts of madness and mental health were affected by the development of lunacy investigation law.

In New Jersey it is possible to trace a two-fold process of understandings of and responses to madness as related to lunacy investigation law. First, we can delineate how the legal process itself had direct effects on conceptualisations of madness. Second, we can see a host of lay understandings of madness that can be gleaned from the testimonials of the lunacy trials. These lay views of and responses to insanity were partially shaped by the encounter with lunacy investigation law, but were also clearly part of much older traditional beliefs and practices. In the setting of New Jersey, the records left behind by the exercise of lunacy investigation law demonstrate the enduring usefulness of this law in negotiating responses to madness. The accounts of relatives and neighbours of the insane offer the historian a rare window onto practices around madness that did not necessarily form part of formal medical or institutional responses. These records also show how informal traditions of understanding and caring for the mad intersected with both legal and, later, institutional responses to madness and the changes wrought as a result of this process.

Over the course of the nineteenth century, the law of lunacy investigation emerged like a web, forming connections both with traditional popular understandings of and responses to madness, and with emerging psychiatric institutional responses. While there is no doubt that after the mid-nineteenth century institutional psychiatry gained pace in its influence in the diagnosis and treatment of madness, in the first half of the century its presence in New Jersey was minimal. Moreover, at mid-century the relationship between lunacy investigation law and the asylum was more complex and significant than historians have thus far considered. This relationship between overlapping and, at times, competing systems of care and treatment of the insane is given due consideration in the rest of this book.

The present chapter examines lunacy trials that highlight the intersections of law, family, property and power in New Jersey. These trials show the effects of mad behaviour on family dynamics, and how families used lunacy trials to help shore up and shape the way that property, inheritance and the care of the mad would be handled in situations that varied widely in late eighteenth- and nineteenth-century New Jersey society. Focusing on familial responses through the use of lunacy investigation law also highlights how gender and socio-economic position affected the progress and outcome of these trials. Although most of the trials centre on families that lived in the rural areas of New Jersey that dominated the landscape during for much of the nineteenth century, two well-documented cases are considered at the end of the chapter, which focus on madness in urban settings and which extend far into other geographic locations. These two cases also highlight how concerns about transgressions of gender and sexual identity figured into the dynamics of lunacy investigation law. Finally, in New Jersey, lunacy trials were not strictly family affairs. This chapter considers how the public and legal authorities weighed in on the trial process.

Safeguarding property and reorganising the care of the mad

In keeping with its English antecedent, lunacy investigation law in New Jersey was employed to safeguard the integrity of property in the face of mental alienation. It is therefore not surprising that the 'wasting' or 'squandering' of property in the face of mad behaviour prompted families to initiate lunacy trials. For example, a father, father-in-law and 'near neighbour' of Peter P. testified that he had formerly been 'very industrious and attentive to his business and the interest of his family', but, for about a year, he had become so neglectful of his farm that 'his property and estate is wasting very fast'. This, along with uncharacteristically violent behaviour, led to a lunacy trial and guardianship arrangements for fear that Peter P. 'and family must shortly come to want.'[1]

Witnesses sometimes cited specific behaviours as proof of the irrational wasting of property. In the view of his neighbours, Robert P. 'suffers persons to go in his woodland and there for a very trifling and wholly inadequate consideration ... cut and destroy the young growing timber in such wanton useless manner as no man who possess his reason would suffer'.[2] John B. unnerved his family and neighbours by 'buying cattle at very extravagant prices and then butchering them and selling the meat for much less that it was worth to any and every person who would buy from him, and to persons wholly unable to pay for it'.[3] Starting in about 1835, Sarah C. 'left her father's house' in the township of Morris to explore New York City. Her visits to New York became more frequent over time and, in the eyes of her family, were responsible for a moral decline that more than once landed her in the New York Penitentiary as a 'vagrant'. The main concern of the lunacy trial which was struck against her in 1855 was that she was 'laying out what property her father has bequeathed to her in the purchase of lottery tickets' as well as openly considering 'destroying herself by suicide'.[4] In these and most other trials, the squandering of property to the detriment of the owner and his/her heirs either was at the core of concern, or formed a major consideration in a host of proofs of insanity.

In the trial of Elizabeth V., the wasting of property is again described as the principal worry. The catalyst of this irrational behaviour, and of the lunacy trial, was the death of her husband. Witnesses at the trial described her as having 'turns of being deranged' for over two decades, 'which have grown worse of late since her husband's death'. Elizabeth

V. had inherited 'a considerable amount of property' from her late husband which, 'in consequence of her deranged condition ... [she] manifests a disposition to waste in the most useless manner'.[5] In this and several other instances, the death of a principal caregiver, or one whose departure fundamentally rearranged the social dynamics of the family unit, was the trigger for a trial in lunacy. The poignancy of loss in this respect, along with the promise of lunacy investigation law, is brought to the fore in the 1831 trial of Samuel P. 'Captain' P. was described as between seventy and eighty years of age and in possession of a 210-acre farm in the township of Bedminster, Somerset County that earned about $200 per year. In about 1824 Samuel P.'s grandson, Samuel Mulford, moved into his grandfather's house to help with the 'management of his affairs', as Samuel P. had become 'unfit by reason of the loss of his mind and mental faculties to take care of himself and to manage his affairs'. Over a seven-year period, Mulford looked after the business of his grandfather's farm while Samuel P.'s wife provided full-time care of her mentally failing husband. However, in 1831 Samuel P.'s wife died. As Mulford put it in his petition to the chancery court, there was thus 'no person but our petitioner and his sister, a small girl of between 12 and 13 years of age, to take care of the said Samuel P.'[6] Under the circumstances, the process of lunacy investigation law formalised Mulford's control over his grandfather's property and set up a guardianship arrangement for Samuel P.'s personal care. This was especially urgent as Samuel P. 'wholly disregards the care of himself and the management of his affairs so ... as not to dress himself or feed himself or to go to bed at times without being aided and directed'.[7] In the case of Anthony B., relatives at his trial in October 1833 claimed that he had been 'of unsound mind' for fifteen years, and behaved in ways that required physical restraint 'from fear of his committing violence and doing mischief'.[8] During this time, his wife 'managed his affairs and had the superintendence and control of all his property'. However, her death in June 1833 left Anthony B.'s 'affairs and property' neglected and 'in want of some person legally authorised to take the charge of them' and, presumably, of his person.[9]

The use of lunacy investigation law in the face of a principal caregiver's death was especially apparent in cases of those considered to be 'idiots'. In an 1841 petition to the Court of Chancery, Nathaniel A. was described by his mother, Mary A., to be 'an idiot and not possessed of mind sufficient for the governance of himself or his property'.[10] While this was the standard legal line in cases such as this, Mary A. went on to state that for the last eight months, since the death of her husband, Joshua A., 'Nathaniel has had no person [of] authority to take the care of his person or estate.'[11] Nathaniel was, she asserted, 'harmless and able to work and in part to earn his support – that his labours together with the avails of his property being a small farm worth fifty dollars per year would be sufficient for his support both now and in his old age'.[12] The problem, according to Mary A. and other witnesses was that, in the absence of his father, the principal regulatory force in his life, the fifty-year-old Nathaniel A. and his property were in danger of being exploited. As one neighbour put it, 'the avails [of Nathaniel's property] cannot be collected for want of a competent authority to demand' them.[13] In this situation, the guardianship protection designed through the Orphans Court would presumably serve as a substitute for the absence of a strong-willed father. In a strikingly similar trial in 1812, Jacob V. explained to the courts that his brother, John V., 'hath from an early infancy been deprived of his reason and understanding' – a situation which was tolerable while 'John V. had been under the care and protection of his father'.[14] But with their father's recent death and Jacob's subsequent inheritance of a portion of his father's wealth, it was deemed necessary by his family to formalise legal protection of his person and property.

If the foregoing examples suggest a relatively uncomplicated use of lunacy investigation law as a solution to the problems created for families by mad behaviour, the case of Elisha A. indicates otherwise. As with other cases of idiocy, James A. explained to the court in 1816 that his uncle, Elisha A., had 'since his birth' been completely deprived of his understanding.[15] On the death of Elisha's father, he inherited a large estate, but it was placed 'under the direction' of Elisha's brother, Isaac A., presumably because of Elisha's mental incapacity.[16] Isaac's subsequent death changed this situation and prompted Elisha's nephew to seek a new arrangement by use of the law of lunacy investigation. However, at the investigation, the jury found that Elisha A. 'is not an ideot and that he is capable for the government of himself, his messenges, lands and tenements'.[17] While there is no supporting documentation with this file to help with an understanding of this verdict, the finding that Elisha A. was not an idiot from birth or from childhood indicates that family perceptions about mental competency were not always in accord with the trial jury. Another possible explanation for the verdict in this case, and one which permeates the contexts of other cases, is that there was disagreement between family members, and/or between family and community, about the mental state of individuals in question, and about how to respond to those deemed insane.

The mix of strategies employed by families in response to madness and their use of lunacy investigation law were closely tied to the family dynamics of individual cases. As many historians have pointed out, a similar mix of elements were in play in the decision of families to commit their relatives to a lunatic asylum.[18] However, in New Jersey, asylum either was not an option or, as was the case later in the nineteenth century, formed only one of many possibilities. Moreover, the law of lunacy investigation had been developed to help satisfy a host of challenges brought on by madness that were not in keeping with the purpose of the asylum. For the most part, New Jersey families had no expectation that one of the outcomes of the lunacy trial would be the removal of their relatives from the household. As can be seen from the following examples, the lunacy trial and the guardianship arrangements that followed suit were embedded in familial efforts to keep property intact, to guarantee control over economic assets, to ensure that economic resources were available for the care and provision of those deemed insane, to re-establish 'normal' or 'functional' domestic social relations, and, in some cases, to provide recourse for recovered individuals to re-establish their positions at the head of their households, or within the family. Not surprisingly, the primary sources reveal that such efforts were frequently fraught with conflict.

Of primary importance to families who made use of lunacy investigation law was the re-establishment of stability for family property, and the care of the individual suspected of insanity. Lunacy trials were thus frequently resorted to in dire circumstances. For example, the eldest son of John M., William M., petitioned that his father had for two months been displaying clear signs of madness. These included alternating convictions on the part of John M. that he needed to 'sell or give away all his property' and that 'his family [was] taking away all his property'.[19] When convinced of the latter, he became abusive to his family, to the point at which 'it was difficult for them to live with him'.[20] John M. also 'very frequently' sent 'his children to the neighbours to borrow different articles of clothing that are not wanted', obliging them to 'go and on their return amuse him by pretending that they cannot get them'.[21] These and other signs of madness became more significant as the forty-seven-year-old John M. had become unproductive on a large farm that needed immediate care in order to provide effectively for his wife and eight children, four of whom were under the age of fourteen. To make matters worse, John M. had accrued several debts owed to his neighbours. In this case, the petition from his eldest son was aimed to create a guardianship arrangement whereby 'the creditors ... may be honestly paid and proper provision may be made for the support of the said John and his family'.[22]

In New Jersey, as in England, it was not uncommon for a wife to make the formal petition for a lunacy investigation when the circumstances of her husband's madness became untenable. In the case of Jacob G., his wife, Jane G., noted that her husband had been of unsound mind for several years. In addition, neighbours testified that although formerly he was 'a man of exemplary moral conduct', as the result of a 'severe attack' of 'inflammatory Rhumatism, or white swelling ... his mind suddenly became impaired' and he became obsessed with the idea that he needed to kill his wife.[23] This was despite the fact that he continuously stated that 'she was a very good woman and kind wife'.[24] In this and other cases, the lunacy trial was conducted in order to confirm the individual's madness so that the guardianship process could help to render farm property productive again, and to consolidate a guardianship process for the financial and domestic maintenance of the mad.

In some cases, the point of initiating the legal process in lunacy was specific. John Ivins initiated a trial into the mental state of James T., in an effort to secure financing for James T.'s care in his own home in Chesterfield, Burlington County. In trial documents and related primary sources, Ivins explained that his wife had been adopted and raised by James T. from her infancy. After the death of James T.'s wife, James T. became 'melancholy', at which point Ivins' wife asked her husband to take James T. into their household so that he could be cared for. According to Ivins, in about 1828 James T.'s melancholy 'continued at intervals of greater or less duration until about two years ago [1833], when his derangement became permanent', accompanied by violent outbursts, threats to burn down the house and wanderings 'in the open fields or woods for several days and nights together'.[25] As a weaver by trade, James T. did not at any point own land, and his property amounted to one bed, one desk, a chest of drawers and an 'old weaving loom'.[26] But, as a participant in the American Revolutionary War, he was entitled to a pension, which, in a guardianship arrangement following the lunacy trial, helped Ivins and his wife to provide more comfortably for James T. The problem was that James T. seemed to have lost proof of his pensionable status. Thus, after successfully convincing the chancery court of New Jersey that James T. was insane, John Ivins appealed to the federal Court of Common Pleas to establish that James T. had been registered in the Revolutionary War. Eventually, the courts acknowledged that James T. had been a private in the Virginia line for three years. James T.'s pension was brought under Ivins' guardianship for the continued care and management of his insane charge.[27]

The use of lunacy investigation law to place families and individuals on a more stable financial footing in the face of mad behaviour was also in evidence in the case of Eunice B. Eunice B. had been considered insane for ten years, since 1822, and was being cared for by her widowed sister, Comfort Brown, in the city of Newark. In 1836 Eunice B.'s brother died, leaving a debt to his sister amounting to $800. Therein lay the problem! When William Tuttle, one of the administrators of the deceased brother's estate, tried to pay Eunice B. back what was owed to her, 'Eunice B. refused to receive payment without rendering any satisfactory reason, calling the Administrators dishonest persons'. In a similar claim, another Newark resident, James Tichenor, stated that he had:

> been indebted for some years past to the said Eunice B., that he has made various offers to settle with her, which she refused without rendering any satisfactory reason for so refusing, that he has frequently offered her small sums of money which she generally refused to receive for which reason he has paid sums of money to the said Comfort Brown for the benefit of the said Eunice B.[28]

At one point, Tichenor thought that he had successfully handed over 'ten dollars partly in a current bank note and partly in specie'.[29] However, a few days later, Eunice B. returned it 'to him saying that she did not want his money'.[30] And, a few days after that, when she met him on the street, she shook her fist and accused him of threatening to kill 'the whole family'. The lunacy investigation trial in this case was established to make legal what, according to witnesses, was already 'current belief of the neighbours in general who know her'.[31] In finding her *non compos mentis* by law, guardianship arrangements were established so that outstanding debts could be collected for Eunice B.'s benefit.

As the foregoing case suggests, women were significant actors in the legal process of New Jersey's lunacy investigations, and in the domestic contexts that gave rise to them. Of major importance was their role in the direct care of those considered to be mad.[32] As well as sometimes being the subjects of lunacy trials, and acting as principal caregivers, they also often initiated petitions for lunacy trials, and were frequently active in taking over from their husbands when these men became mentally incompetent to control their property.[33] Joshua A.'s wife, Phebe A., had taken control of the business side of her husband's farm, off and on, for many years. Witness Major General Clive Moon described the history of Mr. A.'s mad turns as follows:

> In 1803 Mr A. was crazy and continued so for perhaps until about 1805. Mr A. got better and appeared in his right mind and continued so three or four years and then was taken crazy for a second time which lasted about two years and then he got better for about four years and was then taken the third time and remained so until the winter of 1818 at which time I considered him getting better and in August in his right mind.[34]

During these bouts of madness, Phebe A. was sometimes official guardian of her husband's estate and had control of the farm. At other times, she exercised unofficial control of her husband's assets. By 1820, it appeared that Joshua A. was once more demonstrating symptoms of madness. Although the verdict in this latest round of mental trouble is unclear, presumably Phebe A. once more took over the farming business. According to one neighbour, this would have been likely, for even 'while her husband was in his right mind and attending to his concerns of importance and particularly with regard to his contracts for lands I have know him to have her along with him to assist him and consult with her in the contracts'.[35]

In a similar case, Eleanor G. filed the petition and was a key witness in the trial of her husband Benjamin G. Eleanor explained that for about eight months her husband suffered from 'a severe fit of sickness, became disordered in his mind, and seemed at times to have lost all his reason and memory'.[36] Benjamin G. was, she continued, rational at times and mad at others, but 'his spells of imbecility appear to increase and he is

Family, friends and neighbours 149

now more frequently under a deranged and disordered state of mind.'[37] Her main concern, under the circumstances, was that 'he had made a contract for a sale of some lands and the purchasers are willing and ready to pay the money according to this contract, but as no deed can be executed to them, owing to [Benjamin G.'s] insanity', Eleanor G. pressed upon the courts the necessity of a formal legal trial and guardianship process.[38]

Aging and madness

For men and for women, being on the receiving end of a verdict of *non compos mentis* and being tied to the resulting guardianship arrangement could be life altering in several respects. As previous examples (and chapters) have suggested, there was much at stake in being deemed legally insane in terms of landownership, legal status and altered familial and, sometimes, community social relations. Not surprisingly, conflict permeated the process of lunacy investigation law in many cases. These conflicts are clearly apparent in the documents left behind from many trials. Although the circumstances varied greatly from one case to the next, the mental capacity of the elderly was a major source of conflict among family members in New Jersey. For instance, Eleanor C., eighty years old in 1842, became the subject of a petition for a lunacy commission by a son-in-law, John Lloyd, who accused his two sisters-in-law, Mary Murray and Ann Beckman (and their husbands, William Murray and Jacob Beckman), of confining Eleanor C. in the Beckman household for five years without allowing her access to the outside world. Lloyd's complaint was that his two brothers-in-law 'receive the profits of the estate of Eleanor', to the detriment of his wife's inheritance.[39] Making it quite clear why he was petitioning, Lloyd stated that 'he is fearful that the estate of the said Eleanor C. will be dissipated by the said Jacob Beckman and William Murray and in case of her death it will be difficult to get a true and correct statement from them of the estate of said Eleanor C.'.[40] Lloyd's petition for a lunacy trial was strongly opposed by the Murrays and the Beckmans, who counter petitioned with a long list of 'irregularities' and 'illegalities' which they felt were contained in the proceedings.[41] This resulted in a chancery court inquiry into Eleanor C.'s mental state, along with an inquiry into the conditions under which she was being housed and cared for. The resulting testimonials represented a full range of views; from those who considered her having become for the 'second time a child', to those who thought that she was old but not mentally impaired.[42] The final verdict is missing from this file, and the testimonials were equally inconclusive as to whether the Beckmans were confining Eleanor C. against her will.

A more spectacular example of contested views about the mental state of an aging relative involved the trial of Sarah C., a woman living in Eastfield Township, Union County. Sarah C. was the subject of two lunacy investigations, one in 1865 and the other in 1866. In neither trial was Sarah C. found to be mentally incompetent to manage herself or her property, which was remarkable, considering that by the time of the trial in 1866 she was two months away from her one hundredth birthday. The precipitating event of the second trial was the death of her son, Hugh C., who left her a considerable fortune including about $6,000 in personal property and several property rentals in New York, where he had been a very successful carpenter and builder. According to another of Sarah C.'s sons, Noah C., Sarah was not mentally capable of managing this inheritance, and there were several witnesses who agreed that, after the age of ninety, she had suffered a mental decline. However, other witnesses noted that her main problems were that she had become almost blind and that she was also becoming increasingly deaf. It was those declining faculties, some claimed, that made her mental state appear more suspect than it really was. One witness, Henry Marshall, pointed out that she was, in fact, still remarkably erudite in conversation about various subjects, past and present. On the subject of her impending inheritance, she appeared to Marshall to know exactly what she was about to acquire, and was not overly kind about the opinions of her family on the subject. In Marshall's recounting of their conversation, 'she said further[,] "confound them they will not let me enjoy it [the inheritance] in peace in my old days". She said there was not one who had a better right to a share of [her son's] property than she had … that she had furnished him in clothing and washed for him … and took care of him until he was 20 years of age.'[43] Noting that Sarah C. was 'extraordinarily sound for one so old', Marshall gave his opinion was that she was perfectly capable of managing her newly acquired fortune.[44] After considering the weight of many pages of testimony, on 22 January 1867 the chancery court ordered 'that the application for a commission in the nature of a *writ de lunatico inquirendo* of the lunacy of the said Sarah C. be denied and the petition dismissed with costs.'⁴⁵

Madness and community

The structure and use of lunacy investigation law meant that conflict and contest was not merely between family members. As we have already seen, the views of neighbours and local experts who testified were often in conflict with those of family who sought a verdict of *non compos mentis*. Witnesses who lived in the households of those considered to be insane also sometimes voiced opinions in opposition to family. Those appointed as guardians were not always family members and they, too, could be at odds with the wishes of the individuals whose property and person they had sworn to protect. Community members were also challenged in various ways by their association with neighbours and friends sentenced as legally insane. These and other forms of community participation and connection to those involved in lunacy trials ensured that madness and the legal response to it were matters of public concern in New Jersey.

The trials of John L. and Peter C. exemplify, in different ways, how neighbours, friends and local officials formed part of the tension of lunacy investigation law. In December 1822 Elizabeth L. petitioned successfully for a lunacy investigation into the mental state of her son, John L. In her petition, she claimed that heavy drinking was the cause of her son's madness, although there was no mention of this in the verdict of *non compos mentis* that was read at the trial held in the house of the inn keeper at Evesham, Burlington County. Eight and a half months later, John L. petitioned for the earlier verdict to be superseded. He asserted that he had recovered his sanity. However, just as pressing was his assertion that the guardians who had been appointed to take charge of his person and property, Aaron Sippincotte, Thomas Ballenger and Zebedee Wills, 'under pretence that a sale of the real estate of your petitioner was necessary advertised for sale at public vendue ... between 70 and 80 acres of your petitioner's lands which if sold will be very injurious to your petitioner and which is wholly unnecessary in as much as your petitioner will be fully able to pay off and discharge all debts which your petitioner lawfully owes and to support his wife and family'.⁴⁶ Under the circumstances, John L. requested an 'injunction' against his guardians to prevent them from selling his land. The chancery court was convinced both of John L.'s return to sanity and of his right to take over the management of his property, ordering the guardians to be 'restrained from any sale of the property of the petitioner'.[47]

The case of Peter C. underscores how complicated the conflicting concerns of those involved in the lunacy trial process could be. In February 1830 a petition signed by Peter C.'s four sons, one daughter, five grandsons, four granddaughters and two grandsons-in-law claimed that he was 'irrational and incoherent and his conduct indecent'.[48] Although the trial found that he had been *non compos mentis* for five years, by early March Peter C. was petitioning the chancery court, claiming that the lunacy trial had been conducted improperly for many reasons, including the fact that it had been held 'seven miles from his residence'.[49] Peter Gulich, a local land agent, was very interested in helping to prove that Peter C. had in fact been sane, because during the same five-year period Gulich had 'transacted the business of the said Peter C. to a considerable amount'.[50] These transactions included selling Peter C.'s property to various members of the community. Further supporting the claim of Peter C.'s sanity was Gulich's assertion that the verdict of lunacy went 'against [the opinion of] at least eight of the jurors' in the trial. In early April 1830 one of Peter C.'s sons, Peter C. junior, defended the choice of the trial's location, stating that 'the jurors were acquainted with the said Peter C. and came out of the neighbourhood where he resided'.[51] Although he insisted that the verdict of *non compose mentis* was the right one, Peter C. junior argued that 'it is not the wish of the children and the jurors concerned to overturn the sales which have been made of the real estate of the said Peter C. On the contrary,' he noted, 'they are willing to ratify the same and to call the agents who have transacted the business to account for the proceeds.'[52] In mid May 1830 another inquisition was held that found once more Peter C. to be *non compos mentis* and, additionally, that the sale of the five-acre lots that Gulich had sold on Peter C.'s behalf to six local buyers were transactions that had occurred while Peter C. was insane. As such, the transactions were declared illegal.

The cases of John L. and Peter C. demonstrate both the complicated dynamics of family and community relationships as played out in lunacy trials and also the extent to which, in nineteenth-century New Jersey, matters of madness permeated community affairs. Indeed, witness testimonials frequently highlighted this public awareness of who in the community was mad. Courtney Hall, a neighbour to Daniel E., stated that 'in the estimation of the whole neighbourhood the said Daniel E. is of unsound mind'.[53] Similarly, in an 1813 testimonial the neighbours of Jeremiah and Abigail H. asserted that the siblings were 'reputed to be lunatics wherever they are known'.[54] Community opinion clearly counted in the determination of madness.[55] The extent of community awareness about and involvement in those who were considered mad in New Jersey suggests a level of familiarity and comfort that would eventually be drastically altered when the asylum era was fully in place. This does not mean that the eighteenth and first half of the nineteenth centuries should be seen as some sort of golden era for the mad in New Jersey. However, the fact that institutional options for madness did not exist during this time to any considerable extent meant that madness in the community was the norm. If anything, the processes of lunacy investigation law encouraged this community-based sense of awareness about madness and reinforced a community response to it.

Community members could become even more directly involved in the management and welfare of and legal response to those considered to be mad. Huldah P., who by lunacy trial was considered *non compos mentis* in 1826, had been in the care of the trustees of the Baptist Church of the Scotch Plains in Essex County. This was at times clearly challenging to the church officials because, according to witnesses, she was convinced that the church pastor was the 'saviour', and she frequently disrupted service by leaving her seat and running up the pulpit. The lunacy trial in the case of Huldah P. was to investigate whether two lots of land that the community thought she owned could be used to help offset her care and maintenance. The investigation discovered that she had 'alienated her property' in 1818, but that she was still owed money on the sale.[56] In another case, workmates and friends of Edward B., a single male immigrant from Bristol, England who ended up working in the Steam Sugar Refinery in Bergen County, stated that they were forced to 'keep him confined, not allowing him to go at large', on account of his sudden descent into madness.[57] As Edward B. had no relatives in New Jersey, these friends and fellow workers did their best to care for him. However, this was no easy task, for Edward B. had been for some time 'morose and silent', sitting 'with his head bent on his breast almost motionless

– refusing food or nourishment, eyeing his friends and old acquaintances as they approached him with a stealthy and suspicious glance'.[58]

Cases of *supercedeas*

The complicated interplay of family, friends, power and property is especially in evidence in cases in which individuals sentenced as *non compos mentis* petitioned for *supercedeas* to traverse earlier decisions. These cases are so revealing partly because, when a petition for a *supercedeas* was made and a new trial conducted, it was necessary for court officials to have at their disposal a full run of documentation to help them adjudicate a second case. For several individuals, the collected documentation has remained bundled together, presenting detailed accounts. Cases of *supercedeas* are also more revealing because they represent the struggles over the management of and response to madness over a longer period. In some cases, the period was remarkably long, extending over several years. These sustained intersections between madness and the law of lunacy investigation highlight the myriad ways in which civil law was used to help regulate the disruptions of mad behaviour, how the trial process itself shaped perceptions of and responses to madness in particular cases and how families and communities considered the law of lunacy investigation as a useful confirmation of on-going changes in social relationships related to madness.[59]

Abraham W.'s encounters with lunacy investigation law exemplify well the relationship between the legal response to madness and challenging family dynamics. In April 1834 William Stryker, brother-in-law of Abraham W., along with two neighbours, petitioned the chancery court claiming that Abraham W. had been insane for about a year and a half. According to the petitioners, proofs of his insanity included Abraham W.'s convictions that 'a small negro boy owned' his property, that his family was dying and that his children were out to get him.[60] The lunacy trial held in mid May at the house of John Porter, innkeeper in the township of Hillsborough, found Abraham W. insane and thus in need of guardianship in order to provide for himself and his property, which consisted of a 170- acre plantation and two smaller farms. The jury further found that Abraham W. 'hath during his said lunacy to wit some time in the fall of the year 1833 alienated and conveyed to his son Joseph W. one of his said farms'.[61] Abraham W. responded to this trial with a long petition to the Court of Chancery explaining in detail why he thought that the trial and its findings amounted to gross injustice. Abraham W. explained:

> That your petitioner about 36 hours before the taking of the inquisition heard for the first time by one of his neighbours, that some proceedings were to be had at Flagtown about his person and property, but what it was he did not nor could he understand – that the next day after getting the above information he sent his son to [?], to find out if he could what was intended to be done and to employ counsel. That the morning of the day on which the inquisition was taken his son came and informed him that a jury was to be called for the purpose of inquiring whether he was a lunatic – that he had employed counsel and that the counsel had informed him that he (your petitioner) must attend that day at Flagtown. That your petitioner did attend but had no opportunity whatever of defending himself before the jury called upon that occasion – and that he heard with great surprise and astonishment, witnesses testify to lone and isolated expressions made by your petitioner long before the taking of the inquisition, and those expressions cunningly arranged so as to impose upon the jury – your petitioner is well satisfied that if he could have had a proper notice of the taking the inquisition, so that he might have been enabled to have presented the evidence of those with whom he has recently transacted much business the return to the commission would have been entirely different – the jury would have found him of sound mind ...[62]

With this in mind, Abraham W. petitioned for a traverse of the lunacy verdict, this time well armed with testimonials of near neighbours who were willing to testify that he was competent to transact business, and that he was in all other respects a rational person.[63]

The problem for Abraham W. was that, with his property and assets tied up in guardianship protection, and with his person also under the control of a guardian, he did not have the financial means to proceed with the *supercedeas*. To overcome this new obstacle, the resourceful Abraham W. applied for his pension from service in the American Revolutionary War (which he apparently was not hitherto in need of) in order to muster the funds required for the next trial. More struggle ensued because, as he explained to the chancery court, James Randolph, Abraham W.'s 'agent for the purpose of obtaining the pension ... refused to give up the certificate', giving 'as an excuse and reason for the delay that he has heard that your petitioner was a lunatic, and that therefore he ... would not be acting properly by complying with your petitioner's order.'[64] Remarkably, the chancery court approved of Abraham W.'s request to use the arrears of his pension to defray the costs of the court proceedings that he was to incur. On 14 July 1835 the lunacy trial was successfully traversed. Only five and a half months later, on New Year's day 1836, another inquisition was held, this time in the township of Hillsborough, concluding that Abraham W. was once more *non compos mentis*.

In the verdict of the last lunacy trial, the jurors noted that Abraham W. had reached the age of eighty and that his lunacy was the result of 'old age' as well as 'the visitation of God'.[65] The lunacy trials of Abraham W. reflect, on one level, the previously discussed use of lunacy investigation law in New Jersey for those considered to be in a state of mental decline related to their advanced age. But, as we have seen, each case reflects particular vested interests of family, friends, power and property.

In the 1843 case of Abraham R., the initial testimony of family and neighbours depicting him as *non compos mentis* was convincing enough. Led by Daniel Carson, the husband of Abraham R.'s niece, several witnesses claimed that for over a year Abraham R. 'hath altogether given up transacting business ... and that his whole deportment manifests utter imbecility of mind'.[66] The jury found Abraham R. to be *non compos mentis* and Carson assumed guardianship responsibilities of Abraham R.'s large farm property, moving onto the premises in early February 1843. Remarkably, however, Abraham R's wife, Elizabeth R., filed a successful 'caveat against further proceedings' to the court, whereupon Abraham R. petitioned the court to traverse the findings of the first lunacy trial.[67] Shortly thereafter, Abraham R. entered into a legal agreement with Aaron Eldridge by which Eldridge would look after the couple's needs in return for ownership of part of their farm property.

In the ensuing trial of traverse, witnesses were divided as to Abraham R.'s mental state. They all remarked upon his physical weakness due, mainly, to his advanced age, but disagreed about the extent to which these infirmities affected his mental judgement in the everyday running of his farm. When Elizabeth R. testified, she noted that Carson was not treating them properly and that they had made the legal agreement with Eldridge as a result. Possibly affecting the final verdict to the disadvantage of the elderly couple, she added that 'for the last three years I have had the control of the property here pretty much – my husband did not feel very strong and as I was pretty smart he gave it up to me'.[68] Other witnesses agreed with Elizabeth about her role in running the farm, but argued for more guardianship of Abraham's property and person. In the end, Abraham R. was found to be mentally incapable of running his farm and Eldridge was found guilty of 'taking advantage' of Abraham R.'s imbecility in order to exploit his property 'contrary to equity and good conscience'.[69] In this complex case, the husband of Abraham R.'s niece may have initiated lunacy investigation law in part out of concern for the elderly couple, but perhaps also in part as a way to expedite the transfer of property from an older to a younger generation within the family. The response of Abraham R. and his wife to the implications of guardianship after the finding of *non compos mentis* suggests that they were capable of responding, at least as a couple, to organise their affairs in a way that suited them better. Finally, the second lunacy trial, perhaps ironically, took away the couple's power of self-determination, while at the same time possibly taking away the power of an opportunistic neighbour to exploit their vulnerable position.

Daniel V.'s advanced age also served as a catalyst for an extensive engagement with lunacy investigation law. Yet, the circumstances and outcome were very different to those of Abraham R. Daniel V. was placed on trial in April 1854, after an initial petition from his son-in-law, Mark Ayers. The trial witnesses and the jury found Daniel V. to be *non compos mentis*, noting that he was no longer capable of identifying some of his close neighbours and that he displayed a severe loss of memory about the basic functioning of his farm property. One month later, Daniel V. petitioned to traverse this decision, noting that the trial had been held in a different township in order to reduce the number of witnesses who could testify on his behalf, and also that (much like the initial trial of Abraham W.) Daniel V. was given only two days notice before the trial to prepare his defence.

Daniel V.'s trial of traverse was long, including over sixty pages of testimony. What is remarkable about this trial is that a majority of witnesses, although acknowledging his many instances of memory loss and his tendency to be repetitious in conversation, argued that Daniel V. was perfectly capable of managing his farming business. In fact, some took pains to note that, despite his age (not specified), he was as physically capable of conducting the multiple tasks of farm work as he ever had been. One witness, a local cooper, spoke for many in stating that Daniel V.'s 'horses, cows, hogs and his farming all appeared to be conducted with judgement and skill' and 'his conversation is always rational and to the point except the repetition of the same question in some of his conversation'.[70] In this case, the burden of evidence convinced the jury of Daniel V.'s mental soundness, and in October 1854 the verdict of *non compos mentis* was traversed.[71]

Yet, a careful reading of this and other cases indicates an even more complex relationship between family, community, property and lunacy investigation law than the verdicts of such trials suggest. At Daniel V.'s second trial, although he was, from a legal perspective, given a clean bill of mental health, it was pointed out by a few witnesses that 'the business of the farm is carried out by the sons in recent years'.[72] Thus, it is possible to interpret this trial in great measure as the product of familial struggles over inheritance and the passing of wealth and property from one generation to the next. In this case, the advances of an aggressive son-in-law were initially successful, but then in retrial were reversed by witnesses testifying both to the mental soundness of Daniel V. and also to the fact that his two sons were increasingly in charge of the administrative aspects of Daniel V.'s farming business.

Indeed, in several trials, legal verdicts concerning mental capacity can be seen to follow community and familial responses that had already taken place. I have argued elsewhere that in New Jersey there was often a 'lag' between legal response and 'community custom' in matters of madness.[73] For example, in May 1821 Charles B. launched a legal investigation into the mental state of his father, Samuel B., resulting in a verdict of *non compos mentis*. Some residents in the neighbourhood of Gloucester town agreed with Charles B., claiming that Samuel B. had slipped into a 'deep melancholy and depraved state of mind', which had rendered him incapable of conducting the business of his farm.[74] Seven years later, in 1828, Samuel B. petitioned to set aside the earlier verdict. One of his sons testified that 'for more than a year' Samuel B. 'has had the direction and management of his affairs'.[75] Another son, Charles B., claimed that:

> during the time of his insanity, his affairs were carried on by the family in his name – after the inquisition there was some talk of my being appointed to take the management of his affairs – but I never was appointed

to my knowledge – since my father has been restored to his reason which is between one and two years since[,] he has himself had the entire management of his affairs and conducted them with strict propriety.[76]

In their testimony, neighbours confirmed that Samuel B. had been running his farm alone and capably for the two years prior to the trial that aimed to reverse his status as legally mad. Dr Jeremiah Foster added his professional opinion, both as a physician and as a Master in Chancery, that after several conversations with Samuel B., the farmer appeared perfectly sane. Besides, he added, 'I was informed by himself, and his wife, that there had been no medical attendance in the family for a few years past.'[77] In this case, no medical news was good medical news.

Gender, jurisdiction and lunacy investigation law

The preceding cases indicate that the majority of trials took place in rural settings and highlight the importance of the social relations in local settings to the understanding of madness and the use of lunacy trials as a response. However, as the following two mid-nineteenth century cases demonstrate, the circumstances of lunacy trials in New Jersey could extend well beyond the boundaries of local jurisdiction. The cases of Caroline W. and Isaac C. also highlight the extent to which the social expectations of gender were bound up with the meaning of madness and with the use of the lunacy trial as a complicated legal response. Finally, these two trials remind us that those accused of madness could, in some cases, be powerful actors in their struggles with family over the legal process.

The first case involved Caroline W., who, in 1843, married Joseph W.[78] Joseph was at this time starting to make a name for himself as a merchant jeweller with a respectable jewellery firm in Newark. But during the next decade of their marriage, Joseph's health was in continual and steady decline. Finally, in 1855, on the recommendation of his physician, Joseph decided to leave his business and to go on an extended trip to the south of France, in the hopes that the warm, dry climate might help what had been diagnosed as an advanced case of consumption.

Just before leaving, Joseph made his last will and testament, in which he endeavoured to provide for his wife, two small children and Sarah, an orphaned niece who had lived in the family for years. To sum up the contents of a long will, Joseph left a large sum of money for the welfare of his niece. He left all of the household goods and a third of his entire estate to his wife, and the other two-thirds to his children. But until his children turned twenty-one years of age, Joseph appointed his wife as legal guardian of their persons and estates. He made her his executrix and two of his friends executors of the will. Two months after Joseph and his family arrived in France, he died.

One of Joseph's co-workers, John Palmer, was also in Europe at the time of John W.'s death. John Palmer convinced Caroline W., along with her family, to return with him to the United States by steamship in order that he could take proper care of them. But, according to Palmer, once on board the steamer *Pacific*, Caroline W. refused to talk to him or his wife, rebuffing their overtures of sympathy and affection and stating that she never liked them much anyway. Instead, Caroline W. struck up a relationship with an English passenger, Mr Tobin, whom she'd never met before, placing herself under his protection. In fact, she stayed in his cabin for the entire trip. By the time the ship arrived at New York Caroline W. had, by her own admission, fallen in love with Tobin and had resolved to marry him and move with him back to France. When her father, brother and sisters arrived at the New York docks to greet and console her, Caroline W. told them of her plan to return to France with her new lover. At this point, Caroline W.'s father concluded 'that her mind was entirely shattered and unsound'.[79]

But this was only the beginning of an extraordinary turn of events. During the ship voyage back to New York, Caroline W. also had a meeting with her late husband's niece, Sarah, giving her one night to get out of Caroline W.'s house upon their return to Newark. After years of living with the family, Sarah was being evicted. Caroline W.'s decision was made after she had promised to her husband on his deathbed that Sarah could stay at the house to take care of Caroline W.'s children until she was married. Sarah had just become engaged before her adopted family took off for France.

On the journey from New York to Newark, Caroline W.'s family tried to convince her that a marriage to Tobin would be foolish, that her eviction of Sarah was cruel and harsh and that she ought to be mourning for her dead husband. According to one brother, Caroline W. responded by stating that 'Sarah has opposed her intimacy with the strange Englishman, that this Englishman was going to call at her house and she did not want Sarah there to be reporting what took place.'⁸⁰ Then, according to the same brother, Caroline W. looked at him and said '"thank God I am now without any restraint, John has always kept me under restraint, but now I am free with money enough to live independently of you all"'.⁸¹ While these responses appeared to Caroline W.'s family to be sure signs of madness, it is also possible that she was, at least in part, articulating her opinions about her freedom from an oppressive marriage and also her potential to assert, for the first time, her independence from familial control.

But the marriage and escape with Tobin were not to be. Apparently Tobin was happy enough to be Caroline W.'s lover, but not her husband in France. After a few encounters with her in Newark, Tobin steamed back to Europe, leaving her a goodbye letter. According to Caroline W.'s family, this left her depressed for a short while. But she rallied quickly, soon stating her intention to travel to California, where a man she once knew was interested in marrying her. This really upset the family. Caroline W.'s father found a man in the neighbourhood who had been to California and had him visit his daughter in order to convince her otherwise. After several visits and dark, dangerous characterisations of the west coast, Caroline W. finally relented and gave up the idea.

During this time, Caroline W.'s father claimed that she fostered 'the greatest aversion and disgust for all her family and relations except her sister Julia ... [and] in general conversation and deportment she was continually fatuous and strange altogether different from what she had been in the lifetime of her husband.'⁸² According to family and neighbours, yet another episode of the insane behaviour and actions of Caroline W. was her pursuit of a relationship with a Frenchman, Lucien Corvisart. Like Caroline W.'s late husband, Corvisart worked in the jewellery trade. He had moved from Paris to Newark and had been living there for eight years before he met Caroline W. Corvisart claimed that he had fallen in love with Caroline W. before her husband's death and tried to get himself hired under Joseph in order to strike up a relationship with her – but to no avail. So, he had decided to wait it out, knowing that Joseph had not long to live. Some time after her return from France, Corvisart began courting Caroline W. at her house. This made Caroline W.'s father and other family members furious. Caroline W.'s father made investigations into Corvisart's past and warned his daughter that the jeweller was 'a total stranger, his origin and character unknown to her and ... as far as he could ascertain he was a mere adventurer and that his character was very bad.'[83] According to Caroline W.'s father, one of Corvisart's fellow jeweller journeymen noted that Corvisart would 'marry any woman that had money enough, [use her during the trip back to France] and, when she had arrived there, "let her go to the devil"'.[84]

Caroline W. was not convinced. Several weeks after their first meeting, the couple decided to get married in Newark. Caroline W.'s family protested vigorously and, at the point of the marriage ceremony, managed to convince the minister that Caroline W. was 'of unsound mind' and that Corvisart was of 'uncertain' character.[85] The marriage was postponed. In the meantime, Caroline W.'s father filed a *writ de lunatico inquirendo* to try to prevent her from marrying in private, or from taking her children somewhere beyond the control and care of her family. The court's response to the appeal for a lunacy commission was to issue an injunction preventing Caroline W. and Corvisart from social contact before the matter was settled. But Corvisart claimed that they had married successfully just before the injunction was issued and that he had the marriage certificate to prove it. He and Caroline W. thus claimed that they had the legal right to live together. In a crowning symbol of victory, clearly rankling enough for one of Caroline W.'s brothers to note it in his testimony, Corvisart bought a 'door plate' from the local black smith that read 'Lucien Corvisart' and nailed it to the door of Caroline W.'s house.[86]

Although the paper trail is sketchy, it appears that this victory was short lived. In short order, the lunacy trial launched against Caroline W. by her family was successful, but it was followed immediately by Corvisart's attempt to traverse the verdict of insanity. In the last letter in this entry, submitted by Corvisart in mid October, he appeared apologetic (although still defiant) about what was, he claimed, the misconstrued timing of events. He still argued that his marriage with Caroline W., 'the certificate of which appears among the papers before this Honourable Court[,] was only a confirmation of a right which he had acquired before' the court injunction.[87] There is no evidence remaining to suggest that the *supercedeas* was successful or that Corvisart's persistence had paid off at the legal level.

The second case that demonstrates how the intricacies of mid-nineteenth century gender expectations could inform the lunacy investigation process concerns Isaac C.[88] According to Isaac's brother-in-law Ebenezer, Isaac C.'s insanity could be traced back to his early teenage years. Ebenezer described Isaac C. as a 'sprightly little boy [who] was thought to have a better memory than any in the family. He was studious and while his father lived he was kept in school.'[89] But after the death of his father he became less interested in study, and gradually his behaviour changed for the worse. Ebenezer first became concerned when he noticed 'two voices in his conversation', a normal voice and 'a falsetto', which Ebenezer suspected was the result of a 'vicious habit'.[90] According to Ebenezer, 'Dr Bedell was attending him and asked me if I thought he was in this habit, this must have been about 1846. I then paid more attention and watched him and I became satisfied it was so. He grew up week and feeble.'[91] By the time Isaac C. had reached the age of twenty-three he was, according to his family, wild and uncontrollable, threatening his mother physically and, most alarmingly, according to his mother, 'exceed[ing] his income in his expenditures' on frivolous material items.[92]

By the fall of 1851 Isaac C.'s behaviour had, in the eyes of his family, become so bizarre that he was committed to the Standford Hall Asylum, a private institution for nervous and insane patients in Flushing, New York. In the opinion of Stanford's doctors, Isaac C. suffered from acute mania, brought on by his addiction to masturbation. He also had strong delusions that he was going to die immediately and that he had lost his bowels and lungs. Treatment at the asylum included moral therapy (rest, exercise, diet, amusements, voluntary 'work'), liberal amounts of anodyne to calm his excitement and the frequent use of a camisole to prevent his 'vicious' habit. The resident and visiting physicians to Stanford Asylum claimed great improvement in Isaac C.'s condition after about three months. He was no longer experiencing delusions and his behaviour had become more rational. Isaac C. had become convalescent, although not fully recovered. Dr Buel thought he might have recovered completely, had he stayed on at Stanford for another two months. Dr Benjamin concurred. But Isaac C. defied doctors' orders and discharged himself from Stanford.

Both of the asylum's doctors recommended that the best long-term means to end Isaac C.'s onanism, and thus to stabilise his mental condition, was for Isaac C. to find a wife. According to Dr Benjamin, 'physicians generally recommend marriage and it cures the habit in 19 cases out of 20 – intercourse with females whether pure or impure has the same effect'.[93] Much to the dismay of his family, Isaac C. found a way to engage in both the 'pure' and the 'impure' versions of his doctors' medical advice. After leaving the Stanford Asylum, Isaac C. boarded at the house of his brother Andrew for several weeks. During this period, he began to make frequent trips to New York, where, his brother discovered, he was visiting a woman who went by the name of Lizzy Losy. Losy, by all accounts, was a high-society sex worker who worked out of a respectable brothel. After a few weeks of seeing Losy, and against the strong objections of his family, he proposed to her and they were married in New York. Losy and Isaac C. took up residence in a flat that was described by his family as lavishly furnished and decorated with fine art.

It was at that point that Isaac C.'s mother decided to file a *writ de lunatico inquirendo* against her son. On 31 July 1852, while Isaac C. was visiting Morristown in New Jersey, he was issued a summons to appear at a tavern in Morristown for an inquiry into his mental state. Initially Isaac C. responded by drawing up a legal petition protesting the lunacy commission. In the petition he argued that, as he was a resident and originally a native of New York State, New Jersey law had no jurisdiction over his person. But, according to Losy, Isaac C. was prevailed upon by his family to accept the legal summons and lunacy investigation. In her trial testimony Losy claimed that Isaac's family had told him that 'the only object they had in view in [issuing the lunacy commission] was to have his marriage with your petitioner declared null and void by reason of his insanity, that they did not contemplate taking his property out of his control, nor could they do so, if he would withdraw his opposition to the [*writ de lunatico inquirendo*].'[94] It appeared that Isaac C. had struck a deal with his family – one by which he agreed to be found legally insane, and by which his marriage would be thus annulled, in return for continued control of his property. One of the last entries on record in this case is an 1855 petition by Isaac C. stating that he had recovered mentally, subsequently to that recovery had married and as a result needed full control of his property and estate in order to 'make some provision out of his estate for his wife.'[95] The last entry is from his guardians and close family, assenting to his wishes.

Both of these examples say much about the interplay of madness, gender, sexuality and property in mid-nineteenth century North America. In both cases, the legal apparatus of the lunacy investigation is used as a powerful weapon in family disputes over property and in the struggle over the boundaries of acceptable social behaviour. Many witnesses who gave testimony at Caroline W.'s trial were clearly disturbed by her refusal to continue in her role as a good mother and guardian and to take seriously her new role as a respectable widow. Reverend William Stewart, the rector of the church attended by Caroline W. and her family, stated that Caroline W.'s behaviour was 'indecorous in her as a widow, and at variance with her duty as a mother and [with] her modesty as a woman'.[96] Caroline W.'s stubbornness in the face of sensible advice from family and acquaintances was seen as a sure sign of insanity. A member of her husband's jewellery firm, Enos Richardson, warned Caroline W. that taking her children to Paris with a stranger would lead her to ruin. According to Enos, Caroline W. replied that 'she would be ruined then, for she would go to Paris'.[97] Caroline W.'s father described at some length her insistence that, since her husband's death, she felt 'like a bird just let loose from the cage,' that she would 'soar as she pleased' and that 'her talents had never been appreciated'. He considered his daughter's assertions as 'wild, inappropriate and unbecoming'.[98] Her refusal to mourn the loss of her husband, the quick turnaround time between that death and her interest in other men, the character of the men she was interested in and her open animosity towards her family's opinions undermined her position as a female of means in urban New Jersey.

Just as Caroline W.'s insanity was identifiable to her family in her refusal to play out her role as mother and widow, Isaac C.'s family made direct links between his mental trouble and his failings of manhood. The catalyst to his troubles was the death of his father, after which he lost discipline and control. He took to masturbation – considered wasteful, sinful and physically hazardous, and, according to mid-century psychiatrists, a leading cause of madness.[99] His marriage to Losy was potentially curative, according to prevailing medical wisdom. But, as with Caroline W., in the eyes of his family this particular marriage was socially embarrassing and posed a major threat to a large amount of family property. Remarkably, Caroline W. and Isaac C. were both able to resist the full effects of the lunacy commissions launched against them. These cases suggest that, in some instances, the subjects of mental concern could manipulate the legal process of lunacy investigation law, thereby shaping the course and outcome of legal proceedings.

Conclusion

Although these two cases are interesting in the extent to which they reflect the use of lunacy law in more urban contexts and across wider geographical scales, they have much in common with the other cases described in this chapter. The documentation left behind in lunacy trials in New Jersey offers windows into the interplay of civil law and family dynamics in the face of mental instability, real and perceived. Although these trials represent a wide array of familial circumstances, it is nevertheless possible to ascertain key preoccupations that run through many, if not most, of these cases. Not surprisingly, of major concern in most cases was the waste, destruction or unwanted reallocation of family property. Property concerns were built into the laws of lunacy investigation in England from the thirteenth century onward and remained central to the use of this body of law in New Jersey in the colonial period, and even more so in the post-revolutionary period. Family feuds over property were exacerbated by manifestations of madness. Lunacy trials helped to resolve these conflicts in ways that were designed to maintain lines of inheritance and the integrity of property in a developing capitalist society. Permeating many trials were anxieties about the relationship between aging and mental decline, and its effect on property, especially in the agrarian context. As some of the longer cases involving attempts at the *supercedeas* of earlier verdicts of insanity demonstrate, the point at which an individual was no longer mentally capable of managing his/her property was also heavily debated. These debates highlight not only the disagreements between the accused and the petitioners about mental competence, but also the deeper conflicts within families as to how to resolve the disruptive effects of mad behaviour. As lunacy investigation law became more embedded in the understanding of madness and the response to it in New Jersey, the boundary between the concern over property and the impulse to police behaviour became increasingly blurred. Although concerns about property were structured into the law, the use of the law and the testimony that it produced also made clear what New Jersey residents understood as the limits of acceptable behaviour. Chapter 8 further investigates this relationship between law and custom, to more carefully assess the responses to madness in nineteenth-century New Jersey.

Notes

1 NJSA, CC, LCF, Case of Peter P., 1824.
2 NJSA, CC, LCF, Case of Robert P., 1814.

3 NJSA, CC, LCF, Case of John B., 1826.
4 NJSA, CC, LCF, Case of Sara C., 1855; see also NJSA, CC, LCF, Case of William G., 1811.
5 NJSA, CC, LCF, Case of Elizabeth V., 1825.
6 NJSA, CC, LCF, Case of Samuel P., 1831.
7 *Ibid.*
8 NJSA, CC, LCF, Case of Anthony B., 1833. See also the rather complicated trial of Theophilus P., in NJSA, CC, LCF, Case of Theophilus P., 1815.
9 *Ibid.*
10 NJSA, CC, LCF, Case of Nathaniel A., 1841.
11 *Ibid.*
12 *Ibid.*
13 *Ibid.*
14 NJSA, CC, LCF, Case of John V., 1812. See also NJSA, CC, LCF, Cases of Alexander M., 1801; Hannah D., 1822; and Henry K., 1828.
15 NJSA, CC, LCF, Case of Elisha A., 1816.
16 *Ibid.*
17 *Ibid.*
18 As mentioned in Chapter 1, the literature on this subject is extensive. See, for example, Dwyer, *Homes for the Mad*; Tomes, *A Generous Confidence*; Warsh, *Moments of Unreason*; Finnane, *Insanity and the Insane in Post-Famine Ireland*.
19 NJSA, CC, LCF, Case of Jon M., 1807.
20 *Ibid.*
21 *Ibid.*
22 *Ibid.*
23 NJSA, CC, LCF, Case of Jacob G., 1839.
24 See also, NJSA, CC, LCF, Cases of Hiram M., 1832; Jacob V., 1829; Samuel O., 1837, Enoch A., 1840.
25 NJSA, CC, LCF, Case of James Toner, 1835.
26 *Ibid.*
27 *Ibid.*
28 NJSA, CC, LCF, Case of Eunice B., 1836. See also NJSA, CC, LCF, Case of William T., 1844. William T.'s guardians petitioned the court to make use of his mature timber to provide money for his maintenance, and to clear some of his land to cultivate for his financial benefit.
29 Case of Eunice B., 1836.
30 *Ibid.*

31 *Ibid.*
32 The role of women in these respects will be considered more thoroughly in Chapter 8.
33 The implications of the role of women as the principal caregivers of the mad are more fully developed in Chapter 8.
34 NJSA, CC, LCF, Case of Joshua A., 1803–20.
35 *Ibid.*
36 NJSA, CC, LCF, Case of Benjamin G., 1824.
37 *Ibid.*
38 *Ibid.*
39 NJSA, CC, LCF, Case of Eleanor C., 1842.
40 *Ibid.*
41 *Ibid.*
42 *Ibid.*
43 NJSA, CC, LCF, Case of Sarah C., 1865.
44 *Ibid.*
45 *Ibid.*
46 NJSA, CC, LCF, Case John L., 1823.
47 *Ibid.*
48 NJSA, CC, LCF, Case Peter C., 1830.
49 *Ibid.*
50 *Ibid.*
51 *Ibid.*
52 *Ibid.*
53 NJSA, CC, LCF, Case of Daniel E., 1836.
54 NJSA, CC, LCF, Case of Jeremiah and Abigail H., 1813.
55 As Chapter 8 shows, it also counted for much in perceptions of mental recovery.
56 NJSA, CC, LCF, Case of Huldah P., 1826.
57 NJSA, CC, LCF, Case of Edward B., 1837.
58 *Ibid.* Neighbours also tried to help Rebecca L. by washing and cooking for her. NJSA, CC, LCF, Case of Rebecca L., 1829. See also the cases of Mary E., 1836 and Francina D., 1836. The ways in which neighbours contributed to the care of the insane will be explored more fully in Chapter 8.
59 Some of these longer trials involving *supersedeas* will be considered in Chapter 8 for what they indicate about mental recovery and lunacy law.
60 NJSA, CC, LCF, Case of Abraham W., 1834.
61 *Ibid.*

62 Ibid.
63 A typical testimonial read: 'I believe the old man has as sound a mind ... as any man in the neighbourhood – has had frequent dealings with him and has always found him capable of managing his affairs.' See *ibid*.
64 *Ibid*.
65 In most verdicts it was *pro forma* to state that the state of *non compos mentis* had resulted from the visitation of God. Other explanations in the official verdict document were uncommon.
66 NJSA, CC, LCF, Case of Abraham R., 1843.
67 *Ibid*.
68 *Ibid*.
69 *Ibid*.
70 NJSA, CC, LCF, Case of Daniel V., 1854.
71 Another equally long trial and complicated case of traverse can be found in NJSA, CC, LCF, Case of Robert P., 1849–51.
72 Case of Daniel V., 1854.
73 Moran, 'Asylum in the community', pp. 227–9.
74 NJSA, CC, LCF, Case of Samuel B., 1821–28.
75 *Ibid*.
76 *Ibid*.
77 *Ibid*.
78 NJSA, CC, LCF, Case Caroline W., 1856.
79 *Ibid*.
80 *Ibid*.
81 *Ibid*.
82 *Ibid*.
83 *Ibid*.
84 *Ibid*.
85 *Ibid*.
86 *Ibid*.
87 *Ibid*.
88 NJSA, CC, LCF, Case of Isaac C., 1852.
89 *Ibid*.
90 *Ibid*.
91 *Ibid*.
92 *Ibid*.
93 *Ibid*.
94 *Ibid*.

95 *Ibid.*
96 NJSA, CC, LCF, Case of Caroline W., 1856.
97 *Ibid.*
98 *Ibid.*
99 T. Laqueur, *Solitary Sex: A Cultural History of Masturbation* (New York: Zone Books, 2004), pp. 185–227. R. P. Newman, 'Masturbation, madness and the modern concepts of childhood and adolescence', *Journal of Social History*, 8:3 (1975), 1–27.

8

Asylum in the community: managing madness in New Jersey

Chapter 7 highlighted the effect of the complex interplay of family, friends, power and property on legal and social deliberations regarding *non compos mentis* in New Jersey. It was evident in some of these cases that the treatment, care and management of those considered to be mentally unsound varied considerably. This chapter assesses those interventions in more detail. As was the case in England, the lunacy investigation process in New Jersey constituted, in itself, an important response in the identification, treatment, care and management of the mad. The protection of the mad person and his/her property was, in principle, the priority of this law. As such, New Jersey's Masters in Chancery helped to shape the civil legal response to madness by keeping in mind the welfare of those being tried for madness. The detailed trial witnesses' accounts in the New Jersey documents also allow for an analysis of the complex array of treatment, care and management strategies. These included the services of professionalising orthodox medical practitioners and the psychiatric services of fledgling lunatic asylums, on the one hand, and the myriad responses that were grounded in the conventions of popular culture, on the other hand. The trial records reveal the extensive participation of family and friends in the customary responses to madness.

The detail in the New Jersey testimonials also allows for an analysis of the symptoms and causes of madness as understood by the relatives and neighbours of those who were put on trial. The evidence is drawn from a rich sample of 165 cases in which symptoms and signs of madness are described. It indicates that nineteenth-century New Jersey residents had a wide-ranging understanding of madness, but that there were clear signs and symptoms that precipitated the resort to lunacy investigation law, including delusions, incoherence of speech, various forms of violence, unusual silences and suicidal behaviour. The signs of irrationality described by witnesses demonstrate how popular ideas about madness and their articulation were filtered through the prism of trial testimony and the civil law of lunacy investigations. The lay recordings of madness were not just conveniently left behind, uninfluenced by their preservation through the mechanics of legal process. Rather, they were intimately connected to the structuring of perceptions and responses to madness embedded in lunacy investigation law.

This chapter examines the intersections of lunacy investigation law with these lay and medical understandings and responses, including the forms of familial, community and professional care prior to, during and after the trial process. Given the long-standing institutionalisation of lunacy investigation law in New Jersey, the lunacy trial was by far the oldest state-structured response to madness, retaining its importance at least until the late nineteenth century. But it held sway and developed in parallel to, in conjunction with and sometimes in opposition to popular responses to madness. As we will see in this chapter and in Chapter 9, the development of professional medicine and psychiatry initially posed what appeared to be just another set of responses to madness that, in many cases, were integrated into the pre-existing legal and popular armamentarium of approaches. However, with the development of the New Jersey State Lunatic Asylum, by the late nineteenth century the law of lunacy investigation was being used in a manner that signalled a change in the relative importance of responses to madness within the state.

Women as principal caregivers of the mad

One of the least recognised but most obvious and important aspects of the management and care of the mad in New Jersey (and elsewhere) was the central role played by family and community members. Within this group, the lunacy law records demonstrate that women did the lion's share of caring for the mad. As Nancy Osterud has stated in her book, *Bonds of Community: The Lives of Farm Women in Nineteenth-Century New York*:

> The aid women provided to one another in sickness ... illuminate[s] both the nature of women's work and the ties among women that joined

one household to another ... It formed much of the substance of kinship among aunts, nieces, and cousins, between mothers and their sons' wives, and among women who married into the same family. It also created bonds among neighbours resembling those among kin in their intimacy, scope, and duration. It was this sharing of ordinary burdens, this experience of taking up one another's yokes and working for a while in one another's households that created and expressed a sense of commonality among women.[1]

This certainly was so in the case of the mentally troubled. In fact, the death of a principal (usually female) caregiver was cited in many cases as a reason for initiating the lunacy investigation. For example, it is clear from the 1823 lunacy investigation of James V. that for three months he had been behaving strangely. According to his family physician, James V.'s 'disordered state of mind' was made manifest by his insistence on calling himself 'James V. sophisticated James V. prince regent' and 'regent of the universe'.[2] Other neighbours agreed, noting his irrationality of speech. His mother, who had been caring for him in this deranged state, died. As a result, neighbours arranged to take turns watching him, as 'he is sometimes violent in his behaviour so as to alarm persons near him'.[3] But it is clear that this arrangement was no substitute for the care that his mother had provided. Thus, an uncle and brother-in-law soon launched a lunacy commission so that arrangements could be made to safeguard James V. and the considerable property that he had inherited from uncles and his father.

Women were relied upon to care for those whose mental troubles had been of long duration, whether these cases were considered to be instances of idiocy or insanity. When Stephen C. petitioned the chancery court to have the mental state of his thirty-year-old sister examined by trial, he noted that she 'has been all her life under the care of her mother Elizabeth'.[4] Upon her mother's death in 1814, family and friends took her to the 'Hospital of Philadelphia', but 'she would not be relieved of her insanity' through hospital care.[5] As the costs of her care were no longer being absorbed by the free labour of her mother, the lunacy inquisition held at the innkeeper's house at Gloucester was requested, in part, to assess Sarah C.'s property holdings and to determine how they could be put under guardianship in order to provide the means of her continuing care. In a similar but much more confrontational family scenario, Samuel B. petitioned for a commission of lunacy for his father

John B., who, though 'formerly possessed of reason and ordinary good sense',[6] became mentally disturbed as a result of an accident in 1832 in which he broke his thigh. John B., who was 'confined to his bed' for over three months, was cared for principally by his wife. During that time he 'had frequent derangement and insanity of mind', which lasted until the time of the lunacy trial in 1838. In 1836 John B.'s wife died, leaving his care in the hands of two adult daughters who remained at home.[7] As the foregoing examples indicate, lunacy trials were sometimes launched as a way of reorganising familial wealth to finance the care (through guardianship) of the mentally unwell whose principal female caregivers could no longer perform the task. If other women in the family or neighbourhood could not be found to take over this care, the lunacy investigation process and guardianship arrangement provided a surrogate mechanism of management and care.

Although the lines of differentiation were frequently blurred, mental derangement from idiocy – as opposed to insanity – often required care from female family members over extraordinarily long periods of time. Ann K. petitioned the courts that she had been the principal caregiver of her brother, James K., in her home in Trenton from 1816 until the time of her petition for a lunacy commission in 1850. In her testimony, Ann noted that James K. had had 'a defect of speech, eyesight and hearing' since he was a child which 'increased upon him gradually as he grew older'.[8] The trial records suggest that other family members were helping Ann in the care of her brother from time to time. Moreover, one witness, Rachel Stephenson, noted that she had 'lived in the family of Ann K. for twenty eight years ... and during all that time have assisted in attending upon and taking care of her brother'.[9] Whether she was a relative or a neighbour hired to help out is not clear from the records, but she was not included in the long list of family heirs to James K.'s property. Stephenson and Ann K. described caring for James K. as particularly intense during the eight years leading up to the lunacy commission. His worsening condition, along with the fact that he had inherited property from his recently deceased father, resulted in the decision to launch the lunacy investigation. The trial revealed that James K. had inherited farmland outside of Trenton worth $75,000 – a considerable sum – although almost none of it had been under productive cultivation for a long time. As Ann was one of three sisters who stood to inherit from James, it made a great deal of sense to reorganise some of his wealth, under the guardianship arrangements of lunacy investigation law, to help ease the financial burden of James's care.[10]

In some cases, the burden of female caregivers was spelled out in detail. In 1839 James Harris petitioned that his sixty-three year old sister, Elizabeth D., had for about a year and a half been deprived of her 'mental faculties' in consequence of 'one or more paralytic strokes'.[11] Not only had she thus 'ceased to keep house', but she:

> now lives with one of her sisters who has, the said Elizabeth D. under her constant care: That the said Elizabeth D. is in such a state as to require almost as much care and watchfulness at times as an infant, in dressing herself, taking her meals, and in going to bed and rising, and this not from weakness of body, but from infirmity of mind.[12]

In this and similar cases, the lunacy trial was designed to assess the financial means of the lunatic in order to establish guardianship arrangements that would more effectively ensure finances for care. But the likelihood in this and many other cases was that close female relations would continue to provide the same front-line care, regardless of the outcome of the trial process.

Breaking up house

In other cases, the nature of the mental condition of those who came under legal scrutiny severely challenged the long-held traditions of female management and care of the insane. For example, in describing the situation of a relative's madness in 1827, Francis L. and Thomas Grant stated that Barnt L.'s conduct 'had become so extraordinary that in the opinion of his family and friends 'twas necessary to break up House keeping altogether'.[13] In this and other cases, this 'breaking up house' entailed either the removal of the mentally afflicted or the relocation of other family members to another dwelling. The primary concerns were to avoid the escalating violent and/or disruptive behaviour from endangering the rest of the family and to create an environment in which the mad could be more closely and securely supervised. As he approached his mid-thirties, Joseph P., described by his petitioners as 'formerly a man of business and a kind and provident father and husband ... altogether ceased and neglected to attend to his business to make provision for his family, or to hold conversation with anyone in consequence of which it became necessary that he be housed separate from his wife and children who now reside in the state of New York'.[14] In the four years leading to the lunacy commission, Joseph P. was brought under the 'superintendence' of his father and brother.

'Breaking up house' was more urgently necessary in the case of Henry P., a farmer in the township of Bergen, Hudson County. In one deposition, Isaac VanGeisen, one of Henry P.'s farm hands, explained that he saw:

> Henry P. early last spring take his two children aged between four and five year and the other about seven years and tie them with a stout chord to the fence and whip them strongly with a hairy cowskin – the youngest being a delicate girl – and for no other reason than because he found the children playing together the boy having thrown off a part of his clothes. That not long after he saw the said Henry P. take the doors of the dwelling room, where his wife and children were and whilst it was yet cold weather and thro them out upon the ground in the most violent manner without giving any kind of reason therefor – and at the same time took the bed and bedding from the bedstead and threw them with rage and violence upon the floor and around the room and told his wife that if she touched them he would knock her stiff.[15]

This escalating violence climaxed one evening when VanGeisen 'heard the cry of murder from Mrs. P. the wife of said Henry, whereupon deponent jumped up and waked Adrian the son of the said Henry who was obliged to break into the room where Mrs. P. and her husband were',[16] to prevent his father from choking her to death. Henry P.'s wife and family sought refuge in the house of a relative. In another case, Samuel J. of Middlesex County was frequently 'chained' in his own house over a period of five years in an effort to 'prevent his doing injury to himself and family' as a result of his declining mental condition.[17] Eventually, however, his wife and young daughter left for the refuge of Ezekiel Ross, the father of Mrs J. In 1810, a lunacy commission found Samuel J. to have been *non compos mentis* for a period of five years. Remarkably, by March 1812, Samuel J. had launched a successful *supercedeas* of this earlier decision, gaining full control over his property and, for better or for worse, 'his family and family concerns'.[18]

Violent male behaviour connected to madness was not the only precipitant to 'breaking up house' in New Jersey. In 1811 Samuel Harris, the brother of Mary B., petitioned for a lunacy commission, claiming that his sister had been of unsound mind for the past four years. Further testimony from a neighbour, Samuel Watson, indicated that Mary B.'s mental disturbance was preventing her from taking care of her children properly. Watson stated that he had taken in one of Mary B.'s children for safety and that, over the past eighteen months, Mary B. 'frequently came to his house and would ... endeavour to prevent him from eating his necessary food, alleging it would be the death of him'.[19] In this case, the breaking up of the family meant removing Mary B.'s children from her control, at least one of whom ended up under the care of a neighbour.

The roles of neighbours and friends

Indeed, neighbours figured prominently in the response to madness in New Jersey, both as key witnesses in lunacy trials and also through their various interventions in the day-to-day responses to those considered mentally unwell. Neighbours were frequently called upon to visit those considered insane to try to talk them into more rational states, to help to rescue the mentally unwell from varying states of danger and distress and, most commonly, to watch over and provide for them.[20] In many of these cases those considered to be mad interacted directly with neighbours to a considerable extent during the course of their madness. In his 1844 testimony John Decker, of the township of Wantage in the County of Sussex, describes one of his neighbours, David C., as having been mad, off and on, over a six-year period. Decker established his credentials for knowing about his neighbour by noting that he had 'resided in the same neighbourhood with him', for 'about thirty years.'[21] For Decker, David C.'s mental unsoundness was made manifest by his 'hallowing' and his wandering from neighbour to neighbour talking in nonsensical ways. In one instance, recounted Decker, 'about a week ago, at Mr Ports – a neighbour of his – he commenced cursing and swearing and would not be pacified – but walked the floor & kept muttering something over to himself and would not talk to us.'[22] Jacob Dewitt, another neighbour to David C. for twenty years, described a more difficult experience. On the first day of David C.'s mental degeneration, 'he remained in an insane state and his neighbours had to stay with him day and night. I was sitting up one night with him. I became sleepy and laid [by him] during the night. While asleep David C. jumped on me and caught me by the throat and endeavoured to choke me – and he talked about everything unconnectedly not having any meaning to it.'[23] Although he appeared to make a partial mental recovery in the springtime, by the summer of 1843 he began to 'call himself the Russian General ... to sing and endeavour to make words rhyme, kept running around the fields and travelling around the neighbourhood without any particular object in mind.'[24] At the inquisition taken at the house of Horace Vibbert, David C. was found insane without lucid intervals and in need of guardianship to protect him, his 220-acre farm and his wife and eight children.

The case of William S. gives an indication not only of the close connections between family and local community in the response to madness, but also of the weight of community disapproval of poor guardianship practices by family in the aftermath of a trial. In his 1800 affidavit, Abraham S. described his brother William as having been insane for over ten months, manifested by incoherent speech and conduct, by violent behaviour towards friends and by his conviction that he was bewitched. The lunacy trial found William S. to be *non compos mentis*. The guardianship of William's person was given to one of his brothers (Thomas S.), while the guardianship of his considerable property holdings was delegated to another brother (Joseph S.). Within the next five years, it became clear that neighbours were unhappy with the way that William S. was being managed under guardianship. In a letter to the New Jersey state chancellor, seven neighbours protested that:

> William S. now of the said county a lunatic under the care of your Excellency ... has for a considerable time been going at large, in this Town; That his conduct at times is very offensive and alarming, particularly to the female part of the inhabitants, and that his general behaviour is so indicative of a confirmed mental derangement as to excite just apprehensions of his committing some violence on the person or property of the citizens. That his guardian if any he has appears to neglect all care of him. That he wanders about apparently destitute of the necessary clothing to cover him from the inclemency of the season, and dependent on the charity of individuals for food. They therefore pray that your Excellency to whom the law has committed the custody of such unhappy beings would take the necessary measures in the premises, either by compelling his guardian, if he has any, to take proper care of him, or by appointing some other suitable person for the purpose.[25]

In this letter, Salem residents made it clear that they understood the important links between the civil law of lunacy investigation and guardianship processes for the mad. Although willing to offer William S. *ad hoc* charity, the seven signees of this letter were clearly asking the Court of Chancery to compel Sharp's guardian to do his job. Some indication of the on-going challenges of guardianship in this case appears in another appeal to the chancery court in 1809, this time written by Joseph S., who had originally been granted guardianship of his brother William's estate. In this letter Joseph notes that 'Thomas S. departed this life about one year ago, by which means your petitioner's unhappy brother William is without a guardian of his person.'[26] Joseph S. asked the Court of Chancery that he be appointed guardian in his deceased brother's place, but whether this happened (and, if so, whether this improved the situation) is unclear from the available records. In these and several other cases, it is clear that madness in nineteenth-century New Jersey was no solitary affliction, in so far as the mad were almost always in close proximity to family and neighbours. The response to those considered mad also included the direct and indirect involvement of family and friends on a scale that reflected an essentially non-institutional environment.

Signs and symptoms of madness

Evidence from the lunacy trials indicates that family and community considered a wide range of behaviours as signs of madness. Not surprisingly, the most common sign of madness, as made manifest by the mere initiation of a trial, was the incapacity to manage oneself or one's property. A familiar and routine passage in all petitions stating that an individual was 'rendered altogether unfit and unable to govern himself or to manage his/her estate' was, after all, the long-held purpose of the trial itself, dating back to thirteenth-century England. It continued to be a chief determinant of madness in New Jersey throughout the nineteenth century. There is no question that lunacy trials in England and in New Jersey were focused on madness in complex relationships to property and, by extension, to inheritance, to economic power and to the wellbeing of those struggling over the mental incapacity of their relations. But how did New Jerseyites describe and understand the signs and symptoms of those considered to be in mental decline?

A sample of 165 commissions in which clear descriptions of madness are available helps to answer this question. As Table 8.1 shows, certain indications of madness were listed more often than others. In grouping descriptions of insanity into the following thirty-eight symptoms, I have tried to stay as faithful as possible to the language used in the documents. The very nature of the lunacy commission raises the possibility that signs of insanity might have been embellished or even worked up entirely to substantiate the claim that an individual was no longer able to govern him/herself or his/her estate. As is well documented in this book, in England and in New Jersey, it is certainly possible to establish serious family disputes over property as the basis of several lunacy commissions. However, this in itself does not throw the reliability of these documents into question. At the very least, even if the motivations behind some of the *writs de lunatico inquirendo* were occasionally suspect, the descriptions of insanity would have been consistent with prevailing understandings. Moreover, during the period under study the descriptions of insanity in the lunacy commissions never became formulaic. Some investigations briefly cited only a few indications to prove the existence of insanity, while others were long and detailed. This suggests that a petition's successful outcome was not contingent upon the elaborate descriptions of insanity that were often given. On the whole, the lunacy commissions reveal those indications and forms of behaviour that lay individuals in New Jersey thought demonstrated insanity.

Table 8.1 gives a list of thirty-eight indications of insanity described in the documents.[27] At a quick glance, the importance of violence as an indicator of insanity is clearly evident. The various forms of violence found in the commissions have been separated because lay witnesses were usually very specific about the kind of violence in question. Taken together, the various manifestations of violence appear as a sign of insanity in 45 per cent of the lunacy commissions in this study. Like most of the other indicators of insane behaviour, violence needs to be put into context. Many assumed that the types of violence they were describing were obvious signs of mental instability and they let their descriptions stand on their own. In these cases, either the form of violence was considered completely irrational, or it was perhaps indicative of an assumed understanding among the participants in the commission (who were invariably from the same community) that the violence was a sign of insanity for the individual in question. In other cases, witnesses were at pains to

Asylum in the community

Table 8.1 Symptoms described in the lunacy commissions in order of frequency (N = 165)*

Symptom	No.	%	Symptom	No.	%
Unable to conduct self/property	165	100	Uniquely unusual behaviours	7	4.2
Delusions	69	41.8	Refusal of food	7	4.2
Incoherence of speech	39	23.6	Second childhood	6	3.6
Violence toward others	25	15.1	Immoral conduct	6	3.6
Unusual dress	23	13.9	Pacing	5	3
Wandering from home	21	12.7	Nocturnal antics	5	3
Violence to property	21	12.7	Refusal to move	5	3
Threatens violence	18	10.9	Unusual religious beliefs	5	3
Refusal to talk	18	10.9	Self-injury	4	2.4
Suicidal	17	10.3	Filthiness	4	2.4
Wasting property	15	9	Fits of insanity	4	2.4
Impaired memory	13	7.8	Emotional shifts: glad to sad	4	2.4
Persecution	12	7.2	Talking in excess	3	1.8
Lack of judgement/ understanding	11	6.6	Laughing without cause	3	1.8
Mental imbecility	9	5.4	Unusual physical appearance	2	1.8
Melancholy	8	4.8	Strange dancing	2	1.2
Violent language	8	4.8	Unusual body motions	2	2.2
Vulgar language	8	4.8	Frothing at the mouth	1	.06
Hiding from others	7	4.2	Strange noises	1	.06

Source: NJSA, CC, LCF.

Note: Figures indicate the number of lunacy commissions in which the type of symptom was mentioned by a lay member of the community. As each investigation usually recorded several symptoms, the percentage of symptoms does not add up to 100%.

explain that the violent behaviour was out of character, and thus a sure indication of insanity. For example, James T.'s family noted that he 'was always a peaceable kind and friendly man ... [but] during the last 2 years [he] has frequently and without apparent or known cause, except his derangement used violent and angry language and threats towards this deponent and the members of his family'.[28] Likewise, the brothers-in-law of Joseph F. noted that he 'hath frequently committed violence upon his wife – being when in his right mind remarkably kind and affectionate'.[29]

In only 4 of the 165 investigations are instances of violence reported as the sole indicator of insanity. This suggests that violence in itself was not considered a sufficient indication of mental derangement. It is possible that violent behaviour was considered the final blow to a family's tolerance of an insane individual, precipitating the call for a lunacy commission. But there is no indication of this in the records. Unlike petitions for committal to an asylum, these documents were not created to facilitate institutional confinement. Most individuals who were found to be insane by lunacy commission were subsequently cared for at home and in the community.

Violence as an indicator of insanity gains more meaning when it is examined in relation to the other signs of derangement described in such cases. Examining clusters of descriptions, which include violence, reveals common contexts for the manifestation of violent behaviour. In one context, a cycle of increasing derangement resulted from the confinement of the individual after an initial period of violence. For example, according to his two sons, the Reverend Jacob S. began destroying various items in his house and throwing them out of the door without any prior sign or warning. His destructive tendencies continued for several months until they finally decided to confine him to his house with chains to prevent further damage and to avoid injury. Once he was chained, the Reverend S.'s derangement worsened and, according to his family, he developed the delusion that his wife was having 'criminal connection with every person who comes to the house or lives in the neighbourhood, black or white'.[30] This jealousy led him to threaten his wife with violence, and to make several attempts at suicide.

In another common context, violent displays were linked to concentrated outbursts of insanity. For example, all of Phenon S.'s violent behaviour, whether it involved swearing profanely, threatening to kill relatives or to destroy her clothing, was attributed by friends and neighbours to her 'fits of violent passion'. Isaac C. was said to have lucid intervals, but could become violent when 'labouring under excitement'. In other cases, 'fits of derangement', 'spells of derangement', 'crazy fits' and 'raves' were believed to account for violent actions.[31] In these cases, witnesses described violence as a kind of side-effect of a severely deranged moment.

Witnesses at the lunacy commissions also made connections between violence and mental delusion. John B.'s family thought that the source of his animosities toward them lay in his convictions that the devil had inhabited his house, occupying the body of his son-in-law.[32] John L.'s conviction that there was a conspiracy to get his property out of his hands was highlighted by his neighbour as the reason for his sudden destruction of several thousand dollars in bank stocks and railway notes. Here, delusions were seen as the catalysts to violent behaviour.[33]

Another indication of insanity frequently cited in the lunacy commissions was that of unusual dress. As with violence, the issue of dress and its relationship to insanity was also specific to particular social contexts. One concern (familiar enough to historians of mental illness who cover the eighteenth to twentieth centuries period) was the perceived indecency and immorality of wearing too few clothes. But there were only four lunacy commissions in this sample in which indecent exposure was seen as an indication of insanity. And in two of these four cases the circumstances were complicated by the clusters of indications into which unusual dress fitted. In one case, it was made clear that at the age of eighty-seven, Abagail G. was suffering from the effects of old age. Her neighbours noted that she had outlived all of her relatives and was no longer capable of taking care of herself. Her long-term habit of 'strip[ping]' off her clothes and expos[ing] herself in the daytime in the presence of any person', although probably embarrassing, was considered an indication of feeble-mindedness that accompanied old age.[34] In the other case, the parents of Sarah C. considered her insistence on wearing 'poor' and 'wretched' clothing as one indication of 'gross intemperance, weakened intellect, and depraved morals'. Sarah's frequent frolics into New York City, her incarceration in the New York City Penitentiary and her flippant attitude towards her inheritance and to the idea of marriage confirmed her madness in the eyes of her family. Her inappropriate dress was but one indication of a deep-seated derangement.

It is possible that in New Jersey, in this largely pre-asylum period, the spectacle of the naked lunatic had not yet become an especially worrisome image.[35]

A more frequently cited concern in the testimonials related to unusual dress was the refusal to wear clothing appropriate to the prevailing weather conditions. Walking in the rain without a hat, going out 'bare headed' or 'bare footed'[36] and 'sleeping out in exposed situations at night'[37] were all seen to reflect a loss of reason. In some cases, a direct connection was made between this form of exposure and mental illness. For example, Jacob D.'s mother explained that 'by exposing himself to the inclemency of the weather ... he has ... impaired his constitution, weakened his understanding and deranged all the faculties of his mind'.[38] Prevailing assumptions about the close relationship between health, illness and the weather, likely drawing on enduring humoral understandings of disease, partly explain why this form of unusual dress was taken as a common sign of derangement in antebellum New Jersey.

Delusions were among the most important indicators of insanity for the lay population of New Jersey. They appear in almost 42 per cent of the cases examined in this sample. Unlike violence, it is clear that a delusion could, in many instances, stand alone as a symptom significant enough to determine insanity. In 20 of the 165 investigations, there is no other explanation for insanity but the individual's delusions.

Table 8.2 lists the types of delusion in order of frequency. As with the table of symptoms, I have tried to list categories that reflect as closely as possible the language used in the lunacy commissions. The word 'delusion' was occasionally used in the documents to describe the peculiar 'flight of fantasy' or 'altered mental state' of a relative or neighbour. More frequently, it was said that a mentally disturbed individual manifested unusual 'assertion' or 'pretence'. Not surprisingly, the content of delusions was related to the cultural and historical context in which those experiencing delusions lived. As bizarre as they might appear, delusions were in some way grounded in the collective experience of those who considered themselves to be sane. Unusual assertions and pretences related to other peoples' property highlight the context-based nature of the delusions described. Just over 9 per cent of the delusions were related to misconceptions about property ownership. Among the delusions ascribed to David P. was his frequent claim that all of the land around his own farm property was his as well. He would substantiate his claim

Table 8.2 'Assertions and pretences': types of delusion described in the New Jersey lunacy commissions in order of frequency (N = 98)*

Type of delusion	No.	%
Apocalyptic (personal and global)	15	15.3
About persecution	12	12.2
Of Grandeur	11	11.2
About imaginary foes	10	10.2
About other people's property	9	9.1
About the nature of objects	6	6.1
About God	4	4.1
About the devil	4	4.1
About witches/wizards/fairies/spirits	3	3.1
Having supernatural powers	3	3.1
About being ill	3	3.1
About infidelity	3	3.1
About being injured	2	2
About being dead	1	1
About making others ill	1	1
About being someone else	1	1
About the body	1	1

Source: NJSA, CC, LCF.
Note: Figures indicate the numbers of delusions recorded in the 165 lunacy commissions. Some lunacy commissions ascribed more than one delusion to an individual. Others listed no delusions.

(and annoy other farmers) by attempting to 'turn the neighbours' cattle' into his own pastures.[39] Using a different technique, Hezekiah Y. was in the habit of taking down the fences separating his property from that of his neighbours, arguing that the land was all his. Perhaps his assertion about the property of others was related to Hezekiah Y.'s tendency to appear in open fields 'with a stick flourishing it around and striding with great violence and appearing in violent fight and contest with some imaginary person, muttering at the same time incoherent expressions.'[40] Aber H. also caused concern among his neighbours by his pretences about their land. He cut down trees for wood on the property of one neighbour, and planted chestnuts over an already sown field on the property of another. He, like Hezekiah Y., was also prone to moving fence lines to redefine property boundaries to his advantage.[41] What is interesting about delusions over property is that property disputes in nineteenth-century rural New Jersey and elsewhere were commonplace at a time when one's literal and figurative value as a farm owner was based upon the amount of arable acreage one owned. Along with other indications of insanity, it was the exaggerated claims about property and the unusual manner in which an individual acted upon those claims that made these individuals appear mentally unsound.

Also quite common in antebellum New Jersey were delusions of grandeur. This type of pretence can be divided into two categories: those related to God and those related to contemporary earthly figures of authority. The former category included those who thought they were invested with god-like powers and those who thought themselves to be God. Jacob G. told one neighbour that he had had 'an interview with the supreme being in which ... he was made acquainted with the Latin, Greek and Hebrew languages.'[42] Catherine H. believed that she had the power to destroy the whole world.[43] After a period during which he became increasingly absorbed by religion, religious books and the bible, Henry C. began to represent himself 'as the *Deity* and invested with Supreme power and that his commands and wishes must be promptly ... obeyed'.[44]

Among those whose delusions of self-importance were of a more earthly bent, Mathias K. called himself 'Napoleon and threaten[ed] to raise an army and perish all who oppose him'.[45] James V. was frequently heard repeating to himself 'James V., sophisticated James V. prince regent' and 'regent of the universe'.[46] Thomas E. was convinced that he was the Chief Justice of the United States, often signing his name *TECJ* on documents and in an advertisement for a property sale in the *Saturday Evening Post* newspaper.[47] The neighbours of Abraham B. cited his belief that he had the 'power to control the elections held under the general Government' as one of several manifestations of his insanity.[48]

It was possible for both types of grand assertions to appear in the same person, as was demonstrated by William W., who was, according to family, convinced that 'God Almighty stuck pins and irons in him which made him bleed inwardly'.[49] These injuries were the result of 'contests and fights with God Almighty'.[50] William was convinced that if he could meet God 'in an open field and have a fair field battle with him', he could 'get the advantage of God'.⁵¹ But, according to family and neighbours, William W. at other times believed that he was responsible for bringing peace with England and France, and that England had sent him one million dollars as a reward for his efforts.

As the case of William W. suggests, it was not uncommon for an individual to have more than one kind of delusion during a given period of madness. Individuals from twenty-five out of the ninety-eight cases involving delusions, or about one quarter of the sample group, were said to have displayed two or more distinct assertions or pretences. In some cases, there was clearly a connection between the content of one delusion and another. Catherine H. thought that she had the power to destroy the whole world, and, at other times, she was convinced that 'she made every person sick who had anything to do with her'.⁵² Her sense of her own person as lethal seems to have been an underlying subtext for her delusions. In a similar fashion, David B. thought that people were out to deprive him of his property; that a black lamb on his farm caused his horses' eyes to turn to glass and go blind; that a spell had been put upon him by a physician 'to get his body for anatomy'; that he was injured whenever he touched an object made of steel; and that his family 'put salts in his meat and physiked [sic] him nearly to death'.⁵³ Persecution in various forms filled the content of his unusual assertions. Similar connections were also apparent in those whose delusions combined apocalyptic and theistic themes,⁵⁴ or apocalyptic and persecutory themes.⁵⁵ For example, Thomas B., on different occasions, was convinced that there was a man in the corner of the room wanting to kill him; that 'strangers were erecting tents upon a hill in the vicinity of his house ... for the purpose of destroying him ... and his family'; and that 'a man came into his room every night and slept with him against his will, whom he ... represented sometimes as having a head as large as a half bushel, at other times as being without any head, again as having no legs and then again as having but one and that a wooden leg ...'.⁵⁶ Ann W. was described as convinced at various times that the neighbouring town of Key Port had burned to the ground and that its citizens were pressuring her for money to help them; that New York City was burning to the ground and that its citizens wanted Ann to offer all of them accommodation; that people had surrounded her house and were throwing chloroform at her to kill her; that she was 'as big as a house' and could not therefore get in or out of it; and that she had 'lockjaw'.[57]

In some instances, a mixed array of delusions were attributed to an individual. Neighbours of Lewis R. spoke of his intentions to voyage to Europe to bring back with him 'two shiploads of Irishmen to be employed as labourers about Bordentown because he says labourers there are very scarce'.[58] He also insisted that his wife, who had died two years before the lunacy investigation, was still alive, and made frequent plans to visit her. Abraham B. was, according to family and neighbours, under the false impression that 'there were females in pursuit of him who wanted to kill him and who took all his strength from him'[59] by breathing on him in his sleep; that he was a wealthy farmer with a fortune in the Farmer and Merchant Bank of Middletown Point; that he had the power to control lightning; and that he was an important officer of the federal government.

Assertions and pretences about 'imaginary foes' were also seen as important indicators of madness. In some instances, delusions were described as Don Quixote-like. Anna C. made 'violent blows and gestures with her arms, as if in a rage with fighting some person',[60] while Abraham R. wandered the 'Highway … with clubs in his hands swearing, cursing, striking the ground and fence'.[61] In the majority of cases, there were close links between assertions about enemies and assertions about persecution. According to his mother, for years Joseph L. had 'laboured under a very great fear that some persons were taking an opportunity to hang him'.[62] He also believed that he was about to be taken away to the state prison. Daniel E. believed that his township ought to be prepared for an imminent invasion by a 'company of warriors'.[63] Relatives of Zemas W. noted that he feared greatly that strangers designed to kill him by setting fire to the steamboat on which he was travelling.[64]

As Table 8.1 indicates, incoherence of speech was considered by New Jersey's lay population to be a major sign of insanity. It appears in over 23 per cent of the trials under study. This could manifest itself in several ways. Some neighbours and relatives used the word 'incoherence' when referring to the speech of those they considered to be mad.[65] Others described the conversations of the mad as 'wild and incoherent'.[66] Still others described 'strange and incongruous' talk,[67] 'unconnected' speech,[68] 'disordered' conversation,[69] 'disjointed and irrational discourse'[70] or some combination thereof. These descriptions can be broken down into a few general types of verbal incoherence, all of which appeared to disturb those describing it. Some stated that their mad friends or relatives put words together that simply did not make any sense to them. Others described strings of verbal assertions that came out as a succession of disconnected ideas about equally disparate subjects. Finally, others commented on differing degrees of verbal incapacity. Witnesses often connected the loss of verbal capacity to physical decline.

While most descriptions of incoherent speech were short, a few cases gave more detailed accounts of this prominent indicator of insanity. Like other individuals for whom incoherence of speech was a sign of madness, Thomas F.'s 'wild, incoherent and inconsistent conversation'[71] was but one of his mad characteristics. He was also suicidal, delusional and violent to others. Some in his family noted that although he showed some signs of madness a year before the lunacy trial, it was after a more recent 'Methodist Camp Meeting'[72] that he became completely insane. To emphasise the significance of his incoherent speech, a neighbour recalled some recent conversations:

> and upon speaking to him and asking him how he did the said Thomas F. ... immediately said to the deponent 'You had better be dead. We had better be dead, I wish I were dead.' And this he repeated very often – and seemed unwilling or incapable of talking rationally – or upon any subject – the deponent saith that when he told Thomas F. his name he then said 'Oh Gustin – yes I recollect Gustin – you had better be dead, you had better be dead' ... a few days after this he went with his the deponent's wife to the house of Thomas F. – with whom Thomas F. used to be a good acquaintance – and when the deponent asked him if he knew who the deponent's wife was he looked at her and said 'no' – the deponent then said this is my wife – F. then said 'she is most dead'. The deponent said no Tommy she is very well. He replied as before, 'She is most dead' and then immediately said to the deponent, 'you have been with my wife get out of my vessel. I will shoot you you damned brute'. His look was wild and he spoke nothing sensible or rational.[73]

The words spoken at Methodist revival meetings in the early nineteenth century were often considered highly unusual to non-participants in the community. But the nature of Thomas F.'s verbal digressions, along with the manner in which he spoke them, made him appear mentally unstable to family and friends in a way that transgressed the mere religious fervour of Protestant revivalism.

If bizarre verbalisation contributed to a concern over mental stability, so too did the refusal to talk. In some cases, the refusal to talk was mentioned as the only appreciable indication of insanity. For example, according to relatives, John Jordan was known 'not to utter a word for weeks together'.[74] This singularly odd behaviour led to his confinement to the New York hospital for several months but his treatment there seemed not to have improved his mental state. Likewise, Hester C.'s 'strange behaviour is that she rarely answers when spoken to'.[75] It is not hard to imagine how such total withdrawal from social interaction with others might be perceived as a stand-alone indication of madness. Other individuals manifested a mixed bag of indications in addition to their verbal silences. But those who refused to talk tended to display two other indications of madness in common. About 28 per cent of those who refused to talk were described as having attempted or seriously considered suicide, more than double the percentage of suicidal cases described in the sample used for this study. More striking still, 28 per cent of those considered unusually silent were also described as depressed or melancholic, a figure that was much higher than the 4.8 per cent of the entire sample who were described as depressed. In these instances, the refusal to talk formed part of a disturbing mix of suicidal and melancholic behaviour.

Such was the case for Samuel O., whose brother asserted that he had become 'melancholy, low spirited [and] not inclined to conversation' for an eighteen-month period leading up to his insanity trial.[76] By April 1836 Samuel O. was telling his family that 'he had so much trouble that he didn't care about living'.[77] Edward B.'s silent demeanour was a gradual process that, according to friends, bore little relationship to his normally 'communicative and affable'[78] self. After an equally unusual outburst of excited and incomprehensible gesturing and talking, he had descended into a 'silent and morose' state, sitting 'with his head bent on his breast almost motionless'.[79] At the same time, he started to refuse food and nourishment. In equally sudden fashion, on two separate occasions, Samuel O. had come out of this subdued state and beat upon female members of the family. Similarly, friends and relatives described Elizabeth D.'s madness as a mix of 'totally silent and sullen' periods and 'violent passions' during which she threatened them with 'the most ridiculous filthy and scandalous language'.[80] Her mental state was likely not helped by the decision to confine her with chains. Lloyd V. was also forcibly confined by his family for his violent outbursts, which were mainly directed at objects in the house in which he lived. His family also appeared disturbed by his impromptu 'hits of laughter', which were 'unusual to him when of sound mind'.[81] But, leading up to his insanity trial, witnesses described him as mainly disinterested in talking to anyone, disinterested in dressing in the morning and disinterested in eating for days at a time. Most disturbing to one neighbour was his attempt to do himself harm by jumping into a nearby brook on two occasions when the water was 'high and cold'.[82]

A careful examination of the signs and symptoms of madness as described in the testimony of lunacy trials raises familiar debates. It is hardly surprising that the content of mad delusions, for example, would be drawn from the local, national and international contexts of the period. For some researchers these delusions would nevertheless indicate the trans-historical nature of 'mental illness'. For others these same delusions would speak to the complexities of a more nuanced historical epidemiology that considers 'the ways in which different societies have conceptualised diseases, their causes, and modes of transmission, and the ways in which theoretical ideas have been practically applied in the effort to prevent or control' madness.[83] In taking the latter view, the close relationship between the indicators of madness and local context reveals much about the predominantly rural and small-town culture of New Jersey in which instances of mad behaviour were being identified. In a society in which oral communication of knowledge and ideas was crucial, it is not surprising that prolonged silence, verbal incoherence and solitary behaviour were considered as serious signs of madness. Forms of violence that rendered the sociability of close-knit family living arrangements impossible to maintain also, unsurprisingly, indicated madness to relatives and neighbours. 'Flights of fancy', and altered mental states, transgressed social and moral conventions. Clothes frequently worn which were deemed inappropriate to weather conditions raised health concerns connected to long-standing views about exposure and humoral imbalance. These behaviours, usually in combination, were described in trial testimonies as indications of madness. But, as structured around lunacy investigation law, the point at which they were considered extreme was the point at which they rendered the individual incapable of governing self and property. In this respect the measure of madness was not connected to institutional confinement, or the sequestering out of the familial and community context for specialised medical treatment.

Forms of confinement

As the case of Lloyd V. and others suggest, various forms of confinement were part and parcel of the response to madness in New Jersey. Although the trial records do not give the same kind of detail as they do for the signs and symptoms of madness, there is still a relatively full listing, and sometimes a fuller description, of how family and community responded to madness. One of the more common responses was varying forms of attendance. As we have seen earlier in this chapter, the bulk of the front-line care – including providing company, feeding, washing and other forms of immediate management – was done by female relatives and neighbours. Neighbours, physicians and other family members were also called upon to look after those experiencing bouts of mental distress. John Heritage, a neighbour to Samuel B., 'at the request of the family where the said Samuel B. lodged, sat up with the said S. B., to prevent [him] from doing any mischief to himself or others'.[84] This appeared to be a common form of watching, or overseeing, of those whose madness was creating anxiety.

In cases in which the behaviour of the mad was considered dangerous to family members, an alternative to 'breaking up house', as described earlier in this chapter, was the confinement of the individual at home. In many testimonials clear references to confinement are made, but the actual means of confinement are not always specified. However, in these instances the reasons for confinement are made explicit. In 1850, petitioners in the township of Morris noted that Charles C. 'has been so violent and dangerous that it has been necessary to confine him and keep him secure from doing harm to himself or others'.[85] Extraordinarily, in this case, Charles C. had been confined 'for the last ten years'.[86] In some cases, family and neighbours considered it necessary to confine those considered to be mad in a room of the house.[87] The extent of confinement depended on the circumstances described by witnesses. In 1825 Ann H. was periodically confined when she became 'violent and threatening in her actions and words'.[88] As her tendency to be violent increased, 'on the advice of her physician [she was] constantly confined, it not being considered safe that she should be at liberty'.[89] Ann D. was 'locked up'

Asylum in the community

in a room in her home in Washington Township in 1851 'to keep her from injuring herself, and others, and to prevent her from injuring her own child, which she appeared to want to kill'.[90]

In other cases, 'chaining' is described as a means of last resort to prevent self-harm or injury to others. The most dramatic description of this response comes from the testimony of John L., who explained at the inquest at the house of Perez Knowley, innkeeper in Princeton, that his son John L. junior had suffered on and off from mental distress since 1776. By 1812, John L. junior had clearly reached a climax of unhappiness, attempting to end his life by cutting his throat. In response, John L. the father, with the assistance of a neighbour, used a 'straight jacket' to 'prevent him from mangling his throat', and 'chain[ed] him to keep him at home as he appeared determined to end his life by any means in his power.[91] Although his father was successful in preventing suicide, John L. junior continued to 'be in the utmost distress almost continually walking backwards and forwards the length of his chain often observing that his farm was barren and everything belonging to him was going to ruin'.[92] Anna D. explained that her son, Jacob D., 'by exposing himself to the inclemency of the weather when not restrained by chaining ... has so impaired his constitution weakened his understanding and deranged all the faculties of his mind that ever since January last his insanity has rendered him wholly unfit to manage his business and estate'.[93]

Adding even more texture to these descriptions of confinement is the detailed witness testimonies about Daniel H., a forty-five-year-old farmer in Wantage Township, Sussex County. According to his brother Lewis H., Daniel began to show 'symptoms of insanity' in 1821, including 'hallowing aloud, and complaining of pain, while he would at the same time be at work' on his 220-acre farm.[94] Yet 'nothing appeared to ail him, as to real pain and sickness'.[95] This odd behaviour was followed by delusions about the devil and everyone around him plotting his destruction. Daniel H.'s brother added that, at about the same time, he became 'ill natured and violent' striking friends and relatives 'without provocation'.[96] Much like the explanation of Anna D. about the need to confine her son so as to avoid exposure, Lewis H. noted that his brother 'was permitted to go about until the weather became so cold that it was unsafe and improper to permit him to be at large, lest he might perish by exposure to the weather. It then became necessary to confine him in the House, and for this purpose a strong pen or partition was put up in his house, in which he was confined and where he has been kept and confined during the last winter.'[97] Adding more detail, a neighbour, Daniel Moses, noted that Daniel's 'wife and friends have been obliged to have him ... confined pretty constantly in a kind of Pen put up in his house in the room, where the family sit, and near the fire so as to make him as comfortable as possible.'[98] On one visit, Moses was warned by Daniel's wife, 'not to sit within his reach lest he might strike the deponent which he could do as the grating of the Pen were so wide apart that the said Daniel could put his hand and arm through.'[99] Although he was encouraged to 'perform the necessities of nature' outside, Daniel H.'s brother noted that Daniel preferred to do this in his pen, refusing 'any vessel for the purpose'. He also took his meals in the enclosure.[100]

The domestic impact of this kind of arrangement is hard to fathom. But the desire to have Daniel H. among the sane, to the extent that his family thought possible, is notable and consistent with other indications of the relatively open interactions of those considered to be mad with family and neighbours. As I have discussed elsewhere, this was to an extent built into the nature of the lunacy trial process itself – a process that was held publicly, often at the local tavern keeper's establishment, and with the testimony of neighbours and family members being evaluated by a jury of local property-holding men. Moreover, evidence from several trials strongly suggests that those considered to be mad were more often than not moving through public and private spaces relatively freely, so long as their behaviour did not become too threatening.[101]

Asylum in the community

In a small number of cases in which the verdict of *non compos mentis* was successfully traversed or superseded, it is possible to get some idea of how family and community responded to madness over much longer periods of time. It is remarkable how long a period of time could elapse between the initial decision of *non compos mentis* and the use of *supercedeas* to traverse it. Mary A., of Alexandria Township, was found to be *non compos mentis* in March 1807, largely based on testimonials describing her persistent delusion that 'she has ruined herself and her children.'[102] Eleven years later, in August 1818, Mary A. was petitioning to the Court of Chancery that she had recovered and was ready to take back legal responsibility for herself and her property. In the case of Craig L., twelve years separated his trial that found him insane in 1808 and the *supercedeas* that deemed him mentally sound in 1823.[103]

In such cases, how did family and community respond to the madness of their charges during these often long periods of recovery? The evidence suggests an informal combination of responses – some of which we have already encountered in this chapter – that, for some individuals, created the space and time for mental recovery. This kind of response can be seen over the long period of convalescence of Peter D., first considered insane by lunacy trial in July 1834. Neighbours of Peter D., a twenty-five-year-old bachelor farmer in the township of Shrewsbury, described him as violent and deranged in equal measure over a period of three months. Yet, he was, during this period, still freely moving around the neighbourhood. By the account of Joseph Daly:

> On Wednesday or Thursday of last week he … came to the house of this deponent at Eaton town and appeared to be quite deranged that this deponent's wife who is his cousin set him some dinner after eating which he took a cake knife and took a gun in the room and took it to pieces … when asked what he was doing he said he was cleaning it … upon this deponent's asking him what he done with the knife he answered he kept it for opening people that he had opened several and intended to open others that it was a disagreeable business but he said he must do it.[104]

These and other bizarre forms of behaviour led to Peter D.'s family hiring a man 'to take charge of him and prevent his doing mischief to himself and others',[105] and eventually filing for a lunacy commission.

Despite these serious signs of mental instability, seventeen years later Peter D. made an appeal to traverse the earlier finding of *non compos mentis*. In a relatively common practice, the appointed guardian of Peter D.'s farm property hired a series of tenants to keep the farm operational and to generate an income, partly to be used for Peter D.'s maintenance and partly to maintain the profitability of his land holding. In testimony of the last tenant, Rulif Smith, it becomes clear that Peter D. stayed on at the farm, partially under the control of the man hired to take charge of him. But, over the course of Smith's six-year lease of Peter D.'s property, it is also clear that Smith paid Peter D. to perform various farm tasks on his own farm, including planting corn and potatoes, killing hogs and harvesting hay. Rulif explained that 'Mr D. was not of course a regular hand with me', but, rather, 'worked for me occasionally when I was short of help'.[106] Rulif added that Peter D. 'kept an account' of his work and that 'in performing the work for the past few years I have discovered nothing like insanity or derangement in him'. Rulif concluded that Peter D. was, by 1851, 'capable of taking charge of his farm and managing it himself'.[107] Peter D.'s appeal for *supercedeas* was successful.

Lewis P. also had someone hired to keep him under his watch 'day and night'.[108] In his testimony, Joseph Pemmock described himself as Lewis P.'s 'nurse or keeper', a difficult job in this case, for Lewis P. had for one year been suffering the extreme mental effects of alcoholism.[109] This was made manifest in the form of severe memory loss, disorientation and 'extremely strange and violent' behaviour towards 'former friends'.[110] In this case Lewis P. was taken in by the guardian appointed to be in charge of his person after the verdict of *non compos mentis* at his lunacy trial. Witnesses agreed that 'within the last three or four years his mental capacity has been improving', and his 'health during his residence with his guardian has materially improved'.[111] Finally, and maybe most importantly, witnesses noted that 'he has been perfectly temperate since he has resided with his guardian'.[112]

In these and other cases to be discussed in the next chapter, it appears that the potential for recovery was built both into the spirit and structure of the law of lunacy investigation, on the one hand, and into the New Jersey community's more traditional responses to madness, on the other hand. It was known in the community that this kind of recovery might take varying lengths of time, and that the guardianship process created a context that allowed for this to occur. Unlike the extant records for England, the testimonials in the New Jersey records allow for a more detailed consideration of this 'asylum in the community', whereby individuals could be cared for, managed and allowed the time to recover mentally. This could include spending time on the property of a neighbour or a relative, or allowing those considered to be mad to work at farming tasks in order to recover the physical condition, the mental capacity and the acumen required to prove in a court of law that mental control over property and person had been regained.

The role of the community in this process of recovery is in plain view in the case of Francis F., who also experienced asylum confinement. In 1857 Francis F.'s nephew petitioned for a lunacy commission to inquire into the mental state of his uncle. According to one witness, Dr John

Honeyman, Francis F. had been 'bitten by a mad dog and was soon after attacked with strong symptoms of the Hydrophobia', which accounted for 'the derangement of his mind'.[113] This left Francis F. incapable of managing his 380-acre farm in Hunterdon County, New Jersey and another 200-acre property in Seneca County, New York. Francis F.'s process of recovery included a stay at the Canandaigua Asylum. The records do not state when he arrived at the asylum, but he returned to the town of Covert, Seneca County, in July 1868, where he 'boarded just opposite to'[114] one witness, John Rafferty. From there he made frequent trips to work on his farm in New York. Over the next four years he integrated himself back into the community and slowly took over increasing responsibility for his farm. As part of his own attempts to convince those around him that he had regained his sanity, he put his mental state up for community consideration. As Peter Minor, a merchant in Covert put it:

> [Francis F.] had lived under the eyes of the community for a number of years ... he drew up a statement with a view to getting the opinion of the public. In a few days he brought in the store this paper, I think he had the names of over one hundred persons, afterwards he got a great many more, five or six hundred I think, he then said that it appeared to be the general impression that he was sane, and that he did not see any reason why he should not get the possession of his property – the list of names was almost universal in the neighbourhood.[115]

Armed with this community sanction of his return to reason, Francis F. went on to petition successfully to retake control over his property and person in New York and, shortly afterward, in New Jersey.

Conclusion

Whether Francis F. continued to operate his property and person in a state of mental soundness is impossible to say.[116] Nevertheless, a careful examination of what these legal records do indicate about understandings of and responses to madness – more or less fragmented, depending upon the quality of the documents – reveals an exceptionally rich repository of recorded observations. This legal record is itself the product of a legal inheritance from England, adopted into the colonial setting of New Jersey and developed in the post-revolutionary context of the new fledgling state. However, unlike in England, the relatively complete archival series of New Jersey case files allows for a more nuanced description of what a wide range of individuals thought about madness, and how they attempted to respond to it in a largely pre-institutional era.

This evidence reveals, among other things, that women predominated in the day-to-day care, management and convalescence of the mad. This long list of direct care included cleaning the domestic settings of the mad, keeping the mad clean, feeding them, dressing them, consoling them and managing the social relationships between the mad and other members of the household and the wider community. As some examples have demonstrated, these responsibilities could last for weeks, months and sometimes years. Women also figured prominently as witnesses in lunacy trials, offering information and opinion of major concern that weighed in heavily on verdicts of *non compos mentis*. Moreover, they were appointed as guardians through the Orphans Court, usually over the person, but sometimes also over the property of those deemed legally insane. Evidence from the lunacy trials indicates that the bulk of the management and care of the mad took place in domestic settings. The full spectrum of familial relations is on display in these trials, and the testimony suggests an equally wide range of domestic responses, from compassionate care to coercion. Yet, how madness was accepted in New Jersey did not necessarily correspond to specific interventions. As some examples have suggested, forms of confinement, including tying and chaining, could represent a desperate attempt to temper self-harm or the abuse of another family member, just as often as it could signal the injudicious shuttering-up of the mad.

Furthermore, lunacy investigations reveal that women and men in the neighbourhood could be considered as important as family members in the response to madness. Neighbours were predominantly called upon to 'watch over' those whose madness had made them more dangerous either to themselves or to others. Neighbours also attempted to make those living nearby who appeared to be mentally unsound listen to reason. They talked to them and offered them company and sociability in their own homes, in farmers' fields or in town. Neighbours were also solicited by families to help to confine, subdue and sometimes rescue the mad from difficult situations. They participated heavily in trial testimony – their explanations and opinions often being crucial to the determination of *non compos mentis* and also to the determination of mental recovery in civil trials in lunacy. Community opinion – a kind of collective understanding based on long-term association with an individual whose mental condition was under scrutiny – was also central to the outcome of trials, to the determination of mental recovery and to the shaping of madness at a broader remove.

Just as popular responses to madness can be gleaned from the legal records pertaining to lunacy trials, so too can the signs and indications of behaviour that most likely indicated mental instability. Among these it is clear that unusual demonstrations of violent behaviour were near the top of the list, but the list also includes a broad range of delusions that appeared to New Jersey residents to place their friends and relatives beyond the normal boundaries of identity and behaviour. An extraordinarily rich description of altered mental states also included verbal incoherence, unusual silence, impaired memory, inappropriate dress, melancholy and a host of other less frequently cited although significant indicators. Occasionally, local physicians and other community leaders were called upon to testify in these cases. However, the vast majority of key witnesses were those who had been in close approximation to and in close association with those on trial for madness. In this respect, the signs of madness that counted most were those articulated by friends and family.

The testimony of family and community members enables the historian to add considerable substance to what historian David Wright has identified as 'centuries-old cultural and popular ideas about insanity'.[117] While historians have recognised that this culture must surely have existed, it has tended either to be dismissed as 'primitive' and unworthy of study, or elusive – largely beyond the historical record. Moreover, if there were popular ideas about and responses to madness, most historians have written them off as swept away under the doormat of institutionalisation and professional psychiatry. The foregoing analysis of lunacy trial testimony does some justice to the complex culture of madness in pre-/proto- institutional New Jersey.

However, it is also important to consider how these testimonials produced a complex relationship with the legal process of which they formed a part. As an element of a very long-standing legal response to madness, the growth of lunacy investigation law in New Jersey made its mark in the determination of and understanding of madness. By tying witnesses' accounts to a legal definition of madness grounded in property ownership and self-control, the familial and community view of madness was profoundly shaped by lunacy investigation law. The close connections of witness testimony, lunacy investigation law and the practical use of the law by families who initiated proceedings is of major significance. Communities gathering, watching and discussing cases at local tavern owners' establishments, where most of the trials took place, further demonstrate the interconnectedness of lay ideas about madness and the development of lunacy investigation law. This strong, centuries-old amalgam of customary approaches to madness and lunacy investigation law was affected by the introduction of the lunatic asylum in complex ways that will be assessed in the next chapter.

Notes

1 N. Ostreud, *Bonds of Community: The Lives of Farm Women in Nineteenth-Century New York* (Ithaca: Cornell University Press, 1991), p. 193. Thierry Nootens also discusses the role of women in this regard in T. Nootens, '"For years we have never had a happy home": Madness and families in nineteenth-century Montreal' in J. Moran and D. Wright (eds), *Mental Health in Canadian Society: Historical Perspectives* (Montreal: McGill Queen's University Press, 2006), pp. 49–68.
2 NJSA, CC, LCF, Case of James V., 1823.
3 *Ibid.*
4 NJSA, CC, LCF, Case of Sarah C., 1814.
5 *Ibid.*
6 NJSA, CC, LCF, Case of John B., 1838.
7 During this two-year period, after his wife's death and under the care of his daughters, John B. sold his farm to one of his sons, John B., Jr.. This passing on of his property to another son, apparently in a state of insanity, was what spurred Samuel B. to initiate the lunacy investigation. Although the circumstances are unclear from the trial transcript, the verdict was that John B. was indeed insane, but that the selling off of his farm occurred just prior to the start of his madness. This verdict is completely inconsistent with the earlier verdict and suggests that the courts wished for John B.'s brother John Jr. to take over the family farm. For other instances of female family care of the insane, see NJSA, CC, LCF, Case Rachel P., 1820; Case of Jacob W., 1825.
8 NJSA, CC, LCF, Case of James K., 1850.
9 *Ibid.*

10 Another case of constant familial care of a relative described as 'insane from his childhood' can be found in NJSA, CC, LCF, Case of Mahlon H., 1828.
11 NJSA, CC, LCF, Case of Elizabeth D., 1839.
12 Ibid. Joshua Sutterthwaite of Burlington County made a similar case in his petition for a lunacy investigation of his sister in law, Ann B. in 1849. He noted that 'her circumstances are such as to forbid her from living comfortable and at other times she fancies that she has been making large purchases of property which has greatly impaired her mind, which facts exit only in her own disordered imagination, as she has sufficient property for her comfortable maintenance'. NJSA, CC, LCF, Ann B., 1849. See also NJSA, CC, LCF, Case of George S., 1836.
13 NJSA, CC, LCF, Case of Barnt L., 1827.
14 NJSA, CC, LCF, Case of Joseph P., 1835.
15 NJSA, CC, LCF, Case of Henry P., 1841.
16 Ibid.
17 NJSA, CC, LCF, Case of Samuel J., 1810.
18 Ibid. See also NJSA, CC, LCF, Case of George T., 1833.
19 NJSA, CC, LCF, Case of Mary B., 1811.
20 See for example, NJSA, CC, LCF, Case of Alberta P., 1839; Case of George F., 1829; and Case of Phebe M., 1853.
21 NJSA, CC, LCF, Case of David C., 1844.
22 Ibid.
23 Ibid.
24 Ibid.
25 NJSA, CC, LCF, Case of William S., 1800.
26 Ibid.
27 The following section on indications of insanity is reproduced, with minor changes, from J. Moran, 'The signal and the noise: The historical epidemiology of insanity in antebellum New Jersey', *History of Psychiatry*, 14:3 (2003), 281–301.
28 NJSA, CC, LCF, Case of James T., 1835.
29 NJSA, CC, LCF, Case of Joseph F., 1828. In a similar manner, the brother of Marmaduke A. noted that 'when any other person except the family in which he resides come into his presence or offer to converse with him he frequently swears in a very violent manner – although when he was in his right mind he cautiously abstained from the use of such language'. See NJSA, CC, LCF, Case of Marmaduke A., 1821.

30 NJSA, CC, LCF, Case of Jacob S., 1939.
31 NJSA, CC, LCF, Case of Phenon S., 1834; Case of Isaac C., 1852; Case of Susanna P., 1837; Case of Hannah S., 1842.
32 NJSA, CC, LCF, Case of John B., 1860.
33 NJSA, CC, LCF, Case of John L., 1860.
34 NJSA, CC, LCF, Case of Abagail G., 1823.
35 NJSA, CC, LCF, Case of Sarah C., 1855. Some witnesses saw the wearing of too many clothes as a possible indication of insanity. This indication was described as an irrational insistence on wearing hat and shoes to bed, on keeping an overcoat on during the whole summer, etc.
36 NJSA, CC, LCF, Case of Hannah S., 1842; Case of Mathias K., 1821.
37 NJSA, CC, LCF, Case of Joseph P., 1834.
38 NJSA, CC, LCF, Case of Jacob D., 1808.
39 NJSA, CC, LCF, Case of David P., 1803.
40 NJSA, CC, LCF, Case of Hezekiah Y., 1809. See also, NJSA, CC, LCF, Case of Thomas F., 1832. One witness asserted that Thomas 'would frequently say he owned no land, no property – that he had sold his land and then immediately he would say that he had not sold his lands – sometimes he would say that he owned the farm belonging to one of his neighbours, and would move on that – then on some other farm of another neighbour'.
41 NJSA, CC, LCF, Case of Aber H., 1824.
42 NJSA, CC, LCF, Case of Jacob G., 1827.
43 NJSA, CC, LCF, Case of Catherine H., 1799.
44 NJSA, CC, LCF, Case of Henry C., 1855.
45 NJSA, CC, LCF, Case of Methias K., 1819.
46 NJSA, CC, LCF, Case of James V., 1823.
47 NJSA, CC, LCF, Case of Thomas E., 1836.
48 NJSA, CC, LCF, Case of Abraham B., 1854.
49 NJSA, CC, LCF, Case of William W., no date.
50 *Ibid.*
51 *Ibid.*
52 NJSA, CC, LCF, Case of Catherine H., 1799.
53 NJSA, CC, LCF, Case of David B., 1851.
54 See, for example, NJSA, CC, LCF, the Cases of Jacob L., 1814; Case of Mary H., 1833.
55 NJSA, CC, LCF, Case of Samuel S., 1826.
56 NJSA, CC, LCF, Case of Thomas B., 1831.

57 NJSA, CC, LCF, Case of Ann W., 1858.
58 NJSA, CC, LCF, Case of Lewis R., 1858 (last name illegible in document).
59 NJSA, CC, LCF, Case of Abraham B., 1854.
60 NJSA, CC, LCF, Case of Anna C., 1815.
61 NJSA, CC, LCF, Case of Abraham R., 1843.
62 NJSA, CC, LCF, Case of Joseph L., 1819.
63 NJSA, CC, LCF, Case of Daniel E., 1836.
64 NJSA, CC, LCF, Case of Zemas W., 1841; see also NJSA, CC, LCF, Case of Daniel A., 1830.
65 See, for example, NJSA, CC, LCF, Case of William S., 1800.
66 NJSA, CC, LCF, Case of John R., 1808.
67 Witnesses explained that Anna A. talked 'in a very strange and incongruous manner at times presenting that her name is Anna Beekman and that she has a husband in Barbadoes, and a female child with her – which is known to everybody to be destitute of all foundation in fact'. NJSA, CC, LCF, Case of Anna A., 1812. See also NJSA, CC, LCF, Case of Elizabeth D., 1815.
68 NJSA, CC, LCF, Case of Thomas B., 1842.
69 NJSA, CC, LCF, Case of Phoebe P., 1843.
70 NJSA, CC, LCF, Case of David R., 1823.
71 NJSA, CC, LCF, Case of Thomas F., 1832.
72 *Ibid.*
73 *Ibid.*
74 NJSA, CC, LCF, Case of John J., 1821.
75 NJSA, CC, LCF, Case of Hester C., 1853.
76 NJSA, CC, LCF, Case of Samuel O., 1827.
77 *Ibid.*
78 NJSA, CC, LCF, Case of Edward B., 1837.
79 *Ibid.*
80 NJSA, CC, LCF, Case of Elizabeth D., 1815.
81 NJSA, CC, LCF, Case of Lloyd V., 1846.
82 *Ibid.*
83 Elizabeth Fee et al., 'Introduction', in Y. Kawakita, S. Sakia and Y. Otsuka (eds), *History of Epidemiology: Proceedings of the 13th International Symposium on the Comparative History of Medicine – East and West* (Tokyo: Ishiyaku EuroAmerica, Inc., 1993).
84 NJSA, CC, LCF, Case of Samuel B., 1815.

85　NJSA, CC, LCF, Case of Charles C., 1850.
86　Ibid.
87　See, for example, NJSA, CC, LCF, Case of Samuel E., 1856.
88　NJSA, CC, LCF, Case of Ann H., 1825.
89　Ibid.
90　NJSA, CC, LCF, Case of Ann D., 1851. See also NJSA, CC, LCF, Cases of: Samuel T., 1849; Timothy C., 1841; and Zaccheus D., 1809.
91　NJSA, CC, LCF, Case of Jacob L., 1814.
92　Ibid.
93　NJSA, CC, LCF, Case of Jacob D., 1808. Chaining was also considered necessary in the following cases: NJSA, CC, LCF, Case of Jacob S., 1812; Case of Elizabeth D., 1815.
94　NJSA, CC, LCF, Case of Daniel H., 1822.
95　Ibid.
96　Ibid.
97　Ibid.
98　Ibid.
99　Ibid.
100　This example, extraordinary in its detail, begs the question of how common such enclosures were in New Jersey as a means of confinement. Although several cases mention confinement, this is the only case that explains it in depth.
101　See J. Moran, 'The architecture of madness: Informal and formal spaces of treatment and care in nineteenth-century New Jersey', in L. Topp, J. Moran and J. Andrews (eds), *Psychiatric Spaces: Architecture and the Built Environment, 1600–2000* (Abingdon: Routledge, 2007), pp. 153–72'.
102　NJSA, CC, LCF, Case of Mary A., 1807.
103　NJSA, CC, LCF, Case of Craig L., 1808. Although longer periods were common between the first and second verdict, the length of time varied greatly from one case to the next. For Zadock A., only eight months separated the verdict of *non compos mentis* from his gaining a clean bill of mental health. See NJSA, CC, LCF, Case Zadock A., 1836. For Joseph A., it was seven years. See NJSA, CC, LCF, Case of Joseph A., 1832.
104　NJSA, CC, LCF, Case of Peter D., 1834.
105　Ibid.
106　Ibid.
107　Ibid.
108　NJSA, CC, LCF, Case of Lewis P., 1841.

109 *Ibid.*
110 *Ibid.*
111 *Ibid.*
112 *Ibid.*
113 NJSA, CC, LCF, Case of Francis F., 1857.
114 *Ibid.*
115 *Ibid.*
116 As we shall see in the next chapter, however, the mental life-course of a very few individuals is, spectacularly well documented in the State's lunacy law records.
117 Wright, 'Getting out of the asylum', p. 144.

9

Orders of insanity: lunacy investigation law and the asylum reconsidered

In his account of his tour of the Boston State Hospital for the Insane in 1842, Charles Dickens made the following observation to his readership:

> 'Evince a desire to show some confidence, and repose some trust, even in mad people,' – said the resident physician, as we walked along the galleries, his patients flocking round us unrestrained. Of those who deny or doubt the wisdom of this maxim after witnessing its effects ... I can only say that I hope I may never be summoned as a Juryman on a Commission of Lunacy whereof they are the subjects; for I should certainly find them out of their senses, on such evidence alone.[1]

In this passage Dickens makes curious connections between the benevolent psychiatric care of mad asylum patients at mid-century and the position of a juryman in a lunacy trial. When Dickens visited the Boston asylum, it was in its third year of operation. His descriptions indicate that the optimism of moral therapy and of non-restraint were in full swing in the United States and, certainly in Dickens' view, in England. In his observations Dickens linked the 'enlightened principles of conciliation and kindness' governing the Boston institution to those in place in England's Hanwell asylum.[2] The mid-century master of social criticism also likened his experience at the asylum to being a witness at a trial of *non compos mentis*, not only suggesting his familiarity with lunacy investigation law but also indicating that asylum development and lunacy investigation law operated in tandem in England.

In both Massachusetts, where Dickens took his tour of the Boston State hospital, and New Jersey, to the south, one can trace parallel trajectories of institutional and legal responses to madness. However, it took longer for asylum development to take root in colonial America and the United States, leaving lunacy investigation law to play a more prominent role. Gerald Grob states: 'By the outbreak of the Civil War, the mental hospital had become a familiar and accepted institution to Americans everywhere. With a few exceptions, most states had at least one (and some had more than one) public institution.'[3] But this statement holds true only if one gives a generous definition of both 'familiar' and 'accepted'. There is no doubt that from the post-bellum period onward, asylums played an increasingly prominent role in the lives of Americans as a response to madness; but to claim that the asylum was a ubiquitous institution by the time of the American Civil War is erroneous. Asylums were simply not entrenched enough in the United States to have taken centre stage by 1865. In New Jersey, for example, there were many rural and urban areas in which individuals who were considered to be mentally unwell were not committed to the asylum. This was partly the result of the lack of an asylum option for many areas of the United States, but also reflects the ambivalence towards and criticism of the asylum as late as the period of the Civil War.[4]

In the period from early colonial settlement until the 1830s, those considered 'crazy brained' were responded to in a variety of pre-asylum ways, including the application of lunacy investigation law.[5] From the 1830s to the Civil War period, an interplay of private and public asylum care, along with the use of lunacy investigation law and more traditional informal responses to madness, is in evidence. In this period, asylum officials encouraged families and communities to consider the asylum as the response of choice for family and neighbours whom they considered to be mentally unstable. This selling of the asylum, including the individual efforts of asylum superintendents, and the legendary reform efforts of Dorothea Dix in her home state of New Jersey and elsewhere, further suggest that the American public (as well as politicians) needed to be convinced that the asylum was the most logical response to madness.[6]

In the first section of this chapter, a focus on some of the longer lunacy trials in which the asylum experience was carefully considered by trial witnesses allows for some conclusions to be drawn about the role of the lunatic asylum in the broader web of approaches to madness in the nineteenth century. This analysis reveals a range of reactions to the asylum by family and community – from outright rejection, to ambivalence, to a belief that treatment there had positive effects. On the one hand, it is clear from these cases that the asylum was but one

Table 9.1 Patient population of the New Jersey State Lunatic Asylum, 1848–60

Year	Patients	Year	Patients
1848	86	1856	263
1852	171	1857	279
1853	205	1858	293
1855	233	1860	310

Source: Annual Reports of the New Jersey State Lunatic Asylum.

possible alternative to the nineteenth-century communities of New Jersey. On the other hand, it is also clear that, over the course of the century, especially after the opening of the New Jersey State Lunatic Asylum in 1848, the asylum was an increasingly attractive option. Established in 1848, during its first year of operation the institution had a modest population of eighty-six patients. As Table 9.1 indicates, this number grew steadily during the 1850s, reaching 334 by 1860. This 'warming up' to the asylum was partly the result of asylum officials, including those at the New Jersey asylum, promoting their institutional response as a better bet for the insane and their families.

The second section of this chapter explores some examples in which the traditional application of lunacy law was combined with regulatory responses that were designed primarily for more socio-economically marginalised citizens. This mix of poor law responses with lunacy investigation law highlights the range of civil law responses at the disposal of communities that were trying to manage mad behaviour. The last section of the chapter examines the emergence of a legal mechanism that appears to have been an adaptation of the earlier trial process in lunacy. While this new legal response continued to operate under the authority of civil law, it also facilitated the admission of larger numbers of patients to the asylum each year. This hybrid legal process, while not displacing the fuller application of lunacy investigation law completely, was nevertheless an indication that, in an increasingly populated and socio-economically stratified state, the asylum was impressing upon lunacy investigation law to expedite the institutionalisation of the mad. By the end of the nineteenth century, it is clear that lunacy investigation law was being shaped by the increasing demands of asylum admission.

Evaluating the asylum option

As some cases in the previous two chapters have suggested, during the first half of the nineteenth century those considered to be mad in New Jersey were occasionally committed to the asylum or some other form of institutional care. Before the opening of the New Jersey State Lunatic Asylum in 1848, some were sent to institutions in neighbouring states, including the Friends Asylum and the Blockley Asylum in Pennsylvania, the Hartford Retreat in Connecticut, the private house of William Adams in Pennsylvania, the New York Hospital and the Bloomingdale Asylum in New York.[7] After its opening in 1848, most, but not all, of the asylum stays recorded in the lunacy trials were at the asylum in Trenton, New Jersey.[8]

Although the records are incomplete, it appears certain that, once sent to the asylum, some of those deemed mad at lunacy trials likely remained under institutional management for indefinite periods of time. For example, after a prolonged period of care by his sister at her house, George W. was committed to the Pennsylvania Hospital for the Insane from June 1842 to July 1843. At the asylum, superintendent Thomas Kirkbride considered George W. to be 'laboring under that form of insanity known as dementia or weakness of mind and afforded but little reason for hope that he would ever recover'.[9] Between 1843 and 1850, George W. was once more in the care of his sister, after which time he was committed to the New Jersey State Lunatic Asylum, where superintendent Horace Buttolph arrived at the same diagnosis. Henry C. experienced a remarkably similar multi-institutional confinement, being cared for by his family for several years, then being sent first to the New Jersey State Asylum for two years, followed by a prolonged stay at the Brattleborough Retreat in Vermont.[10] In some cases, the asylum stay was followed by more permanent care back home, as was the case for Joel D., who spent three months in the New Jersey asylum but whose family took him back, 'since which time he has not [become] better but [appeared] to be worse and excited'.[11] Likewise, Jane C., a twenty-six-year-old woman from the township of Union, Essex County, was confined in 1843 to the Bloomingdale Asylum for six months on the advice of

Dr George Chetwood, her family physician. According to Chetwood, 'she was so sent to the asylum and remained there about six months, when she was brought home without being cured'.[12] Two years later, a successful lunacy commission was filed against her, but there is no indication that this legal action was accompanied by an effort to put her back into the care of an asylum.

These glimpses of the role of the asylum in nineteenth-century approaches to madness in New Jersey are more fully developed in a few cases of traverse, or *supercedeas*, in which the detail of trial testimony is especially rich. As explained earlier in the book, since the fourteenth century, in theory, the English civil law of lunacy held out the promise that a state of madness was temporary. The right to supersede the verdict of *non compos mentis* was open to those who thought that they had recovered enough mentally to call for a new trial. Although *supercedeas* attempts were few, they tended to create longer paper trails, at times documenting in great detail the histories of those considered to be insane, as well as the familial and community dynamics in which these individuals lived. Like all sources, trials of *non compos mentis* followed by attempts at *supercedeas* have their limitations. But, as the following examples suggest, the detail that they offer on the minutiae of madness in local context offers great insight into the role of the asylum as understood by family, neighbours, doctors, asylum superintendents and, sometimes, by those being tried for madness.

The case of John B. demonstrates just how complex the interplay between the law of lunacy investigation and the asylum could be, as understood through the lens of community understandings of madness and customary responses to the insane.[13] John B.'s wife initiated lunacy proceedings against her husband on 29 December 1865. In an accompanying petition, John B.'s son-in-law, Peter Larne, noted that B.'s behaviour was violent enough to require the family to chain him inside the house. Larne was asked to 'keep watch' over John B. during his violent turns, at which times John B. also appeared to make wild accusations about the presence of the devil in the room. The trial, held one month later on the premises of innkeeper Robert Thatcher, found that John B. had been *non compos mentis* for nine years. His property was valued at about $150 per year, with an additional $190 worth of personal property.

One and a half years later, on 10 June 1867, John B. applied to 'set aside and vacate' the findings of the lunacy commission that had been launched against him. John B.'s appeal for traverse was a contested five-day trial with witnesses testifying to three separate lines of argument: that John B. had recovered mentally; that he was still mentally unstable; and that he had never been mentally unwell in the first place. Much of the testimony revolved around whether John B.'s mental condition had improved (or not) after he was released from the Trenton Asylum. Upon his release, John B. took the train from Trenton to Copper Hill, where he was met by one of his guardians, Robert Thatcher, along with Thatcher's son. They took John B. home in their carriage. On the same evening of his release from the asylum, John B. spent time at the local supply store, a gathering place where the men of the neighbourhood tended to socialise. John B. bought tobacco at the store and joined in the conversation that evening. Some of the questioning of witnesses revolved around who had said what about John B.'s mental state at the Copper Hill store during a several weeks' period between his release from the asylum and his retrial.

Many witnesses testifying on behalf of John B. asserted that he was, at the time of the trial, mentally capable of conducting himself and his affairs. These witnesses argued that he had always been in control of his mental faculties, as far as conducting his business was concerned. For example, Judiah Kuhl, the Copper Hill storeowner, testified that 'in reasoning with him and talking with him I cannot see but that his mind is just as strong as it ever was. I should say that his reasoning powers are just as strong as they ever were'.[14] William Daily, a local blacksmith who had conducted business with John B. before and after his stay at the Trenton Asylum, spent considerable time with him, including a day-long excursion back to the Trenton Asylum to 'get some clothes he had left there', followed by dinner in downtown Trenton and a visit to the nearby fairgrounds.[15] On these and other occasions, Daily stated, 'he was right, rational' on every occasion that they met.[16]

Other witnesses concurred that John B. had never actually been insane, while at the same time describing his state of mind as strained or unusual at times. Henry Rockefeller, a long-standing neighbour and employee of the Flemington railroad depot, had this to say in answer to questions put to him:

> Q. Have you not at any time discovered anything strange or unusual in his speech or conduct? ... A. No Sir. Q. Have you at any time during all

your acquaintance with him discovered anything strange or unusual or that looked like insanity in his speech or conduct? A. I have seen him when he looked to me like a man that had a good deal of trouble, but I could not attribute it to insanity. Q. You have never considered him insane then? A. I never knew that he was.[17]

Stacy Bray, the superintendent of the wood department of the Belvedere Delaware Railroad Company, who hired John B. to work for him from April to October 1865, stated that John B. was 'as rational now as at any time since I have known him.'[18] However, Bray also stated that he thought that he 'discern[ed] a decided improvement in Mr B. every time I seem him', and that John B. appeared 'irritated and excited at times', when discussing political matters with the other workers at the wood lot.[19] Another neighbour, George Wills, explained that, upon John B.'s release from the asylum, he had discussed with him a conversation in which John B. had become excited 'on the morning he was taken to the asylum.'[20] Not only did John B. remember the conversation but he '[talked] over some of the points that he had held at that time in his conversation. I remember that we agreed upon those points and the conversation was changed.'[21] This, for Wills, proved both that he was mentally excitable before his asylum committal, but also that he was, since his release, more in control of his mental powers. Wills also added, with humour, that John B. had had conversations with him about 'his college home', by which he meant his asylum stay, which held 'enlarged opportunities' for John B., including 'reading, getting hold of the papers, and the like.'[22]

For Hiram Siraphin, a prominent witness who was not convinced that John B.'s legal status should be changed, John B.'s quips about his having 'graduated from college' were one of many signs of a mentally unsound individual. But most of what Siraphin took for mental unsoundness was bizarrely connected to his own father's stay at the same Trenton Asylum, a stay that lasted for roughly the same period as that of John B. It was John B.'s descriptions of his and Siraphin's father's asylum experience that convinced Siraphin that John B. had not yet recovered. In one part of the testimony, Siraphin explained that John B. had asked when Sirpahin's mother was next 'going to the asylum' to visit her husband. 'He said he had left a pair or two of stockings there, and wanted to know if she would get them for him when she went down. He said they were very good ones and they would wear them out if he did not get them away from there. That the keepers would wear out other peoples [sic] clothes whenever they would get a chance. He said that the keepers were a regular set of rascals.'[23] On another occasion, Siraphin explained, he was at the asylum and overheard John B. speaking increasingly loudly in his father's room. When Siraphin went in to investigate, he found John B. 'berating the [asylum] keepers', threatening to 'smash one of them over the head with a chain when they undertook to abuse'[24] his father. Still later, John B. inquired to Siraphin about his father and he 'asked me whether we had any Doctor to examine his bruises.'[25] John B. then explained to Siraphin that, 'they didn't abuse [B.] any. He said they undertook to [but] he told them if they did, he would smash them as flat as pancakes.' According to Siraphin, John B. walked down the road after their conversation, 'shaking his fists.'[26]

Although for Siraphin these accounts of John B.'s behaviour in relation to the asylum were signs of mental instability, the difficulties of interpretation for the historian are rendered still more challenging (and perhaps telling) by the last lines of Siraphin's testimony: 'Re examined in chief: Q. Do you know how your father received the bruises spoken of? Objected to. A. No Sir. Q. How long has your father been insane? Objected to. A. About two years.'[27] This account suggests that John B.'s asylum stay had its ups and downs, but also that he was far from the passive victim of the institution's unequal relations between attendants and patients. His 'graduation from college' may have been considered one measure of his mental recovery, but in his New Jersey community the burden of testimony from community and family members who could testify to his sanity was equally if not more important. It is also significant that several witnesses considered him to have been of sound mental judgement in his farming business before the lunacy trial filed successfully against him, and before his committal to the Trenton Asylum. From the familial and community perspective, the asylum was an option – but only one – that figured, to varying extents, in the local struggles over madness and what to do about it.

The uneven track record of asylum management and care in the eyes of the community is also evident in the case of John L. However, in this case the asylum and its superintendent figured prominently and, in so doing, highlight how awkwardly the legal and mental institutions could be intertwined in the response to madness. By all accounts John L., from Ocean Township, Monmouth County, was a very successful farmer/

merchant with two prosperous 'plantation tracts of land' and stocks, bonds and bank notes amounting to tens of thousands of dollars. The precipitating event of his committal to the Trenton Asylum on 13 November 1860 was his singular act of destroying $11,000 worth of 'vouchers, bonds, railroad bonds, coupons and certificates of stocks' by throwing them into the stove at his house.[28] While he was in the asylum, a petition for a lunacy trial was launched against John L. on 26 December of the same year and the trial was held two and a half weeks later at the house of Samuel Sillick, innkeeper at Eatontown. At the trial, John L.'s spectacular act of financial destruction and his asylum committal, along with testimony asserting that he thought there was a conspiracy to deprive him of is property, were enough to find him *non compos mentis*.

At the Trenton Asylum, superintendent Horace Buttolph described John L. as being 'in an melancholy desponding state of mind', and yet he appeared able to 'talk rationally on business subjects'.[29] This was corroborated by John L.'s guardian, Thomas Cook, who noted that as early as 3 January 1861 John L. appeared 'as sound as ever' in the letters he sent from the asylum to Cook and which itemised the papers that John L. had destroyed in the fire in order that Cook could go to the various banking establishments to have them reissued. At the asylum, John L. explained to Buttolph that 'he was driven to [destroying his financial papers] by an evil spirit'. Dr Buttolph tried anodynes, which did not have the desired effect of inducing sleep in his patient. He also prescribed hyoscyamus (black henbane), which, he noted had a positive outcome. The asylum superintendent gradually weaned John L. off it as his condition improved. Buttolph discharged John L. as 'recovered' on 9 April, with a caution that the earliness of the season might have an adverse effect on a patient who had been institutionally confined for several months.

On 9 June John L. filed a legal challenge to the lunacy commission that had been launched against him. In his petition he noted that since his release from the asylum he had 'had charge and still hath the management and overseeth ... his farm and business relative thereto', but that 'some portion of his property and such as road bonds, bank stocks, insurance stocks &c. are still in the hands and possession' of his guardian.[30] The lunacy trial hinged upon whether or not John L. would continue to be impulsive and irrational with his paper assets. One witness, the brother of John L.'s guardian and a farm hand on John L.'s property, confirmed that 'Mr L. has been in charge of his farm since 9 April last. He takes care of his own horses and cattle himself. He also takes care of his garden himself – except a portion of the digging.'[31] This witness attested both to John L.'s abilities to conduct productive work and also to his competence in managing the work of others on his property. These virtues of rational decision making and productivity were central to testimonials leading to a successful verdict of sanity in many such trials.[32]

Witnesses appeared divided about the effects of asylum treatment on John L.'s state of mind. Dr Thomas Chattle, John L.'s family physician, noted that 'from all the opinions that I can form from all the conversations I have held with him I should say he was as rational as he ever was at any time previous to his sickness' which had resulted in asylum committal.[33] Despite not being convinced that he was ready to take back possession of his paper assets, John L.'s guardian, Thomas Cook, acknowledged in his testimony that 'some of the neighbours who saw him before he was sent to Trenton expressed themselves to be that they thought it was not necessary to send him to the asylum because they did not think anything was the matter with him.'[34] Cook's own concern focused on his charge's management of financial affairs. In a rare glimpse of just how intimate the conflict between guardian and those under guardianship for *non compos mentis* could be, Cook's testimony detailed several fights over access to funds. One that occurred at the neighbourhood supply store is worth quoting at some length:

> [John L.] wanted me to let him have the Bank Books or Bank Book can't say certain which for the purposes of drawing some more money – I don't remember that he said that he had some bills to meet. I had an order presented from him for a lumber bill of his own buying at Ocean Port. I had two orders presented to me from Mr L. for lumber bills ... – one from Ocean Port and one from Branchport – the two bills amounted to about $100.00. I knew that some lumber had been used before this upon this property. I had not paid those orders then and I have not yet paid them. He had had a Bank book before this expressly to get money to pay these bills and some others. I could not say positively when he got the bank book ... When he got the bank book he told me he wanted to buy paint, a Range and that Mrs. L. would want some money to go to New York with and that she wanted an outhouse built and he would want some money for that. I asked him how much money he wanted

and he said about $200.00 or something like that. I told him I hadn't any money in hand to get these things ... and then he asked me for the Bank books and said he could draw it ... When he asked me for it, I told him I couldn't give it or can't give it – I don't think I used the expression 'you can't have it.' I told him he had been buying things which he ought not to. He asked me what and I said lumber and he said very well and wheeled and left [the store] ... I told Mr L. that I would be down and see Mrs. L. – he appeared as if he was not friendly and had not a good feeling ...[35]

It is not hard to imagine that a conversation like this, in the local supply store in front of other customers, caused consternation for both John L. and his guardian. Given the extent to which productive labour and business acumen were measures of success for men in rural New Jersey, it is easy to imagine that being declared *non compos mentis* constituted a major loss of masculine identity. In the case of John L., not only did this entail the loss of control over property that had clearly taken years to amass, but also included belittling contests with his guardian over limited access to his own funds in public spaces in his neighbourhood. In Chapter 5 the parameters of masculinity and *non compos mentis* decisions for English men were explored. The much more detailed accounts of the New Jersey lunacy trials allow, in some cases, for a nuanced consideration of the extent to which lunacy law investigation, guardianship and struggles over the property/gender relationship played themselves out.[36]

A close examination of John L.'s case also gives some indication of how the various responses to his mental state were gauged. In his attempts to prove that John L. had not recovered mentally, William Covert, brother-in-law to John L., noted that John L. 'told me no longer ago than yesterday that he would have got well if they had not taken him to the asylum and that there was no necessity of taking him there.'[37] This statement makes clear how uncertain many were of the efficacy of the asylum. For John L., like some of the other witnesses in this and other trials, the asylum was seen as part of the problem, or at least not particularly useful in the recovery process. For witnesses like Covert, John L.'s criticisms of the asylum were in themselves proof of mental instability!

For his part, Trenton Asylum superintendent Buttolph considered the mental rigours of the trial of lunacy and the trial of *supersedeas* to be largely responsible for a relapse of John L.'s condition that led to his readmission of the Trenton Asylum on 13 December 1861. In Buttolph's view, 'while [John L. was] here before, his property was placed in the hands of a guardian and he has had to resort to legal measures to regain possession of it. A good deal of delay occurred in this proceeding and probably influenced him unfavorably and perhaps caused the present attack.'[38] This episode led to a much longer stay in the asylum. But by March 1865 Buttolph once more considered John L. to have recovered and he was released. There is no legal paper trail indicating whether a lunacy trial to consider his mental capacity was launched against him during this time.

Buttolph's dubiousness about the effects of the trial process on John L.'s mental state went hand in hand with a more general critique of the perils of domestic and community care of the insane. Buttolph and other asylum superintendents could be quite critical and dismissive of families who chose to care for their mentally disturbed at home. This scepticism of family and community management and care formed part of the professionalisation process of early psychiatry. It only made sense for those in charge of the medical affairs of the asylum to promote institutional care as a superior option to that which might be provided in local contexts. As Buttolph put it in 1863,

> in many cases of mental disorder ... caused or perpetuated by unfavorable circumstances and influences connected with home life ... no time should be lost in removing the patient from the sphere of noxious influences that have caused or continued his disorder, and in such cases a well regulated institution for the insane is generally the most favourable for his comfort and restoration.[39]

The extent to which Buttolph and others included the legal trials of lunacy in the list of 'noxious influences' is hard to say, but, at least in the case of John L., we can see a similar kind of scepticism.

The case of Elias B. highlights in detail how the asylum entered into the dynamic of madness and family feuds in New Jersey. Elias B.'s mental state was clearly of concern to family members and neighbours over a long period of time. In 1832, at the age of twenty-two, he experienced a six months' period of mental decline, during which time he was 'so violent as to endanger the members of his family and required to be confined', although the form of confinement was not clear. At the age of forty-nine, his mental troubles had returned, leading his brother, Samuel B., to have Elias confined to the New Jersey Lunatic Asylum on 17 April 1856. Samuel also became guardian of Elias' property and person following the verdict of *non compos mentis* in a lunacy trial shortly thereafter. A contentious ride by wagon to the asylum, where bickering between Elias B. and his two brothers was continuous, started a long debate about the role of the asylum and the causes of Elias' troubled mental state. This debate was fully articulated in Elias B.'s attempt to set aside the verdict of insanity during the traverse proceedings in the month of December 1858.

Witnesses at the trial of traverse testified that Elias B. stayed in the asylum for three months. He left the institution in mid April 1857. This marked the start of a remarkably long eighteen-month set of travels for Elias B. in the states of New Jersey, Washington and New York. First, Elias B. went to Newton, where he stayed at the Cochran Boarding House, situated about ten miles away from his farm property. During his year-long stay in Newton he travelled frequently to within sight of his farm but did not actually visit it. In April 1858 Elias B. left for Washington, DC for three or four months, during which time he stayed at two boarding houses. After a brief return to Newton, he then embarked on a trip to Port Jarvis, New York, where he visited acquaintances and stayed at the 'public house'. Next he stayed in Hamburgh, a small town within three miles of his farm, and finally he resided at the boarding house of 'Mr. Monell', which was less than a mile from his property. At this point he began to visit his farm frequently and to speak with one of his brothers, Jonas B., about regaining legal control of his property. A few weeks before he launched the trial of traverse, Elias B. began to work his farm by himself. The trial was the legal confirmation of the fact that he had regained mental control over person and property.

According to the testimony of his brother, Jonas B., Elias was never a fit candidate for the Trenton Asylum, despite being mentally stressed from time to time. Another witness, physician Franklin Smith, noted that 'during the time I saw him in Newton I never saw anything to induce met to believe that he was really insane but he is a peculiar man'.[40] Witnesses also linked Elias' mental distress, and his committal to the asylum, to the coercive life-long relationship that he had with his brother Samuel. Jonas B. testified that he 'remonstrated with Samuel against taking Elias [back to] the asylum after he had been at the Cocharn House'.[41] One of the proprietors of the Cochran House, John Cougar, described in detail a confrontation between Samuel and Elias about asylum committal:

> Before [Elias] went away [to Washington] he told me he thought he would leave before this year was up because he feared that Samuel would take him back to the Asylum – There had been talk of Samuel's taking him back to the Asylum – Elias told me that Samuel had said he could board him cheaper in the Asylum than here – Samuel had been here for the purposes of taking him to the asylum, but I do not recollect exactly how long before – I do not know why he did not take him at that time – I never saw anything in his conduct that required that he should be restrained of his liberty … I think Samuel made an effort to take him to the asylum – when he came down for that purpose I heard them talking … and heard Elias tell him to keep his hands off – Elias was standing with his back to the wall, Samuel on one side and Jonas on the other and I heard this remark as I was passing – I did not wish to hear or see it and went on.[42]

As Elias was considering his options during his stay at the boarding house of Mr Monell in close proximity to his farm, his brother Samuel 'wanted him to come home and work under him and let him hold the farm and be guardian still and see how he, Elias would mange.'[43] For reasons that his brother Jonas made clearly enough, Elias was not interested in this option. 'Prior to Elias' derangement', testified Jonas, Elias 'mainly depended on Samuel's judgement – Elias would always ask and take Samuel's advice about the purchase of horses and cattle and such things[,] and about other matters [when] he would differ with him [he] allowed Samuel to dissuade him from carrying out his own views.'[44]

The role of the asylum in the response to Elias B.'s mental troubles was significant enough – after all, he spent three months at the Trenton facility. But his medical record suggests some doubt as to his need for being there. This doubt can be seen in comments from his trial testimony. Upon admission to the asylum, he was described as 'eccentric and singular in opinions and manner', but by the end of his stay he was reported to be enjoying 'good health and generally improved in the state of his mind'. Nothing in the medical file suggests major mental illness, except for information that had been gathered from Elias B.'s brother, Samuel, upon admission, which stated that he had been 'deranged for four weeks and is second attack – cause uncertain perhaps ill health – seemed disturbed in his manner and neglected all business.'[45] In this case, asylum committal was entwined within the power struggles between three brothers over control of family farm property. These struggles included mental manipulation and coercion. The lunacy trial became a means for one brother to incarcerate another in an asylum. However, it is clear that, at certain points in this struggle, Elias' confinement in a boarding house was just as economically effective, if not preferable, for his brother. The same legal mechanism was also used by Elias B. to wrestle power back from the guardianship of his brother and to re-establish legal control over himself and his property. In this case, Elias called for the traverse (or *supercedeas*) of the original verdict of *non compos mentis* after he had returned to his property and had proved that he had established partial control of his farming operations.[46]

Overlapping legal responses

If the relationship between asylum committal and the use of lunacy investigation law was varied in mid-nineteenth-century New Jersey, the experiences of madness in local communities in the state were made even more complicated by overlapping legal responses. The poor law, and the law permitting justices of the peace to apprehend 'any lunatic furiously mad or dangerous to be permitted to go at large' and to place him/her 'safely locked up and chained if necessary, in some secure place', were sometimes used in cases that also involved the asylum and the lunacy commission options.[47] The case of David R., whose legal and medical record spans a twenty-eight-year period, captures well the multiple uses of these different responses. David R., a farmer from Medford County, Evesham Township, was investigated by lunacy trial twice and in both cases was considered *non compos mentis*. The first trial, in 1843, resulted in a guardianship arrangement that lasted until David R. successfully traversed his status of *non compos mentis* in 1845. The second trial, in 1861, resulted in guardianship arrangements that remained permanent despite David R.'s efforts to have them set aside in another trial of traverse in 1867.[48]

Throughout this nearly three-decade period, the trial evidence is marked by uncertainty about the mental state of David R. All witnesses agreed that he was consistently 'sharp' in his abilities to bargain and to run the day-to-day activities of his successful farm, but there also was general agreement that his eccentricities of behaviour sometimes placed him on the margins of mental instability. This uncertainty as to David R.'s mental state and how to respond to it coincides with the equally ambiguous response of witnesses to his committal to the Friends Asylum in Pennsylvania in February 1843. Neighbours and relatives considered David R. to be more or less as 'sane' though 'eccentric' after his four-month stay at the asylum as he was before being institutionalised. His asylum stay was also marked by multiple attempts to escape. His last attempt was successful and it appears that neither the asylum authorities nor his family thought it was worth sending him back.

Between the first lunacy trial to evaluate his mental capacity and his committal to the asylum, David R. had encounters with the poor law official and the local justice of the peace (JP). George Haywood, a JP from Mount Holly, testified that David R.'s brothers had convinced the local overseer of the poor, Daniel Zelley, to take David R. to Haywood. The JP testified that David R.'s brothers had tried to convince him that David R.'s 'state of mind was in such a situation that he could not with safety be permitted to go at large, that he had threatened them with injury to their persons and property and that he had by force carried from the house of one of them an iron chest containing papers and vouchers ....'[49] After a three-hour examination of David R., Haywood found that he 'did not manifest any dangerous or violent symptoms.'[50] However, he noted, David R.'s claim that the papers in the chest 'relating to his estate' were his property, and his insistence that 'he was not bound to abide by the inquisition' (the verdict of the lunacy trial) convinced Haywood that David R. was mentally unbalanced enough to be sent to the asylum.[51] Much later, in 1867, several years after David R. had regained control over his person and property, he was observed fishing in local 'mud holes' without his clothing. Despite the fishing area being some distance from the public road, his nakedness offended enough passers-by to cause one witness, who kept a hotel in the area, to complain about it to the local JP. The JP duly wrote up a notice 'forbidding him to expose himself again'. The hotel owner acknowledged that David R. fished naked in this way so as not to 'dirty clothes', and he also testified that, upon being served notice, 'he did not fish naked afterwards'.[52] However, this encounter with local justice was used as evidence that, at the age of seventy, and with David R. now sharing control over the farm property with his son, the most judicious response by 1867 was to let the second determination of *non compos mentis* stand.

In the case of David R., the legal interventions of the JP and overseer of the poor seemed to complement the use of the asylum and lunacy investigation law in a collective effort to manage the behaviour of a farmer who, although capable of managing himself and his property most of the time, was nevertheless considered by some to warrant those regulatory responses to his mental eccentricities that were at the disposal of the community. Archival evidence about those whose social and economic condition was much worse also suggests that lunacy investigation law was used in conjunction with other legal responses in an effort to shore up more desperate situations. For example, in the fall of 1836 two JPs confined Obadiah M. to the Poor House of Monmouth County. Because of his aggressive and violent behaviour, the steward of the poor house, Francis Parker, and the keeper, William Parker, recommended that he not be released, despite internal tensions to their institution caused by Obadiah M.'s threats to the washerwoman and to other poor house inmates. They also claimed that there was nowhere else for Obadiah M. to go because 'his brothers and sisters have abandoned [him] and have refused to keep him on account of his madness'.[53] Under these circumstances, a lunacy trial was filed against Obadiah M., not so much to determine his mental state (which was already clear to local JPs and poor house officials) but, rather, to provide the grounds for a legal investigation into Obadiah M.'s property and to establish a guardianship arrangement in order to secure funds for his management in the poor house. The trial found that Obadiah M. was entitled to several hundred dollars in property that had been sold off from the estate of his late father. Although the records in this case are unclear, the trial would presumably have enabled authorities to secure this money for Obadiah M.'s maintenance in the poor house. In a similar case, in 1805, Henry Vanderveer, an overseer of the poor in Somerset County, noted that Thomas R. 'has been for a long time past and now is chargeable to the said township of Bridgewater as a pauper'.[54] Vanderveer argued that Thomas R. 'is possessed of lands and tenements in … Somerset sufficient to maintain him during life if properly disposed of' by a committee appointed at the end of a successful lunacy trial.[55] The same situation was described in 1833 by John Williams, the farmer of the poor for Union Township, Essex County, in the case of Jacob S., and in 1836 by

John Myers, the overseer of the poor for Hackensack Township, Bergen County, in the case of Mary G.[56]

The extent to which familial and community responses combined with the law in the management of those whose situations had rendered them poor and mentally troubled can be understood from the case of Mary P. A resident of 'New Ark', Essex County, Mary P. was considered by family and neighbours to be an 'idiot' from her infancy, requiring constant care from her mother, Pamela Drake.[57] Mary P.'s father died in 1777 and her mother remarried shortly thereafter. However, the second husband died shortly after the marriage, 'leaving [the] wife in distress and unable to take care of' her daughter.[58] At this point 'one friend after another voluntarily took care of the infant'.[59] Moreover, when 'the rent of the [house] proved deficient for the maintenance of the child', the difference 'was made up by the friends of the father'.[60] However, at the age of twenty-five, on the death of her mother, local authorities petitioned the chancery court for a lunacy trial, over concern that Mary P.'s property was 'going to waste daily' and that without legal intervention 'the unhappy girl must become a town charge'.[61] In the petition for a lunacy trial the 'memorial of the subscribers, inhabitants of New Ark', went so far as to recommend 'Silvanus Baldwin of New Ark, who has from motives of compassion taken the care of her for some time as a proper person to be appointed by your Excellency to have the care of the person and property' of Mary P.[62]

Orders of insanity

By the 1850s, it appears that a combination of poor law, lunacy investigation law and asylum committal had been formalised into a procedure that facilitated the movement of individuals with lesser means and deemed to be insane to the New Jersey State Lunatic Asylum. It is possible that this 'hybrid' legal process evolved to meet the needs of a state whose economic development at mid-century, and changing social relations, led to an increasing willingness to consider the asylum as an option.[63]

This hybrid process, referred to as 'orders of insanity' in some counties, was applied to individuals of varying social and economic backgrounds, but all were struggling economically in one way or another. This can be seen in the extant documentation for Essex County. As Table 9.2 demonstrates, the population of Essex County, including the

Table 9.2 Population of Newark County, New Jersey, 1840–80

Year	Population
1840	44,621
1850	73,950
1860	98,877
1870	143,839
1880	189,929

Source: *Population of States and Counties of the United States, 1790-1990*, comp. and ed. R. L. Forstall, Department of Commerce, U.S. Bureau of the Census Population Division (Washington, DC: U.S. Government Printing Office, 1996), p. 109.

industrialising city of Newark, increased markedly, from 44,621 in 1840 to 143,839 in 1870.

The hybrid process was clearly designed to facilitate asylum committal in the face of the rapid population increase and an increased willingness for economically challenged families to consider the asylum alternative. However, this process still bore the markings of the earlier lunacy investigations. An examination of fifty orders of insanity from Essex County from 1853 to 1855 reveals a relatively consistent pattern. In every case, the process was brought forward through the Court of Common Pleas and included an official petition, either from a poor house official, from an overseer of the poor or, less commonly, from a relative of the individual whose admission to the Trenton Asylum was sought. In every case a signed letter from a licensed doctor testifying to the mental condition of the individual was also necessary. Finally, a judge of the Court of Common Pleas summarised the findings of the written evidence and granted approval for asylum committal.

An important part of this process was to confirm the location of the township in which the person deemed insane had been residing for the past year, so that the township officials would bear the financial responsibility for the asylum committal of the indigent, mentally troubled individual. This helped to ensure that the asylum would obtain the necessary support, but the extent to which it guaranteed, in principle, a certain level of care in the asylum is an open question. Unlike the intimate guardian arrangements of a lunacy trial, once an individual considered mad by order of insanity was committed to the asylum, his/her experience formed part of a much larger process of institutionalised management and care. Although asylum officials constantly complained that many indigent poor patients were not being financially supported by their families and that townships were not paying their share, it is unclear how this may have affected the treatment of specific patients in the asylum.

Much like the trials from the chancery court in the case of lunacy investigation law, the orders of insanity varied in terms of the extent of documentation and the number of testimonials that were included in each case. Not surprisingly, many of the orders of insanity came from Newark, a growing urban centre in mid-century New Jersey. For example, in March 1853 judges of the Court of Common Pleas Stephen Haines and Moses King requested an investigation into the mental state of Margaret H. Margaret's father, Thomas H., noted in his letter that his twenty-three-year-old daughter had become too difficult for him to manage. The problem, as he outlined it, was that her mental derangement, which had lasted 'about five weeks … is such a condition as to prevent this applicant from attending to his daily labour, the said Margaret requiring his almost constant attendance, to prevent her from doing injury to herself or others'.[64] Although Margaret normally supplemented the family income through her trade as a 'tailoress', she was no longer able to do so. In Thomas's view, 'unless he can be relieved from the care and support of the said Margaret, he [would] be unable to support the other members of his family', which consisted of his wife and two other children.[65] A letter from Thomas H.'s employer in Newark, and another letter from a city alderman, confirmed his story. Two physicians testified to the medical certainty of Margaret's insanity. Under the circumstances, the judges of the Court of Common Pleas reported that they 'have not deemed a jury in the above named case necessary'.[66] This was an acknowledgment of the longer, more expensive lunacy investigation process and a confirmation that, in this case, the abbreviated order in lunacy would be sufficient.

Except for some details, the order of insanity for Eva D. resembled a more traditional lunacy trial process. In his petition, Eva's father, Carl D., explained that he had come first to New York from Germany as an immigrant in 1844 and that in 1852 he had moved with his wife and five children to Ralway Township, Essex County, New Jersey. According to Carl D., his nineteen-year-old daughter was so violent towards his other children, and destroyed household furniture to such an extent, that it became 'unsafe to allow her to go without being watched and restrained by force'.[67] She was eventually confined to a separate room in the farmhouse. Petitions from neighbours confirmed that they were 'sent for in the night time to assist in caring for her [as] she was very violent and uncontrollably insane'.[68] According to a local physician, Samuel Abernethy, who attended to Eva D. frequently over a six-week period, her insanity was connected to 'an irregularity and suppression of the menses'.[69] A judge of the Court of Common Pleas verified that Carl D. was not in a financial position to support her daughter 'without putting himself and his family to great straits and inconvenience'.[70]

In the case of Rachel C., it is clear that the asylum was not the place of first resort for her family. Rachel C., from Plainfield Township, Essex, had already been a patient at the Trenton Asylum for six months when the order of insanity was launched against her in May 1853. Before her committal she stayed at the home of her brother for six to eight months, but a combination of family poverty and her brother's inability to 'curb her tendency to wander'[71] resulted in her asylum committal. An uncle from Rochester, New York paid for the first six months of her asylum stay but refused to maintain his financial support thereafter. In this case, a great deal of the investigation was spent in figuring out if there was property in the family that could be used to partially offset the cost of asylum care. Although the documentation is not clear, it appeared that there was a family farm upon which judges of the Court of Common Pleas were attempting to draw in support of Rachel C.'s maintenance.

The most common orders of insanity were ones initiated by officials of the city poor house, or other overseers of the poor. Poor house officials requested that individuals like Benjamin B., a hatter who, at the age of forty-three had already been committed to the Newark poor house for several months, be moved on to the asylum. In such petitions it was rare for there to be evidence drawn from family or neighbours, as the chances were very high that the insane individual was already 'a pauper chargeable' to the township or city in which he/she resided. The point of the order of insanity in the case of Benjamin B., as with others, was to establish that 'he cannot be provided for by the overseer of the poor [or] at the poorhouse ... with comfort and without danger to himself and others'.[72] Often, doctors whose work included attendance at the poor house wrote brief testimonials certifying the insanity of those who were en route to the Trenton Asylum.

Conclusion

Although the orders of insanity were shaped to fit the circumstances of a growing number of poor individuals who were considered to be suitable candidates for the Trenton Asylum, this legal process did not become the only mechanism by which the difficult response to madness was met. As we have seen, throughout the nineteenth century in New Jersey, lunacy investigation law continued to play an important role for many property-holding families in the state. This chapter has assessed the role that the civil law played in relation to the asylum option. It is clear that some individuals who were subjected to trial under the auspices of lunacy investigation law were also committed to the asylum in the nineteenth century. This was especially the case when increasing numbers of New Jersey residents had access to this option with the opening of the New Jersey State Lunatic Asylum in 1848. However, as this and previous chapters have demonstrated, the early to mid-nineteenth-century period was one in which a considerable range of legal and non-legal responses to madness was also in play.

The depth of detail provided by lunacy trials for New Jersey allows for a close study of how these various responses were used and considered. Moreover, the trials reveal the circumstances 'on the ground' that led to the decision to try either the mechanism of civil law or that of institutionalisation – resorts that were considered in addition to an already complicated host of domestic responses. In a given situation, the response to madness in nineteenth-century New Jersey could include: the employment of attendants or nurses, the oversight and care of family members and neighbours, various forms of domestic confinement, the care of an attending local physician, the use of lunacy trials and trials of traverse, the interventions of local justices of the peace, the local poor house, private houses and committal to the asylum. The options that were chosen to respond to madness depended on the socio-economic circumstances of the family, the nature of the mental trouble of the individual considered to be mad, the application of lunacy investigation law, the course of the asylum stay, the power relations between family members, community perceptions and the extent to which the mad individual could impose some will in the process.

At least until mid-century, given the complicated world of responses to madness that the testimony of lunacy trials reveals, the asylum was not considered to be a stand-alone option in New Jersey but, rather, one of many potentially compelling responses. Moreover, as trial witnesses explained in their testimonials, the asylum was considered in a variety of ways – with optimism as a potential answer to the problem of mental trouble, with scepticism as to its necessity and with ambivalence as to its efficacy. For their part, asylum doctors such as New Jersey asylum superintendent Buttolph were inclined to be critical of most if not all other responses to madness as they attempted to convince state officials, local authorities and families that institutionalised moral therapy was the superior option to all others, including the use of lunacy investigation law. In these respects, the asylum did not really complement legal and non-legal responses to madness but butted up against them. Nevertheless, from the mid-nineteenth century onwards the asylum was incorporated by family members, and by local overseers of the poor and JPs, as an increasingly viable option. This likely explains the evolution of responses like the orders of insanity that more effectively combined the earlier traditions of lunacy investigation law with the newer option of asylum committal.

Notes

1 C. Dickens, *American Notes for General Circulation* (New York: Random House, 1996), p. 60.
2 *Ibid.*
3 G. Grob, *Mental Institutions in America: Social Policy to 1875* (New York: Free Press, 1973), pp. 130–1. See also Rothman, *Discovery of the Asylum*, p. 130.
4 A. Cellard and M-C. Thifault, 'The uses of asylums: Resistance, asylum propaganda, and institutionalization strategies in turn-of-the-century Quebec', in J. Moran and D. Wright and (eds), *Mental Health and Canadian Society: Historical Perspectives* (Montreal: McGill Queen's University Press, 2006), pp. 97–116.
5 L. Eldridge, '"Crazy brained": Mental illness in colonial America', *Bulletin of The History of Medicine*, 70:3 (1996), 361–86.

6 D. Gollaher, 'Dorothea Dix and the English origins of the American asylum movement', *Canadian Review of American Studies*, 23:3 (1993), 149–76; D. Gollaher, *Voice for the Mad: The Life of Dorothea Dix* (New York: Free Press, 1995); T. Brown, *Dorothea Dix: New England Reformer* (Cambridge, MA: Harvard University Press, 1998).
7 See, for example, NJSA, CC, LCF, Case of Aaron R., 1837; Case of Samuel S., 1826; Case of Thomas B., 1822; Case of Franklin K., 1837; Case of George M., 1855; Case of Zemas W., 1841; Case of Andrew L., 1835; Case of Aaron O., 1810; Case of Albert B., 1848; Case of William A., 1846; Case of John J., 1821.
8 See, for example, NJSA, CC, LCF, Case of Margaret C., 1853; Case of Lydia V., 1855; Case of George A., 1856.
9 NJSA, CC, LCF, Case of George W., 1842.
10 NJSA, CC, LCF, Case of Henry C., 1853.
11 NJSA, CC, LCF, Case of Joel D., 1852.
12 NJSA, CC, LCF, Jane C., 1846.
13 NJSA, CC, LCF, Case of John B., 1867.
14 *Ibid.*
15 *Ibid.*
16 *Ibid.*
17 *Ibid.*
18 *Ibid.*
19 *Ibid.*
20 *Ibid.*
21 *Ibid.*
22 *Ibid.*
23 *Ibid.*
24 *Ibid.*
25 *Ibid.*
26 *Ibid.*
27 *Ibid.*
28 NJSA, CC, LCF, Case of John L., 1860.
29 *Ibid.*
30 *Ibid.*
31 *Ibid.*
32 See, for example, J. Moran, 'Travails of madness: New Jersey, 1800–70', in W. Ernst (ed.), *Work, Psychiatry and Society, c. 1750–2015* (Manchester: Manchester University Press, 2016), pp. 77–99.

33 Ibid.
34 Ibid.
35 Ibid.
36 See also the case of Isaac C. in Chapter 7.
37 Ibid.
38 Ibid.
39 NJSA, John Buttolph, 'Annual Report of the New Jersey State Lunatic Asylum', 1863.
40 NJSA, CC, LCF, Case of Elias B., 1859.
41 Ibid.
42 Ibid.
43 Ibid.
44 Ibid.
45 NJSA, New Jersey State Lunatic Asylum, Case Book A, Elias B., patient file 946.
46 For other cases that include complex combinations of asylum committal and legal investigation law, see NJSA, CC, LCF, Case of Lloyd V., 1846; Case of Lukas H., 1831.
47 See the discussion in Chapter 5.
48 NJSA, CC, LCF, Case of David R., 1843 and 1861.
49 Ibid.
50 Ibid.
51 Ibid.
52 Ibid.
53 NJSA, CC, LCF, Case of Obadiah M., 1837.
54 NJSA, CC, LCF, Case of Thomas R., 1805.
55 Ibid.
56 NJSA, CC, LCF, Case of Jacob Stookey, 1833; and Case of Mary G., 1836.
57 New Ark would eventually become Newark.
58 NJSA, CC, LCF, Case of Mary Plum, 1804.
59 Ibid.
60 Ibid.
61 Ibid.
62 Ibid.
63 The combination of socio-economic changes at mid-century that led some families to consider the newly established New Jersey State Lunatic Asylum as a viable option awaits further historical research along the lines of John

Walton's exemplary work on Lancaster, England. See Walton, 'Lunacy in the Industrial Revolution'.
64 NJSA, Essex County, Court of Common Pleas (hereafter EC, CCP), Certificates of Lunacy/Non-Criminal Commitments, Case of Margaret H., 1853.
65 Ibid.
66 Ibid.
67 NJSA, EC, CCP, Certificates of Lunacy/Non-Criminal Commitments, Case of Eva D., 1853.
68 Ibid.
69 Ibid.
70 Ibid.
71 NJSA, EC, CCP, Certificates of Lunacy/Non-Criminal Commitments, Case of Rachel C., 1853.
72 NJSA, EC, CCP, Certificates of Lunacy/Non-Criminal Commitments, Case of Benjamin B., 1853. For an excellent analysis of the wide array of responses to madness, and their interdependence, in seventeenth- and eighteenth-century north-east England, see P. Rushton, 'Lunatics and idiots: Mental disability, the community, and the poor law in north-east England, 1600–1800', Medical History, 32:1 (1988), 34–50.

Conclusion

In 2001 Peter Bartlett observed that the 'study of the determination of civil competency has been marginal in the history of modern law and madness to the point of being almost ignored'. This despite the fact that 'wherever there is law, there is madness [and] ... similarly, wherever there is madness, the law is usually close by'.[1] This book adds to the expanding but still modest body of historical work that considers the role of civil law in shaping the understanding of madness and, in turn, the responses to it. The approach of this book has grown, in part, out of a desire to exploit the potential of an excellent collection of civil trials in lunacy in the state of New Jersey. As the colonial connections between North American and English civil law in the response to madness came increasingly into focus, what was originally conceived of as a regional case study grew into one that was transatlantic. This transatlantic turn evolved out of an interest in tracing the origins of New Jersey's lunacy investigation law. Historiographically, the transatlantic casting of this book has also been guided by the flourishing of social history that is oriented toward transnational and imperial perspectives. On the subject of madness, most such work has been focused on the asylum's imposition and integration, along imperial pathways, into colonial settings, including British India, South Africa, Nigeria and the British Caribbean. Contrastingly, this book has sought to demonstrate how interpretations of the history of madness might be altered with due attention to the importance of civil law and to a transatlantic perspective that focuses on the development of English lunacy investigation law both in England and in the white settler colony of New Jersey.

Several opportunities arise from such a study. First, it helps us to 'get out' of the asylum in our investigation of the history of madness – not

Conclusion

because the asylum was unimportant but, rather, because the asylum's long shadow becomes shorter and more geographically restricted when one is able to uncover and analyse pre-asylum understandings of and responses to madness that continued to thrive long after the asylum's introduction. In 1987 Roy Porter identified what he called 'the "institutionalization" viewpoint'.[2] He noted that 'because of the intensity of today's debates about the future of mental hospitals within psychiatry, the history of psychiatry as it has recently been written has been monopolised by assessments of the history of the asylums'.[3] At the beginning of the twenty-first century, this situation has not changed. This is partly because, as the fate of the mental hospital has become increasingly obvious since Porter's publication, a strong emphasis in historical writing has been placed on the process of deinstitutionalisation. This is fascinating and necessary work and, since the second half of the twentieth century, has resulted in considerable historical investigation into the end of the asylum era.[4] However, perhaps ironically, with this emphasis on deinstitutionalisation, the asylum remains the pivot around which most historical investigations turn. This book has argued that the 'institutionalization viewpoint' may not always give us the clearest view into the history of madness. A close look at the development of civil law in relation to madness indicates that over a five-century period lunacy investigation law grew into an important response to madness that needs to be considered in relationship to other histories of madness, including histories of the rise and demise of the asylum.

Lunacy investigation law was a structured response to madness that tied lunacy to English citizens' mental competencies to govern their property and person. This law developed into a complex mechanism through the participation of legal expertise, a trial process, the right of traverse and the legal restraints and protections (guardianship) placed upon those found to be *non compos mentis*. The role of legal precedent in shaping this law was important. So too were the limitations to the law's development and deployment that resulted from the participation in this legal process of family members whose interests were not always consistent with those who regulated the law. In England, and in the American region of New Jersey, lunacy investigation law reflected powerful legal perceptions of madness and resulted in important responses to madness that were legally bound. However, this legal tradition played out differently in each setting, according to broader political, social and economic realities. In England, the influence of lunacy investigation law was, by and large, restricted to those with considerable property at stake. This did not completely exclude those of lesser means from the influence of this legal process, as legal authorities sought to extend the protection and regulation that this law provided to those with more modest amounts of property. While lunacy investigation law was a powerful force for centuries in England, by the beginning of the nineteenth century the increasingly complex asylum response, along with the process of lunacy inspection, shaped and, in some respects, curbed the powers of this legal process. In New Jersey, this transplanted body of law was subject to colonial and post-revolutionary influences that greatly affected the ways in which it operated. In the North American context, the civil law provided a structured response to madness for a much broader socio-economic spectrum of colonists and, later, American citizens. In so doing, this successful legal transplant delayed the need for asylum provision in this part of the United States.

The paucity of available source material on this subject in England, and the embarrassment of archival riches in New Jersey, result in an asymmetry of opportunity for historical investigation. Nevertheless, recognising lunacy investigation law as a major influence on madness in England, despite the fact that trial material has not weathered well the test of time, encourages the historian to look harder for relevant sources – in the case of this book, at case reports of lunacy trials. The extant English trial evidence indicates that complex and often conflictual interactions occurred among family members and legal experts in the response to madness. The ways in which the relatives of the mad attempted to use lunacy investigation law to resolve difficulties arising in their domestic and economic affairs were not always consistent either with the spirit of the law or with legal experts' views on the proper use of the law. What we can glean from English lunacy trials demonstrates how lay ideas about gender, class, power, property and madness intersected with, and were partially conditioned by, the standards of lunacy investigation law upheld and enforced by legal authority.

Lunacy investigation law was even more influential in New Jersey. But, from the outset, the use of lunacy investigation law in England's colonial contexts was at least partially rationalised through a combination of abstract concepts of governance, mental incompetence and colonisation. Law's empire, in this case, included an understanding of lunacy investigation law that would both serve the needs of New Jersey's English colonists and partially justify the dispossession of lands occupied by indigenous peoples. As the colony developed and evolved through the post-Revolutionary era, it is clear that this law was fundamental to how madness was managed, treated and understood. The extensive and detailed surviving New Jersey trial testimonies also reveal the traditions and customs of familial and community management and care of the mad. Finally, the richness of detail from these documents allows for an understanding of how these traditions and customs were tightly woven into the structure of lunacy investigation law. This fabric of civil law and custom, established over several generations in New Jersey, was unlikely to be torn apart quickly by reform efforts or by the introduction of the asylum. Instead, the asylum, and its novel set of ideas about madness and what to do about it, was brought into the fabric of civil law and custom at mid-century. More dramatic changes in the balance of custom, law and institutionalisation were delayed until the latter part of the nineteenth century.

It is clear that histories of the role of civil law in lunacy bear much relevance to contemporary concerns. The emergence of the United Nations' Convention on the Rights of Persons with Disabilities has led to a remarkable focus on mental capacity and human rights at the national and international levels over the fifteen years since 2004. A resolution of the Committee on the Rights of Persons with Disabilities (CRPD), adopted by the UN General Assembly in 2006, included a strong set of principles on the rights of persons with disabilities, including mental disabilities.[5] In 2014, the eleventh session of the CRPD stated that '"unsoundness of mind" and other discriminatory labels are not legitimate reasons for the denial of legal capacity (both legal standing and legal agency) ... [P]erceived or actual deficits in mental capacity must not be used as justification for denying legal capacity.'[6] Moreover, according to the Committee, 'mental capacity is not, as is commonly presented, an objective, scientific and naturally occurring phenomenon [but rather it] ... is contingent on social and political contexts, as are the disciplines, professions and practices which play a dominant role in assessing mental capacity'.[7] Although the countries that form the focus of this study – England (United Kingdom) and the United States – were both signatories to the Convention when it came into effect in 2008, the United Kingdom signed with some reservations, and the United States has not, as of the publication of this book, indicated its formal confirmation, accession or ratification of the Convention. As scholars like Sheila Wildeman have demonstrated, the 'social model' of mental disability adopted by the CRPD has created both opportunities and challenges in the implementation of Convention principles that could be considered as consistent with existing laws, policies and practices in the United Kingdom, the United States and elsewhere.[8] An appreciation of historical context contributes significantly to these contemporary discussions and debates by explaining how the long-standing and complex legal traditions relating to mental capacity were created in the first place, how they were consolidated over time and space, and how they continue to shape and challenge present-day reconceptualisations of the relationship between madness and mental capacity.

Notes

1. Bartlett, 'Legal madness', pp. 117, 107.
2. Porter, *Mind Forg'd Manacles*, p. 227.
3. *Ibid.*
4. A. Klein, H. Guillemain and M-C. Thifault (eds), *La fin de l'asile? Historie de la déshospitalisation psychiatrique dans l'espace francophone au XX siècle* (Rennes: Presses Universitaires de Rennes, 2018); D. Kritsotaki, V. Long and M. Smith (eds), *Deinstitutionalization and After: Post-War Psychiatry in the Western World* (London: Palgrave Macmillan, 2016); A. Parsons, *From Asylum to Prison: Deinstitutionalization and the Rise of Mass Incarceration after 1945* (Chapel Hill: University of North Carolina Press, 2018).
5. Committee on the Rights of Persons with Disabilities, https://treaties.un.org/doc/source/docs/A_RES_61_106-E.pdf (accessed 22 September 2018).
6. See CRPD, Eleventh session, 31 March–11April 2014, General comment No. 1 paragraph 13, https://documents-dds-ny.un.org/doc/UNDOC/GEN/G14/031/20/PDF/G1403120.pdf?OpenElement.
7. *Ibid.*, paragraph 14.
8. S. Wildeman, 'Protecting rights and building capacities: challenges to global mental health policy in light of the convention on the rights of persons with disabilities', *Journal of Law, Medicine and Ethics*, 41:1 (2013), 48–73; S. Wilson, 'Mental capacity legislation in the UK: Systematic review of the experiences of adults lacking capacity and their carers', *British Journal of Psychiatry Bulletin*, 41:5 (2017), 260–6; J. Craigie, 'A fine balance: Reconsidering patient autonomy in light of the UN convention on the rights of persons with disabilities', *Bioethics*, 29:6 (2015), 398–405.

Bibliography

Primary sources

Archival sources

Norfolk Record Office
  WKC 7/17, Folder of notes about the Ashe family
New Jersey State Archives
  1776 State Constitution, http://www.nj.gov/state/archives/docconst76.html
  Chancery Court, Lunacy Case Files, 1796–1912
  Essex County, Court of Common Pleas, Certificates of Lunacy, 1853–1903
  John Buttolph, 'Annual Report of the New Jersey State Lunatic Asylum', 1863
  Trenton Psychiatric Hospital Annual Reports, 1848–1973
  Trenton Psychiatric Hospital Case Books, 1848–1910

Printed primary sources

Brydall, J., *Jura coronae. His Majesties royal rights and prerogatives asserted, against papal usurpations, and other anti-monarchical attempts and practices. Collected out of the body of the municipal laws of England* (London: G. Dawes, 1680).
Brydall, J., *Non compos mentis: Or, the Law Relating to Natural Fools, Mad-Folks and Lunatick Persons, Inquisited, and Explained, for Common Benefit* (London: Richard and Edward Atkins, 1700).
Brydall, J., *Speculum juris anglicani, or, A view of the laws of England as they are divided into statutes, common-law and customs: incidently, of the customs appertaining to the famous city of London, never before printed; together with resolutions on several of them, given by the reverend judges at Westminster* (London: John Streater, Eliz. Flesher and H. Twyford, assignes of Rich. Atkyns and Edward Atkyns, for Thomas Dring, 1673).
Cheyne, G., *The English Malady, or, a Treatise of Nervous Diseases of All Kinds* (London: 1733), reprinted with an Introduction by R. Porter (London: Routledge, 1991).

Edmonds, J., *The Apology, or Vindication of Sir Cleave More, Bart. Upon the Suing forth a Commission of Lunacy against Joseph Edmonds, Esquire* ... (London: George Croom, 1711).

Elmer, J., *An Outline of the Practice in Lunacy under Commissions in the Nature of Writs de Lunatico Inquirendo* (London: V. & R. Stevens and G. S. Norton Publishers, 1844).

English Reports (London: Stevens & Sons, 1900–32, 178 vols) (accessed via justis.com).

Fry, D. P., *Lunacy Law: The Statutes Relating to Private Lunatics: Pauper Lunatics: Criminal Lunatics: Commissions of Lunacy: Public and Private Asylums: And the Commissioners in Lunacy* (London: Knight and Co., 1890).

Grotius, H., *On the Law of War and Peace*, ed. Stephen Neff (New York: Cambridge University Press, 2012).

Honeyman, A. (ed.), *Documents Relating to the Colonial, Revolutionary and Post Revolutionary History of the State of New Jersey, Volume IV 1761–1770* (Somerville: Unionist-Gazette Association Printers, 1928).

Journal of the House of Lords, vol. 17 (1701–5) (accessed via British History Online, www.british-history.ac.uk).

Murphy, J. L., *Revision of the Statutes of New Jersey: Published Under the Authority of the Legislature by Virtue of an Act Approved April 4, 1871* (Trenton: 1877).

Nelson, W. (ed.), *Documents Relating to the Colonial History of the State of New Jersey* (Patterson: The Press Printing and Publishing Company, Vol. 21, 1899).

Pitt-Lewis, G., R. Smith and J. A. Hawke, *The Insane and the Law: A Plain Guide for Medical Men, Solicitors and Others* (London: Sweet and Maxwell, 1895).

Pope, H. M. R., *A Treatise on the Law and Practice of Lunacy* (London: Sweet and Maxwell, 1890).

Ricord, F. and W. Nelson (eds), *Archives of the State of New Jersey, First Series, vol. X, Documents Relating to the Colonial History of the State of New Jersey, Administration of Governor William Franklin, 1767–1776* (Newark: Daily Advertiser Printing House, 1886).

Urban, S., *The Gentlemen's Magazine and Historical Chronicle for the Year 1797* (London: John Nichols, 1797).

Secondary sources

Adair, R., J. Melling and B. Forsythe, 'Migration, family structure and pauper lunacy in Victorian England: Admissions to the Devon county pauper lunatic asylum', *Continuity and Change*, 12:3 (1997), 373–401.

Anderson, M., *The Battle for the Fourteenth Colony: America's War of Liberation in Canada, 1774–1776* (Hanover: University Press of New England, 2013).

Andrews, J., 'Begging the question of idiocy: The definition and socio-cultural meaning of idiocy in early modern Britain', *History of Psychiatry*, 9:33 (1998), 65–95.

Bibliography

Andrews, J., 'Begging the question of idiocy: The definition and socio-cultural meaning of idiocy in early modern Britain', *History of Psychiatry*, 9:34 (1998), 179–200.

Andrews, J. and A. Scull, *Customers and Patrons of the Mad-Trade: The Management of Lunacy in Eighteenth-Century London: With the Complete Text of John Monro's 1766 Case Book* (Berkeley: University of California Press, 2003).

Andrews, J. and A. Scull, *Undertaker of the Mind: John Monro and Mad-Doctoring in Eighteenth-Century England* (Berkeley: University of California Press, 2001).

Bartlett, P., 'Legal Madness in the Nineteenth Century', *Social History of Medicine*, 14:1 (2001), 107–131.

Bartlett, P., *The Poor Law of Lunacy: The Administration of Pauper Lunatics in Mid-Nineteenth-Century England* (London: Leicester University Press, 1999).

Bartlett P. and D. Wright (eds), *Outside the Walls of the Asylum: The History of Care in the Community, 1750–2000* (London: Athlone Press, 1999).

Bjornlie, M. S., *Politics and Tradition Between Rome, Ravenna and Constantinople: A Study of Cassiodorus and the Variae, 527–554* (Cambridge: Cambridge University Press, 2012).

Borschberg, P., *Hugo Grotius, the Portuguese and Free Trade in the East Indies* (Singapore: National University of Singapore Press, 2010).

Brown, T., *Dorothea Dix: New England Reformer* (Cambridge, MA: Harvard University Press, 1998).

Bushman, R. L., 'Farmers in court: Orange County, North Carolina, 1750–1776', in C. Tomlins and B. Mann (eds), *The Many Legalities of Early America* (Chapel Hill: University of North Carolina Press, 2001), pp. 388–413.

Cellard, A., *Histoire de la folie au québec de 1600 à 1850* (Montreal: Boréal, 1991).

Cellard, A. and M-C. Thifault, 'The uses of asylums: Resistance, asylum propaganda, and institutionalization strategies in turn-of-the-century Quebec', in J. Moran and D. Wright (eds), *Mental Health and Canadian Society: Historical Perspectives* (Montreal: McGill Queen's University Press, 2006), pp. 97–117.

Coleborne, C., *Insanity, Identity and Empire: Immigrants and Institutional Confinement in Australia and New Zealand, 1873–1910* (Manchester: Manchester University Press, 2015).

Coleborne, C. *Madness in the Family: Insanity and Institutions in the Australasian Colonial World, 1860–1914* (Hampshire: Palgrave Macmillan, 2010).

Craigie, J., 'A fine balance: Reconsidering patient autonomy in light of the UN convention on the rights of persons with disabilities', *Bioethics*, 29:6 (2015), 398–405.

D'Antonio, P., 'The need for care: Families, patients, and staff at a nineteenth-century insane asylum', *Transactions and Studies of the College of Physicians of Philadelphia*, 12:3 (1990), 347–366.

Dickason, O. P., 'The sixteenth-century French version of empire: The other side of self-determination', in G. Warkentin and C. Podruchny (eds), *Decentering*

the Renaissance: Canada and Europe in Multidisciplinary Perspective, 1500–1700 (Toronto: University of Toronto Press, 2001), pp. 87–109.
Dickens, C., *American Notes for General Circulation* (New York: Random House, 1996).
Digby, A., *Madness, Morality and Medicine: A Study of the York Retreat, 1792–1914* (Cambridge: Cambridge University Press, 1985).
Doerner, K., *Madmen and the Bourgeoisie: A Social History of Insanity and Psychiatry* (Oxford: Basil Blackwell, 1986).
Dwyer, E., *Homes for the Mad: Life Inside Two Nineteenth-Century Asylums* (New Brunswick: Rutgers University Press, 1987).
el-Khayat, G., *Une psychiatrie modern pour le Maghrib* (Paris: Harmattan, 1994)
Eldridge, L., ' "Crazy brained": Mental illness in colonial America', *Bulletin of the History of Medicine*, 70:3 (1996), 361–386.
Erickson, A. L., *Women and Property in Early Modern England* (London: Routledge, 1993).
Ernst, W., *Mad Tales from the Raj: The European Insane in British India, 1800–1858* (New York: Anthem Press, 1991).
Ernst W. and T. Mueller (eds), *Transnational Psychiatries: Social and Cultural Histories of Psychiatry in Comparative Perspective c. 1800–2000* (Newcastle: Cambridge Scholars, 2010).
Fee, Elizabeth et al., 'Introduction', in Y. Kawakita, S. Sakia and Y. Otsuka (eds), *History of Epidemiology: Proceedings of the 13th International Symposium on the Comparative History of Medicine – East and West* (Tokyo: Ishiyaku EuroAmerica, Inc., 1993).
Finnane, M., 'Asylums, families and the state', *History Workshop Journal*, 20:1 (1985), 134–148.
Finnane, M., *Insanity and the Insane in Post-Famine Ireland* (London: Croom Helm, 1981).
Fitzpatrick, P., 'Terminal legality: Imperialism and the (de)composition of law', in D. Kirby and C. Coleborne (eds), *Law, History, Colonialism: The Reach of Empire* (Manchester: Manchester University Press, 2001), pp. 9–25.
Forstall, R. L. (ed.), *Population of States and Counties of the United States, 1790–1990* (Washington, DC: U.S. Government Printing Office, 1996).
Fox, R., *So Far Disordered in Mind: Insanity in California, 1870–1930* (Berkeley: University of California Press, 1978).
Freemon, F., 'The origin of the medical expert witness: The insanity of Edward Oxford', *Journal of Legal Medicine*, 22:3 (2001), 349–373.
Fur, G., *A Nation of Women: Gender and Colonial Encounters Among the Delaware Indians* (Pennsylvania: University of Pennsylvania Press, 2009).
Gollaher, D., 'Dorothea Dix and the English origins of the American asylum movement', *Canadian Review Of American Studies*, 23:3 (1993), 149–176.

Bibliography

Gollaher, D., *Voice for the Mad: The Life of Dorothea Dix* (New York: Free Press, 1995).
Grob, G., *Mental Institutions in America: Social Policy to 1875* (New York: Free Press, 1973).
Hanly, C., 'The decline of civil jury trial in nineteenth-century England', *Journal of Legal History*, 26:3 (2005), 253–278.
Hatch, R., *Thrust for Canada: The American Attempt on Quebec in 1775–1776* (Boston: Houghton Mifflin, 1979).
Horden, P. and R. Smith (eds), *The Locus of Care: Families, Communities, Institutions and the Provision of Welfare Since Antiquity* (London: Routledge, 1998).
Houston, R. A., *Madness and Society in Eighteenth-Century Scotland* (Oxford: Clarendon Press, 2000).
Hunt, R. A. and I. McAlpine (eds), *Three Hundred Years of Psychiatry, 1535–1860: A History Presented in Selected English Texts* (London: Oxford University Press, 1963).
Jiminez, M., A. *Changing Faces of Madness: Early American Attitudes and Treatment of the Insane* (Hanover: University Press of New England, 1987).
Jones, K., *Lunacy, Law, and Conscience, 1744–1845: The Social History of the Care of the Insane* (London: Routledge and Kegan Paul, 1955).
Keller, R., 'Madness and colonization: Psychiatry in the British and French empires, 1800–1962', *Journal of Social History*, 35:2 (2001), 295–326.
Kelm, M-E. 'Women, families and the provincial hospital for the insane, British Columbia, 1905–1915', *Journal of Family History*, 19:2 (1994), 177–193.
Kiralfy, A. K. R., *Potter's Historical Introduction to English Law and Its Institutions* (London: Sweet and Maxwell Limited, 4th edn, 1958).
Kirby, D. and C. Colborne (eds), *Law, History, Colonialism: The Reach of Empire* (Manchester: Manchester University Press, 2001).
Kingsbury, B. and B. Straumann (eds), *Roman Foundations of the Law of Nations: Alberico Gentili and the Justice of Empire* (New York: Oxford University Press, 2010).
Klein, A., H. Guillemain and M-C. Thifault (eds), *La fin de l'asile? Historie de la déshospitalisation psychiatrique dans l'espace francophone au XX siècle* (Rennes: Presses Universitaires de Rennes, 2018).
Klinck, D. R., 'Lord Nottingham and the conscience of equity', *Journal of the History of Ideas*, 67:1 (2006).
Kritsotaki, D., V. Long and M. Smith (eds), *Deinstitutionalization and After: Post-War Psychiatry in the Western World* (London: Palgrave Macmillan, 2016).
Laqueur, T., *Solitary Sex: A Cultural History of Masturbation* (New York: Zone Books, 2004).

Levine-Clark, M., 'Dysfunctional domesticity: Female insanity and family relationships among the West Riding poor in the mid-nineteenth century', *Journal of Family History*, 25:3 (2000), 341–361.

McCandless, P., *Moonlight, Magnolias and Madness: Insanity in North Carolina form the Colonial Period to the Progressive Era* (Chapel Hill: University of North Carolina Press, 1996).

McCulloch, J., *Colonial Psychiatry and 'the African Mind'* (New York: Cambridge University Press, 1995).

MacDonald, M. *Mystical Bedlam: Madness, Anxiety, and Healing in Seventeenth-Century England* (Cambridge: Cambridge University Press, 1981).

MacDonald, M. and T. Murphy, *Sleepless Souls: Suicide in Early Modern England* (Oxford: Clarendon Press; 1990).

McGlynn, M., 'Idiots, lunatics and the royal prerogative in early Tudor England', *Journal of Legal History*, 26:1 (2005), 1–24.

Mills, J. H., *Madness, Cannabis, and Colonialism: The 'Native Only' Lunatic Asylums of British India, 1857–1900* (New York: St Martin's Press, 2000).

Moran, J., 'Asylum in the community: Managing the insane in antebellum America', *History of Psychiatry*, 9:34 (1998), 217–240.

Moran, J., *Committed to the State Asylum: Insanity and Society in Nineteenth-Century Quebec and Ontario* (Montreal: McGill Queen's University Press, 2000).

Moran, J., 'The architecture of madness: Informal and formal spaces of treatment and care in nineteenth-century New Jersey', in L. Topp, J. Moran and J. Andrews (eds), *Psychiatric Spaces: Architecture and the Built Environment, 1600–2000* (Abingdon: Routledge, 2007), pp. 153–172.

Moran, J. , 'The signal and the noise: The historical epidemiology of insanity in antebellum New Jersey', *History of Psychiatry*, 14:3 (2003), 281–301.

Moran, J., 'Travails of madness: New Jersey, 1800–70', in Waltraud Ernst (ed.), *Work, Psychiatry and Society, c. 1750–2015* (Manchester: Manchester University Press, 2016), pp. 77–99.

Moran, J. and L. Chilton, 'Mad migrants and the reach of English civil law', in M. Harper (ed.), *Migration and Mental Health: Past and Present* (Basingstoke: Palgrave Macmillan, 2016), pp. 149–170.

Neugebauer, R., 'Mental Illness and Government Policy in Sixteenth and Seventeenth Century England' (PhD dissertation, Columbia University, 1978).

Newman, R. P., 'Masturbation, madness and the modern concepts of childhood and adolescence', *Journal of Social History*, 8:3 (1975), 1–27.

Nootens, T., '"For years we have never had a happy home": Madness and families in nineteenth-century Montreal', in J. Moran and D. Wright (eds), *Mental Health in Canadian Society: Historical Perspectives* (Montreal: McGill Queen's University Press, 2006), pp. 49–68.

Nootens, T., *Fous, prodigues et ivrognes: familles et déviance à Montréal au XIXe siècle* (Montreal: McGill Queen's University Press, 2007).
Oda, A. M., C. Banzato and P. Dalgalarrondo, 'Some origins of cross-cultural psychiatry', *History of Psychiatry*, 16:2 (2005), 155–169.
Osterud, N., *Bonds of Community: The Lives of Farm Women in Nineteenth-Century New York* (Ithaca: Cornell University Press, 1991).
Parle, J., 'Family commitments, economies of emotions, and negotiating mental illness in late-nineteenth to mid-twentieth-century Natal, South Africa', *South African Historical Journal*, 66:1 (2014), 1–21.
Parle, J., *States of Mind: Searching for Mental Health in Natal and Zululand, 1868–1918* (Scottsville: University of KwaZulu-Natal Press, 2007).
Parry-Jones, W., *The Trade in Lunacy: A Study of Private Madhouses in England in the Eighteenth and Nineteenth Centuries* (London: Routledge and K. Paul, 1971).
Parsons, A. *From Asylum to Prison: Deinstitutionalization and the Rise of Mass Incarceration after 1945* (Chapel Hill: University of North Carolina Press, 2018).
Philo, C., *A Geographical History of Institutional Provision for the Insane from Medieval Times to the 1860s in England and Wales: The Space Reserved for Insanity* (Lampeter: Edwin Mellen Press, 2004).
Porter, R., *Mind-Forg'd Manacles: A History of Madness in England from the Restoration to the Regency* (Harvard: Harvard University Press, 1987).
Prestwich, P., 'Family strategies and medical power: "Voluntary" committal in a Parisian asylum, 1867–1914', *Journal of Social History*, 27:4 (1994), 799–818.
Rawlyk, G., *Revolution Rejected, 1775–1776* (Scarborough: Prentice-Hall, 1968).
Reaume, G., 'Mental hospital patients and family relations in Ontario, 1880–1930', in L. Chambers and E-A. Montigny (eds), *Family Matters: Papers in Post-Confederation Family History* (Toronto: Canadian Scholar's Press, 1998), pp. 271–287.
Rosenberg, C. E., 'The therapeutic revolution: Medicine, meaning and social change in nineteenth-century America', *Perspectives in Biology and Medicine*, 20:4 (1977), 485–506.
Rosenberg, C. and J. L. Golden (eds), *Framing Disease: Studies in Cultural History*, (New Brunswick: Rutgers University Press, 1992).
Rothman, D., *The Discovery of the Asylum: Social Order and Disorder in the New Republic* (Boston: Little Brown, 1971).
Rushton, P. 'Lunatics and idiots: Mental disability, the community, and the poor law in north-east England, 1600–1800', *Medical History*, 32:1 (1988), 34–50.
Sadowsky, J., *Imperial Bedlam: Institutions of Madness in Colonial Southwest Nigeria* (Berkeley: University of California Press, 1999).

Scull, A., *Museums of Madness: The Social Organization of Insanity in Nineteenth-Century England* (New York: St Martin's Press, 1979).

Scull, A., *The Insanity of Place/The Place of Insanity: Essays in the History of Psychiatry* (London: Routledge, 2006).

Scull, A., *The Most Solitary of Afflictions: Madness and Society in Britain, 1700–1900* (New Haven: Yale University Press, 1993).

Sloan, M. and M. Vaughan, *Psychiatry and Empire* (Basingstoke: Palgrave Macmillan, 2007).

Smith, L., *Insanity, Race and Colonialism: Managing Mental Disorder in the Post-Emancipation British Caribbean, 1838–1914* (Hampshire: Palgrave Macmillan, 2014).

Sprunger, K. L., *The Learned Doctor William Ames* (Urbana: University of Illinois Press, 1972).

Stanley, G., *Canada Invaded, 1775–1776* (Toronto: Hakkert, 1973).

Stansfield, C. A., *A Geography of New Jersey: The City in the Garden* (New Brunswick: Rutgers University Press, 1998).

Staves, S., *Married Women's Separate Property in England, 1660–1833* (Cambridge, MA: Harvard University Press, 1990).

Suzuki, A., 'Lunacy in seventeenth and eighteenth-century England: Analysis of Quarter Session records, Part I', *History of Psychiatry*, 2:8 (1991), 437–56.

Suzuki, A., "Lunacy in seventeenth and eighteenth-century England: Analysis of Quarter Session records, Part II," *History of Psychiatry*, 3:9 (1992), 29–44.

Suzuki, A., *Madness at Home: The Psychiatrist, the Patient, and the Family in England, 1820–1860* (Berkeley: University of California Press, 2006).

Swartz, S., 'Madness and colonial spaces: British India, c. 1800–1947', in L. Topp, J. Moran and J. Andrews (eds), *Madness, Architecture and the Built Environment: Psychiatric Spaces in Historical Context* (Abingdon: Routledge, 2007), pp. 215–38.

Tomes, N., *A Generous Confidence: Thomas Story Kirkbride and the Art of Asylum Keeping, 1840–1883* (New York: Cambridge University Press, 1984).

Tomlins, C., 'Law's empire: Chartering English colonies on the American mainland in the seventeenth century', in D. Kirby and C. Coleborne (eds), *Law, History, Colonialism: The Reach of Empire* (Manchester: Manchester University Press, 2001), pp. 26–45.

Tosh, J., *Manliness and Masculinities in Nineteenth-Century Britain* (Harlow: Pearson, 2005).

Turner, W. J., 'Town and country: A comparison of the treatment of the mentally disabled in late medieval English common law and chartered boroughs', in W. Turner (ed.) *Madness in Medieval Law and Custom* (Boston: Brill, 2010), pp. 17–38.

Bibliography

Veeder, V., 'The English Law Reports, 1292–1865', *Harvard Law Review*, 15:2 (1901).
Wacker, P., *Land and People: A Cultural Geography of Preindustrial New Jersey: Origins and Settlement Patterns* (New Brunswick: Rutgers University Press, 1975).
Walkowitz, J., 'Science and the séance: Transgressions of gender and genre in late Victorian London', *Representations*, 22 (1988), 3–29.
Walton, J., 'Lunacy in the Industrial Revolution: A study of asylum admissions in Lancashire, 1848–1850', *Journal of Social History*, 13:1 (1979), 1–22.
Warsh, C., *Moments of Unreason: The Practice of Canadian Psychiatry and the Homewood Retreat, 1883–1923* (Montreal: McGill Queen's University Press, 1989).
Weaver, J., *The Great Land Rush and the Making of the Modern World: 1650–1900* (Montreal: McGill Queen's University Press, 2003).
Weslager, C. A., *The Delaware Indians: A History* (New Brunswick: Rutgers University Press, 1972).
White, G. E., *Law in American History, Volume I* (Oxford: Oxford University Press, 2012).
Wildeman, S., 'Protecting rights and building capacities: Challenges to global mental health policy in light of the convention on the rights of persons with disabilities', *Journal of Law, Medicine and Ethics*, 41:1 (2013), 48–73.
Wilson, S., 'Mental capacity legislation in the UK: Systematic review of the experiences of adults lacking capacity and their carers', *British Journal of Psychiatry Bulletin*, 41:5 (2017), 260–266.
Wright, D., 'Family strategies and the institutional confinement of "idiot" children in Victorian England', *Journal of Family History*, 23:2 (1998), 190–208.
Wright, D., 'Getting out of the asylum: Understanding the confinement of the insane in the nineteenth-century', *Social History of Medicine*, 10:1 (1997), 137–155.
Wright, D., 'The certification of insanity in nineteenth-century England and Wales', *History of Psychiatry*, 9:35 (1998), 229–267.
Wright, D., J. Moran and S. Gouglas, 'The confinement of the mad in Victorian Canada', in R. Porter and D. Wright (eds), *The Confinement of the Insane, 1800–1965: International Perspectives* (Cambridge: Cambridge University Press, 2003), pp. 175–222.

Index

Act Concerning Idiots and Lunatics (1820) 132
Act for Supporting Idiots and Lunatics and Preserving their Estates (1794) 129–32
Act for the More Effectual Punishment of Rogues, Vagabonds, Sturdy Beggars and Vagrants (1714) 31–3, 41, 131
Act for the Regulation of Proceedings Under Commissions of Lunacy (1853) 42–3
Act for the Regulation of the Care and Treatment of Lunatics (1845) 41
Adair, Richard 10
aging *see* elderly
Albemarle, Duke of 53
American Revolutionary War 129
  pensions 147, 155–6
Andrews, Jonathan 36, 99–100
Ashe, Anne (later Packer) 73–8, 92
asylums
  Bethlem Hospital 54, 99
  Boston State Hospital for the Insane 206
  colonialism and 232
  community care vs. 6
  David R. 221
  Elias B. 217–20
  in England 206
  families and 6–11, 13–15, 145
  Francis F. 196–7
  George W. 209
  Hanwell Asylum 206
  Henry C. 209
  as historiographical pivot 233
  home care vs. 182, 217
  James B. 2, 11
  Jane C. 209–10
  Joel D. 209
  John B. 210–13
  John L. 213–17
  Long Island Home, Amityville 2, 3, 11
  lunacy investigation law and 15, 24, 141, 172, 227
  Morris Plains Lunatic Asylum 2, 11, 28n.32
  New Jersey State Lunatic Asylum 15, 24, 133, 134, 172, 209, 223, 227
  orders of insanity and 223–7

Index

overseas 101–3
patient population numbers 208–9
Pennsylvania Hospital for the Insane 9, 209
poverty and 224–7
Rachel C. 226
reactions to 207–8
and recovery process 216
reform 207
in traverse/*supersedeas* 210–13
in US 206–7
Asylums Act (1845) 41
Audley, Thomas 86–7

Bariatinski, Princess 123–4, 126
Barker, Frances 103–5
Barnsley, William 57, 69n.20
Bartlett, Peter 14, 232
Battie, William 99–100
Bennet, John 106
Bennet, Mr 83–4
Bergen, Frank 3–4
Beverley v. Snow 39
Binfield family 82
Bird, Samuel 64, 65, 67
Bonds of Community (Osterud) 172–3
borderlands of madness 20, 49–50, 66–8
  Cranmer 57–9
  Donegal 55–7
  Kendrick 56–7, 59
  Leigh 50–3, 67
  physical debility and 62–5
  Sherwood 59–60
  Standard 53–4
  Topp 54

breaking up house
  Barnt L. 175
  confinement as alternative to 192–3
  Henry P. 176
  Joseph P. 175–6
  Mary B. 176–7
Brown, Edward 107–9
Brydall, John, *Non Compos Mentis* 118–20
Bumpton, Mr (case) 82
bureaucratisation 42–3, 133
Buttolph, Horace 209, 214, 216–17, 228

care/treatment
  asylum vs. home/community 14, 15, 182, 217
  central role of family/community 172
  community 194–7
  complications of 107–10
  family-based 6, 13
  financing 108–9, 146–7
  lunacy investigation law and 21–2
  payment for 105, 111
  property used for costs 111, 173, 174, 175, 226
  use of inheritance for costs 110, 174–5
  use of property for 167n.28
  variety of interventions 171
  see also protection of person; welfare/wellbeing; women as caregivers
caregiver's death 173–4
  Anthony B. 143
  James V. 173

John B. 174
John V. 144
Nathaniel A. 143–4
Samuel P. 143
Cheyne, George 99
children's welfare
   Henry P. 176
   Mary B. 176–7
Coke, Sir Edward 34, 39–40, 58–9
Coleborne, Catharine 17
colonialism
   American Revolutionary War and 129
   and asylums 232
   and institutions 17–18
   James B. case and 16
   and lunacy investigation law 15–19, 117–22, 123–4, 125–6, 133, 234–5
   in New Jersey 117
   and property 118–22
commissions 37–8, 40, 110, 113, 117, 128–9
   effects on mental health 95n.49, 97, 100–3
committees 21–2, 38, 41, 86–7
community 151–4, 178
   and asylums 207–8
   central role in treatment/care/management 172
   lunacy investigation law and 12
   opinion 199–200
   see also neighbours
confinement
   alternative to breaking up house 192–3
   Ann D. 192–3
   Ann H. 192
   chaining 176, 190, 193, 210
   Charles C. 192
   Daniel H. 193–4
   Elizabeth D. 190
   forms of 192–4, 198
   Jacob D. 193
   John L. 193
   Lloyd V. 191, 192
   in New Jersey 132–3
   poor laws and 220
   Samuel B. 192
   Samuel J. 176
   see also asylums
Court of Chancery 1, 40
Court of Common Pleas 224, 225, 226
Court of Exchequer 40
Court of Wards and Liveries 35, 37–8, 40
Cranmer, Henry 55, 57–9, 67

D'Antonio, Patricia 10
De Indis (de Vitoria) 118
De Jure Belli et Pacis (On the Law of War and Peace) (Grotius) 119–20
de Vitoria, Francisco, De Indis 118
delusions 181, 182, 183, 184–8, 191, 194–5, 199
   Aber H. 185–6
   Abraham B. 186, 188
   Abraham R. 188
   Ann B. 201n.12
   Ann W. 187–8
   Anna C. 188
   Catherine H. 186, 187
   Daniel E. 188

Index

David B. 187
David P. 184–5
of grandeur 186–7
Henry C. 186
Hezekiah Y. 185
Jacob G. 186
Rev. Jacob S. 182
James V. 186
John B. 183
John L. 183
Joseph L. 188
Lewis R. 188
Mary A. 194–5
Mathias K. 186
regarding property 184–6, 201n.12
Thomas B. 187
Thomas E. 186
William W. 186–7
Zemas W. 188
Dickens, Charles 206
division of labour 113
Dix, Dorothea 207
Donegal, Lord 55–7
Dormer, Sir William 85–6
dress *see* clothing
D'Vebre, Deborah 115n.15

elderly 149–51
Abagail G. 183
Abraham R. 156–7
Abraham W. 156
Daniel V. 157–8
Eleanor C. 149–50
Sarah C. 150–1
Eldon, John Scott, Earl of 56–8, 59–60, 79–80, 81, 87–8, 105, 123

Erickson, Amy Louise, *Women and Property in Early Modern England* 76–8
Erskine, Thomas 58–9, 83, 125–6
Eyre, Sir James 84

families
ability vs. willingness to care 13
and asylums 6–11, 13–15, 145, 207–8
borderlands of madness and 50, 60, 67
breaking up 175–7
central role in treatment/care/management 172
and commissions of lunacy 98, 113, 114
dynamics, Abraham W. case 154–6
finances, Eunice B. case 147–8
financial stability 145–8
interests vs. interests of insane 88–9, 92, 93
Lord Chancellors and 20–1, 22, 72, 92, 93
lunacy investigation law and 20–1, 71, 92–3, 98, 144–5
neighbours vs. 151
non compos mentis verdict and 71–2
opinion 199–200
perceptions regarding mental competency 144–5
and property 71, 73–4, 84–5, 166
and property wasting/squandering 142–3, 145–6
and welfare of mad 71
see also breaking up house

Ferrers, Earl 54–5, 66, 107
Finnane, Mark, *Insanity and the Insane in Post-Famine Ireland* 8–9
Fitzherbert, Anthony 34
Fitzpatrick, Peter 118
Forsythe, Bill 10
Foucault, Michel 17
Fox, Richard 7–8
Franklin, William 128
Fry, Danby P. 31, 33
   Lunacy Law 32
Fust, Fanny 78

Gandy, Joseph 82
gender
   lunacy investigation law and 72–3, 92
   see also masculinity; *entries beginning* women
gender expectations
   Caroline W. 159–62, 164–5
   Isaac C. 159, 162–4, 165
   see also women as caregivers
Gentili, Alberico 118
'Getting out of the asylum' (Wright) 13
Goodwin, Ann (later Ferne) 55, 60–2
Grant, Sir W. 88–9
Great Land Rush and the Making of the Modern World, The (Weaver) 122
Grimstone, Bridget 87
Grob, Gerald 207
Grotius, Hugo 118
   De Jure Belli et Pacis (On the Law of War and Peace) 119–20

guardianship
   aging and 149–51
   borderlands of madness and 67
   committees and 38, 41, 86–7
   contestation of 109–10
   David R. 220–2
   Dormer 85–6
   Eunice B. 148
   of indigenous people 17
   Jacob L. 127
   Lewis P. 196
   Lord Chancellors and 41, 93, 111–12, 114
   lunacy investigation law and 12
   and masculinity 89
   neighbours and 151, 178–9
   in New Jersey 1804 Act 130
   non compos mentis verdict and 4–15
   Peter D. 195–6
   property 12, 81–2, 86–7, 173, 174, 175, 198
   Samuel H. 127
   William B. 127–8
   wives' petitions and 146
   women and 21, 82, 112–13, 198

Hamilton, Andrew 127
Hardwicke, Philip Yorke, Earl of 57–8, 102–3
Hartford, Mrs 83–4
Henry of Bracton 39
Houston, R. A. 14
Houstoun, John 123, 126
Hunt, Anne 101

idiocy
   and Crown profit 38
   Elisha A. 144–5

Index

legislation regarding 129–31
lunacy vs. 35–6, 38, 39
Nathaniel A. 143–4
Prerogativa Regis on 35–6
and property 35–6
indigenous people
  guardianship of 17
  lunacy investigation law and 16–17, 18–19
  in New Jersey 121–2
  and property 16–17, 18, 118, 121–2
inheritance
  Brown 107–9
  Daniel V. 157–8
  Elisha A. 144
  family property and 71, 166
  indigenous people and 118
  James K. 174–5
  John V. 144
  Price 110
  Sarah C. 150–1
insanity *see* madness
Insanity and the Insane in Post-Famine Ireland (Finnane) 8–9

Jenkinson, Sir Robert 85
Jones, Mr and Mrs 83
Justices Commitment Act (1744) 32–3, 131–2

Kelm, Mary Ellen 10
Kendrick, Ann 55, 56–7, 59, 67
Kenyon, Lloyd, Baron 104, 106
Kiralfy, A. K. R. 66
Kirkby, Diane 17

Law in American History (White) 121

Law of Nations (Vattel) 124
Le Heup 80
Lee, Sir George 63
Leigh, Sir John 67, 85, 107
Levine-Clark, Marjorie 10
Littleton, Thomas 39, 58
Lord Chancellors
  in Ashe case 76
  in Bariatinski case 123, 124
  and borderlands of madness 20, 53, 55–60, 66–8
  on commissions as detrimental to mental health 95n.49, 97, 100–2
  in Cranmer case 57–8, 58–9
  on creditors' attempts to recoup 87–8
  direct application to 43
  in Donegal case 55–7
  in Dormer case 86
  in Edward Brown case 108–9
  entrusting of lunacy investigation to 40
  and families 20–1, 22, 72, 92
  in Ferrers case 54–5, 66
  in Gandy case 82
  in Goodwin case 61, 62
  and guardianship 41, 93, 111–12, 114
  in Houstoun case 123
  influence 92–3
  and interest/comfort of lunatic 100
  in Kendrick case 56–7, 59
  on legal reach of chancery court 102–3
  and Leigh trials 51–3
  in M'Niven case 105
  in Niell case 88–9

and precedent 49, 53, 65–6, 68
and property 53
and protection/wellbeing of mad 79–80, 85–6, 97–8, 113
and recovery of insane 100, 107
responsibilities 40
in Sherwood case 59–60
in Southcot case 125–6
on testimony from those attending insane person 104–5
and traverse 65–6
in Virgil Parker case 84–5
visitors appointed by 42
in Wenman case 82–3
Loughborough, Alexander Wedderburn, Baron 61, 62
Ludlow, Elizabeth 111–12
lunacy *see* madness
Lunacy Act (1890) 43
lunacy investigation law
  aspects of 34
  asylum admissions and 208–9
  and asylums 15, 24, 141, 172, 227
  colonialism and 15–19, 117–22, 123–4, 125–6, 133, 234–5
  and community 12
  complexity of 113–14
  in England 5, 233–4
  families and 71, 92–3, 98, 144–5
  family/community testimonials and 199–200
  gender and 72–3
  history 31–4
  importance of 11–12
  and indigenous people 16–17, 18–19
  inquisitions in lunacy 40–1
  James B. case and 1–4, 15, 16
  jurisdictional reach 122–6, 159–62
  and masculinity 89–92
  in New Jersey 5–6, 22–3, 44, 126–33, 133–4, 140–1, 233–5
  in North American colonies 25n.11
  origins/history of 34–43, 49
  property and 19–20, 122, 142
  protection/care of mad under 97, 109, 171
  socio-economic status and 11–12, 110–13, 134, 234
  transatlantic nature 4
  and wellbeing of person/property 100
Lunacy Law (Fry) 32
Lunatics' Visitors Act (1833) 42
Lyndhurst, John Singleton Copley, Baron 124

mad-doctors 22, 99–100, 113
madness
  borderlands of *see* borderlands of madness
  definitions of 9, 19–20, 33–4, 49–50, 53, 56, 57, 114, 199–200
  as disease 103–5
  idiocy vs. 35–6, 38, 39
  legal responses to 103–5
  meanings/understandings of 97, 98–100, 140–1, 199–200
  orders of insanity 223–7
  Prerogativa Regis on 35–6
  responses to 227–8
  temporary nature of 113–14, 210

Index

Madness at Home (Suzuki) 14–15, 133
Manliness and Masculinities in Nineteenth-Century Britain (Tosh) 89
masculinity 21, 72–3, 89–92, 216
Masters in Chancery (NJ) 171
medicalisation 42, 97, 98, 99–100
  see also professionalisation
Melling, Joseph 10
Mills, Mary 84–5
Mitchinson, Wendy 10
M'Niven, Margaret 105
Monro, John 54, 55, 99–100, 101, 106, 107, 115n.15
Museums of Madness (Scull) 6

neighbours 151–4, 171–2, 177–9, 192, 198–9
  and Abraham R. 156–7
  and Daniel E. 153
  and David C. 177–8
  and Francina D. 168n.58
  and Jeremiah and Abigail H. 153
  and John L. 151–3
  and Mary E. 168n.58
  and Peter C. 151, 152–3
  and Rebecca L. 168n.58
  and Samuel B. 158–9
  and William S. 178–9
  see also community
Neugebauer, Richard 34–5, 36, 37
Nicholl, Sir John 79
Niell, John 88–9
Non Compos Mentis (Brydall) 118–20
Nootens, Thierry 10, 14, 200n.1

Orphans Court 2, 131, 144, 198
Osterud, Nancy, *Bonds of Community* 172–3

Packer, Philip 73–8
Pargeter, William 98–9
Parker, Thomas, Earl of Macclesfield 82–3
Parker, Virgil 84–5
petitions 40, 130
Philo, Chris 31–2
poor, the 98, 222–7
  Eva D. 225–6
  Margaret H. 225
  Mary P. 223
  poor law/lunacy investigation law responses for 208
  Rachel C. 226
poor houses 226–7
  Benjamin B. 226–7
  Obadiah M. 222
poor laws
  David R. 220, 222
  Jacob S. 222
  Mary G. 223
  Thomas R. 222
Pope, H. R. 40
Porter, Roy 97, 98, 233
precedent (England) 4, 49, 53, 68
Prerogativa Regis 32, 34–6, 39, 40, 86, 125, 128
Prestwich, Patricia 10
Priaux, Elizabeth 110
Price, Elizabeth 110
professionalisation 6, 22, 171, 172, 217
  see also medicalisation

property
　borderlands of madness and 60, 67
　colonialism and 118–22
　committees 38
　concern for, vs. policing of behaviour 166
　delusions regarding 184–6, 201n.12
　families and 71, 73–4, 84–5, 166
　guardians' use of 86–7
　guardianship 12, 19, 38, 41, 81–2, 173, 174, 175, 198
　and idiocy vs. lunacy 35–6
　indigenous people and 16–17, 18, 118, 121–2
　inquisitions into 36
　jointure 77
　lunacy investigation law and 12, 16, 19–20, 122, 142, 171
　married women and 73–80
　and masculinity 90, 216
　patient recovery and regain of control over 4, 19, 86, 129–30
　protection/safeguarding 114
　and signs/symptoms of madness 179
　use for patient care/maintenance 111, 167n.28, 173, 174, 175, 226
　women and 72, 80–1, 148–9
property tampering
　Aber H. 185–6
　Hezekiah Y. 185, 186
property wasting/squandering 166
　Elizabeth V. 142–3
　families and 142–3, 145–6
　John B. 142
　John M. 145–6
　Peter P. 142
　Robert P. 142
　Sarah C. 142
protection of person 85–9
　complications of 107–10
　legal responses 103–7
　lunacy investigation law and 21–2, 97–8, 109, 171
　and nature of lunacy as disease 103–5
　property protection and 114, 171
　supersedeas and 106–7
　use of inquiry 105–7
　see also care/treatment

Randolph, James 155–6
Reaume, Geoffrey 10
recovery
　asylums and 216
　completeness of 107
　Crown profit and 38
　elapse of time to 195
　idiocy vs. lunacy and 38, 129–30
　as legal principle 4, 113–14
　in lunacy investigation law 19, 21–2, 100
　Prerogative Regis and 86
　and safeguarding wellness 113–14
　and *supercedeas*/traverse 210
Romilly, Sir Samuel 57–8, 101
Rosenberg, Charles 98

S., Ahab 130
Sayer, Robert 106
Scott, Sir William 91

Index

Scull, Andrew 99–100
  Museums of Madness 6
Sherwood, Kitty 55, 59–60, 79–80
Shirley, Lady Betty 54–5, 107
Shirley, Lawrence 54–5, 107
signs/symptoms of madness 171–2, 179–92, 199
Smith, Anne 80–1
Smith, Mary 81
Smith, Richard 64–5
Smith, Thomas 80–1
socio-economic status
  Crown's protection duty and 36
  and family-based vs. asylum caregiving 9–10
  and home- vs. asylum-based care 14
  and lunacy investigation law 11–12, 234
  lunacy investigation law and 23, 134
  non compos mentis verdict and 71–2
  and orders of insanity 223–4
  and responses to madness 227–8
  see also poor, the
Somers, John, Baron 74
Southcot, Thomas 101–3, 125–6, 137n.49
speech problems
  Anna A. 203n.67
  Edward B. 190
  Elizabeth D. 190
  Hester C. 190
  incoherence 188–9, 191, 199, 203n.67
  John Jordan 190
  Lloyd V. 190–1
  Samuel O. 190
  silence 190–1, 199
  Thomas F. 189
Spitzka, Edward 3
Standard, Barbara 53–4
Stedman, Jane 62–4, 67
Steed, Elizabeth 64–5
supersedeas see traverse, trials of
Suzuki, Akihito 5, 40, 43, 68n.19
  Madness at Home 14–15, 133

Thurlow, Edward 78, 103, 104–5
Tomes, Nancy 9
Tomlins, Christopher 120
Topp, Sir John 54
Tosh, John 90
  Manliness and Masculinities in Nineteenth-Century Britain 89
traverse, trials of 12, 22, 41, 106–7, 154–9, 166
  Abraham R. 156–7
  Abraham W. 154–6
  Ashe 75–6
  asylums in 210–13
  Bumpton 82
  Caroline W. 162
  Craig L. 195
  Daniel V. 157–8
  David R. 220
  Edward Brown 108–9
  elapse of time to 194–5
  Elias B. 218–20
  Ferrers 54–5, 66
  Fust 78
  Goodwin (Ferne) 61–2
  James B. 2–4, 12
  John B. 210–13
  John L. 214–17

Lord Chancellors and 65–6
Mary A. 194–5
Peter B. 195–6
Samuel B. 158–9
Sherwood 59–60
treatment *see* care/treatment
Tuberville, George Gleane 111
Turner (case) 90–2
Turner, Wendy 37

United Nations Convention on the Rights of Persons with Disabilities 235–6

Vattel, Emer de, *Law of Nations* 124
Vaughan, Megan 17
Veeder, Vecliten 70n.59
violence
  Ann H. 192
  and breaking up house 175–6
  Charles C. 192
  and confinement 192–4, 210
  Daniel H. 193–4
  David R. 221
  Eva D. 226
  Hezekiah Y. 185
  as indicator of insanity 180–3, 191, 199
  Isaac C. 183
  Jacob G. 146
  Rev. Jacob S. 182
  James T. 146, 182
  Joseph F. 182
  Lloyd V. 191
  Marmaduke A. 201n.29
  and neighbourhood watching 198

  Peter D. 195
  Phenon S. 182–3

Wacker, Peter 18
Waddington, Dr 80
Walkowitz, Judith 94n.26
Walton, John 7
watching/overseeing 173, 192, 196, 198–9
Weaver, John, *Great Land Rush and the Making of the Modern World, The* 122
welfare/wellbeing
  families and 71
  guardianship and 41
  Lord Chancellors and 113
Wenman, Lord and Lady 82–3
West, Richard 128
White, G. Edward, *Law in American History* 121
White, Mary (later Reane) 78–9
Wildeman, Sheila 235–6
Wilsey, Orville 3
wives as significant actors
  Eleanor and Benjamin G. 148–9
  Jane and Jacob G. 146
  Phebe and Joshua A. 148
women
  battling each other 80–1
  defiance of commissions 82–3
  as guardians 21, 82, 198
  marriage to those subsequently found mad 83–4
  participation in lunacy investigation law 21, 72
  and property 73–80
  property law and 72

Index

Women and Property in Early Modern England (Erickson) 76–8
women as caregivers 172–5
  Ann and James K. 174–5
  in division of labour 113
  duration of caregiving 173–5, 198
  Elizabeth and Sarah C. 173
  Elizabeth D. 175
  as front-line care 192, 198
  gendered expectation and 112–13
  James V. 173
  John B. 174
  and property 148–9
  see also caregiver's death
Wright, David 10, 14, 199
  'Getting out of the asylum' 13
Wright, Sir Nathan 73
writs *de lunatico inquirendo* 4, 37–8, 164, 180

EU authorised representative for GPSR:
Easy Access System Europe, Mustamäe tee 50,
10621 Tallinn, Estonia
gpsr.requests@easproject.com

www.ingramcontent.com/pod-product-compliance
Lightning Source LLC
Chambersburg PA
CBHW071406300426
44114CB00016B/2198